Digging for the Treasure:

Translation After Pound

Digging for the Treasure: Translation After Pound

Ronnie Apter

PARAGON HOUSE PUBLISHERS
New York

First U.S. Paperback Edition 1987.

Published in the United States by

PARAGON HOUSE PUBLISHERS
2 Hammarskjöld Plaza
New York, New York   10017

Copyright 1984 by Peter Lang.

Library of Congress Cataloging-in-Publication Data

Apter, Ronnie.
  Digging for the treasure.

  Reprint. Originally published: New York : P. Lang, c1984.
  Bibliography:
  Includes index.
  1. Pound, Ezra, 1885–1972—Influence.   2. Pound, Ezra, 1885–1972—Criticism and interpretation.   3. Poetry—Translating.   4. English poetry—Translations from foreign languages—History and criticism.   5. Poetry—Translations into English—History and criticism.
  I. Title.
  PS3531.082Z542   1986   811'.52   86-18724

ISBN 0-913729-50-7

For Rosalind Apter

Contents

Part Three: The Creative Translation as New Poem

Preface and Acknowledgments

This study of the influence of Ezra Pound on the translation of poetry has been limited to translation from older literatures. Although I have primarily considered translations from Latin, Old and Middle English, Old Provençal, and Medieval French, Pound also translated from the classics of Italian, Greek, Chinese, and Egyptian. However, I do not read Greek, Chinese, or Egyptian at all, and, at the time I wrote this book, I read Italian only limpingly. Therefore, I did not discuss Pound's influence on modern translations from these languages, and I relied on other scholars for the limited discussion of the translations by Pound himself.

In a study like this, the author is plunged into a welter of conflicting editions of the original poems. I have usually used, if it was known to me and available, the text followed by the translator under discussion; if not, then the best available modern edition of the text. However, where several translators each used a different text, and these differed in only minor ways, I have simply chosen one text to follow, usually the best available modern edition. I have no idea from what texts Swinburne and Rossetti translated the poems of François Villon. John Payne was in correspondence with Auguste Longnon while Longnon was compiling his edition of 1892, the cornerstone of modern Villon textual scholarship. Modern translators usually follow the fourth edition (1932) of Longnon, revised by Foulet. I chose to use the text edited by Anthony Bonner, since his edition, with its excellent scholarship and helpful notes, is most convenient to an English speaker. In the case of the Latin poet Sextus Propertius, where editions vary greatly, I have followed the Loeb Classical Library version edited by H. E. Butler, but I also give the reading of Lucianus Mueller, whose edition Pound used, if the difference is substantial. Regardless of the text used, the numbering of Propertius's elegies has been converted to Butler's system. The Mueller edition is no longer available, but J. P. Sullivan has reprinted all the sections of it relevant to Pound's *Homage to Sextus Propertius* in an Appendix to *Ezra Pound and Sextus Propertius: A Study in Creative Translation.* Quotations from Pound's *Homage* are also based on Sullivan's Appendix, since he has compiled a variorum edition, and consulted with Pound as to the definitive readings.

The use of different texts by different editors has resulted in inconsistencies in Latin and Provençal orthography.

I wish to express my thanks to my husband, Mark Herman, for his suggestions and corrections, and for typing the original hard-cover edition of this book. Also, I would like to thank L. R. Lind, George Economou, Burton Raffel, J. P. Sullivan, and Paul Properzio, who helped me with translation bibliography and with interpretation of the original poems.

The following persons and publishers have graciously given me permission to reprint from the publications listed below:

William Arrowsmith, trans. *Iliad* 18, in *The Craft and Context of Translation: A Symposium,* ed. William Arrowsmith and Roger Shattuck, © 1961.

Peter Green, trans. *Iliad* 1, in *The Craft and Context of Translation: A Symposium,* ed. William Arrowsmith and Roger Shattuck, © 1961.

University of California Press. *Proensa: An Anthology of Troubadour Poems,* trans. Paul Blackburn, copyright © 1978; *New Approaches to Ezra Pound,* ed. Eva Hesse, copyright © 1969.

The University of Chicago Press. *The Complete Works of the "Gawain"-Poet,* translated and with a critical Introduction by John

Gardner. © 1965 by The University of Chicago. All rights reserved.

The Editor of *Poetry.* "On Translating Poets," by John Peale Bishop. First appeared in *Poetry* 62. © 1943 by The Modern Poetry Association.

Harvard University Press. *The Classic Anthology as Defined by Confucius,* trans. Ezra Pound. Reprinted by permission. Copyright © 1954 by the President and Fellows of Harvard College, © renewed 1982 by Mary DeRachewiltz and Omar Pound.

Bantam Books, Inc. From *The Complete Works of François Villon,* edited and translated by Anthony Bonner. Copyright © 1960 by Bantam Books, Inc. By permission of Bantam Books, Inc. All Rights Reserved.

Black Sparrow Press. *The Journals,* by Paul Blackburn. © 1975.

J. M. Cohen. *English Translators and Translations,* Longmans, Green & Co. Copyright © 1962 by J. M. Cohen.

University of Nebraska Press. "The Seafarer," reprinted from *Poems from the Old English,* translated by Burton Raffel, by permission of University of Nebraska Press. Copyright © 1960, 1964 by the University of Nebraska Press.

The University of Michigan Press. Matthew Arnold, *On Translating Homer* (1860–1861), from Volume 1 of *The Complete Prose Works, Matthew Arnold on the Classical Tradition,* edited by R. H. Super, copyright © 1960 by The University of Michigan; Catullus 13, from *Gaius Valerius Catullus: The Complete Poetry,* translated, with an Introduction, by Frank O. Copley, copyright © 1957 by The University of Michigan. Reprinted by permission of The University of Michigan Press.

Angel Flores. "Assatz sai d'amor ben parlar," by Raimbaut d'Aurenga, translated by Maurice Valency in Angel Flores (ed.): *Medieval Lyrics.* N.Y.: Modern Library, 1962, copyright © 1962 by Angel Flores.

Farrar, Straus and Giroux, Inc. Reprinted by permission of Farrar, Straus and Giroux, Inc. Excerpts from *Imitations* by Robert Lowell. Copyright © 1958, 1959, 1960, 1961 by Robert Lowell. Excerpts from *Collected Poems 1919–1976* by Allen Tate. Copyright © 1952, 1953, 1970, 1977 by Allen Tate. Copyright 1931,

Galway Kinnell. *The Poems of François Villon: A New Translation* by Galway Kinnell, New American Library, A Signet Classic. Copyright © 1965 by Galway Kinnell.

Barnes & Noble Books. *To Homer Through Pope,* by H. A. Mason, copyright © 1972; and *A Literary History of Rome,* by J. Wight Duff, copyright © 1909, 1963. Permission to reprint granted by Barnes & Noble Books, Totowa, New Jersey.

Cambridge University Press. John Speirs, "Mr. Pound's Propertius," *Scrutiny* 3 (March 1935):409–18.

New Directions Publishing Corporation. Excerpts from *ABC of Reading,* copyright 1934 by Ezra Pound; *Cantos of Ezra Pound,* copyright © 1934, 1940, 1956 by Ezra Pound; *Selected Prose 1909–1965,* copyright © 1973 by the Estate of Ezra Pound; *Literary Essays,* copyright 1935 by Ezra Pound; *Selected Letters of Ezra Pound: 1907–1941,* copyright 1950 by Ezra Pound; *Personae,* copyright 1926 by Ezra Pound; *Spirit of Romance,* copyright © 1968 by Ezra Pound, all rights reserved; *Translations,* copyright © 1954, 1963 by Ezra Pound, all rights reserved; *The Collected Longer Poems of Kenneth Rexroth,* copyright 1944 by New Directions Publishing Corporation; *An Examination of Ezra Pound* by Peter Russell, all rights reserved; *The Poetry of Ezra Pound* by Hugh Kenner, all rights reserved. All of the above Pound material reprinted by permission of New Directions Publishing Corporation and Faber & Faber, Ltd. All other material by permission of New Directions.

Faber and Faber Publishers. "The Ghost: After Sextus Propertius," from *Poems 1938–1949,* by Robert Lowell, published by Faber and Faber, copyright © 1946; excerpts from *Imitations* by Robert Lowell, copyright © 1958, 1959, 1960, 1961 by Robert Lowell; excerpts from *Collected Poems 1919–1976* by Allen Tate, copyright © 1952, 1953, 1970, 1977 by Allen Tate, copyright © 1931, 1932, 1937, 1948 by Charles Scribner's Sons, copyright renewed © 1959, 1960, 1965 by Allen Tate.

Viking Penguin Inc. "Pervigilium Veneris," translated by Frank Lucas, in *The Portable Roman Reader,* edited by Basil Davenport, copyright © 1951; Horace Odes 1. 11 and 1. 9, from *The Odes of Horace and the Centennial Hymn,* translated by James Michie, copyright © 1963 by James Michie. Reprinted by permission of Viking Penguin Inc.

. . . the translator . . . can show
where the treasure lies. . . .

Ezra Pound, *Literary Essays*

1

A Renaissance for Translation

The Influence of Ezra Pound

During his lifetime, Ezra Pound made a number of verse translations from classical and medieval literatures. He also wrote many essays on translation and essays incorporating translations. The quality of this array varied greatly, but the best of it began a modern renaissance in English translation. Today the Latin classics are translated by poets like Robert Fitzgerald, W. S. Merwin, John Frederick Nims, and Kenneth Rexroth. Old and Middle English poetry have found translators like Burton Raffel and John Gardner, while Robert Lowell and Paul Blackburn struggle with *langue d'oil* and *langue d'oc*. However greatly these modern translators differ from each other in their styles, they have all made a sharp break with the kind of translation of older literatures current at the turn of the century. Following Pound, they translate using new assumptions about the nature and intent of literary translation.

Pound's major innovations are three: he discarded the Victorian pseudo-archaic translation diction; he regarded each translation as a necessarily limited criticism of the original poem; and he regarded good translations as new poems in their own right.

Translation Diction

The question of translation diction is connected to the question of historical perspective. As J. M. Cohen, author of *English Translators and Translations* points out, Elizabethans tended to view ancients like "Plutarch, Pliny, and Homer as moralists, historians, and story-tellers whose climate of thought and world-picture did not greatly differ from their own."[1] Consequently, they translated the Greek and Roman classics into contemporary Elizabethan English. Victorian translators, on the other hand, translated into a pseudo-archaic diction belonging to no recognizable period of English, which made the past and its poetry seem romantically remote. According to Cohen, they wrote as if "distance of time and place" were "the prime reality of which the reader must be constantly reminded."[2]

Pound espoused neither view. He wished to make the past seem as vividly alive and complex as the present. However, unlike the Elizabethans, he was fully aware that a long-dead writer would have been imbued with a Weltanschauung very different from the modern one. In order to express his historical perspective, he experimented with various dictions ranging from the genuinely archaic to the completely contemporary; he even experimented with a blend of both.

Pound's use of contemporary diction has been vastly influential; his use of mixed dictions less so.

The Translation as Criticism

Victorian translators would have agreed with Pound that a translation of a poem is a criticism of it. Merely to choose a poem for translation is a form of criticism: the chooser singles out the original poem for notice. They would also have agreed that the translator's expression of the content and the various stylistic factors of the original is a form of criticism. However, Victorian translators believed it the translator's duty to express *all* the qualities of the original poem in a near-literal paraphrase while following the meter of the original poem. Even if this proved impossible, it was still the translator's duty to try. Pound was willing to try for only *some* qualities of the original poem, and, as often as not, to translate it into free verse. Moreover, Pound included the literal sense of the poem among the qualities he was willing to scant.

Nineteenth-century translators were agreed that a translation ought to be of the kind John Dryden (1631–1700) termed paraphrase* (although they defined paraphrase more narrowly than Dryden did), while Pound sometimes translated in the mode Dryden termed imitation. Dryden, whose distinctions between the types of translation were often referred to and accepted by Victorian translation theorists, set up three categories:

> All Translation, I suppose, may be reduced to these three heads:
> First, that of Metaphrase, or turning an Authour word by word, and Line by Line, from one Language into another. . . . The second way is that of Paraphrase, or Translation with Latitude, where the Authour is kept in view by the Translator, so as never to be lost, but his words are not so strictly follow'd as his sense, and that too is admitted to be amplyfied, but not alter'd. . . . The Third way is that of Imitation, where the Translator (if now he has not lost that Name) assumes the liberty not only to vary from the words and sence, but to forsake them both as he sees occasion; and taking only some general hints from the Original, to run division on the groundwork, as he pleases.[3]

Dryden was formulating a theory for the translation of poetry into poetry, and thus he dismissed metaphrase with the comment: " 'Tis almost impossible to Translate verbally, and well, at the same time. . . . "[4] He preferred paraphrase. In para-

---

*The exception to this statement, discussed later, is Edward Fitzgerald, translator of *The Rubáiyát of Omar Khayyám*.

phrase, he explained, the translator should never violate the sense of the original, but should have great liberty in choosing English words to express the ideas, for

> ... thought, if it be Translated truly, cannot be lost in another Language, but the words that convey it to our apprehension (which are the Image and Ornament of that thought) may be so ill chosen as to make it appear in an unhandsome dress, and rob it of its native Lustre.[5]

Imitation Dryden condemned, saying,

> I take Imitation of an Authour ... to be an Endeavor of a later Poet to write like one who has written before him, on the same Subject: that is, not to translate his words, or to be Confin'd to his Sense, but only to set him as a Patern, and to write, as he supposes, that Authour would have done, had he liv'd in our Age, and in our Country.[6]

Dryden had some awareness that his definition of imitation embraced too broad a territory; that, in fact, there is a large gray area between paraphrase and imitation, left unmapped by his definition. Having condemned the theory of imitation as set forth by the poet-translators Sir John Denham (1615–1669) and Abraham Cowley (1618–1667), he remarks of their practice:

> Yet I dare not say that either of them have carried this libertine way of rend'ring Authours (as Mr. *Cowley* calls it) so far as my Definition reaches.[7]

In summing up the motive for translating in the mode he calls imitation, Dryden explicates with great fairness what he had previously failed to define:

> But if after what I have urg'd, it be thought by better Judges that the praise of a Translation Consists in adding new Beauties to the piece, thereby to recompense the loss

which it sustains by change of Language, I shall be willing to be taught better, and to recant.[8]

In discussing Pound's work, it becomes convenient to make a distinction between "adding new Beauties . . . to recompense the loss . . . [a poem] sustains by change of language" and "taking only some general hints from the Original." Another term ought to be inserted between paraphrase and imitation. I shall borrow J. P. Sullivan's choice of "creative translation."[9]

Dryden evidently did "recant" and made creative translations, for in his introduction to the translations in *Sylvae,* published in 1685, he wrote:

> Yet, withal, I must acknowledge, that . . . I have both added and omitted, and even sometimes very boldly made such expositions of my Authors, as no *Dutch* Commentator will forgive me. Perhaps, in such particular passages, I have thought that I discover'd some beauty yet undiscover'd by those Pedants, which none but a Poet cou'd have found. Where I have . . . cut them shorter, it may possibly be on this consideration, that what was beautiful in the *Greek* or *Latin,* wou'd not appear so shining in the *English:* And where I have enlarg'd them, I desire the false Criticks wou'd not always think that those thoughts are wholly mine, but that either they are secretly in the Poet, or may be fairly deduc'd from him: or at least, if both those considerations should fail, that my own is of a piece with his, and that if he were living, and an *Englishman,* they are such, as he wou'd probably have written.[10]

Both Victorian theorists and Pound could call on Dryden for support of their views. Pound, never one to appeal to authority, did not bother. However, he clearly believed, as Dryden argued, that his deletions and exaggerations were not arbitrary, but based on a critical apprehension of the original poem. Further, Pound believed that a translation could always and only be *one view* of the original. Therefore, he had the freedom to regard his translation as one criticism among the many possible; if it sacrificed denotation in favor of connotation, deleted a blemish that was another critic's beauty, or exaggerated an undervalued quality—why, some other translation, possibly his own, would redress the balance.

Pound's notion that a translation presents one of many possible critical analyses is now in great favor. Modern translators purposely exaggerate, delete, or sacrifice one quality of the original for the sake of another. In fact, this is the most far-reaching of Pound's re-interpretations of the intent and possibilities of translation.

The Translation as New Poem

Hugh Kenner argues in his book *The Pound Era* that the twentieth century has developed a new conception of the learning process, seeing it as a feedback process. Kenner applies this to the study of the past. He says that we no longer believe that the past is a simple collection of facts to be unearthed and apprehended; rather, we believe that as we seem to approach an understanding of the past, we alter our perceptions of both the past and the present.[11]

Pound saw translations as new poems in two different, but connected, ways. First, he viewed the past as an active participant in the changing of the present. He selected for translation those poems which he felt displayed desirable qualities lacking in contemporary poetry. His translations from Provençal, Chinese, and Latin were deliberate attempts to change the poetic sensibility of his time. Such translations are in themselves new poems as well as reflections of old poems, because they are intended to belong to the body of contemporary poetry.

Second, he believed that a translation cannot be the old poem; it can only be the old poem viewed from the standpoint of the present. Therefore, insofar as a translation is an augmented view of the past, colored by intervening centuries of experience, it is a new poem. Pound made a radical innovation

in translation practice by discussing the simultaneous altera-
tion of present and past within the very language of his poem.
Both Hugh Kenner and Donald Davie have shown that
Pound invented a means of displaying the feedback process of
perception within the context of the translation itself.[12]

No modern translators have been influenced by Pound to
discuss the changing of the present by the past and the past by
the present within the context of their translations, but a number have given evidence that they believe such a process is taking place.

The Present Scene

In contemporary translations, metrical practice and diction
differ greatly from the Victorian. Historical perspective differs
from the Victorian. Even the very concept of the purpose of
translation differs from the Victorian. Naturally, not all contemporary translators make creative translations in modern
diction. Pound himself made various kinds of translations,
some distinctly Victorian. However, due to his influence, new
approaches to translation now exist.

In subsequent chapters, a number of minor, and some major,
Victorian translations are quoted. It may seem unfair to base
an argument on lesser works. Yet, Victorian translators, lesser
and greater, held some principles in common, and the lesser
translators, who were unable even partially to transcend their
theories, in some ways better illustrate these principles than
do the greater translators. Finally, no age produces more than
a few great translations. Time will no doubt prove that many
of the new translations quoted herein are also minor. Comparison of contemporary and Victorian translations, both
greater and lesser, does show that translation now rests on a
new set of assumptions, arising from the theory and practice
of Ezra Pound.

Part One
Historical
Perspective

2

The Victorian Vision of Time: Theory and Practice

Victorian Theory

The two major Victorian translation theoreticians were Matthew Arnold (1822–1888) and F. W. Newman (1805–1897). Their controversy centered on the relationship of an ancient work to the present, with special reference to what diction appropriately conveys that relationship. Both their positions are given in Matthew Arnold's famous essay, *On Translating Homer* (1860–1861), which was originally a series of lectures delivered in response to the publication of F. W. Newman's translation of the *Iliad*. Arnold outlines the controversy thus:

> It is disputed what aim a translator should propose to himself in dealing with his original. Even this preliminary is not yet settled. On one side it is said that the translation ought to be such 'that the reader should, if possible, forget that it is a translation at all, and be lulled into the illusion that he is reading an original work,— something original' (if the translation be in English), 'from an English hand.' The real original is in this case, it is said, 'taken as a basis on which to rear a poem that shall affect our countrymen as the original may be con-

ceived to have affected its natural hearers.' On the other
hand, Mr. Newman, who states the foregoing doctrine
only to condemn it, declares that he 'aims at precisely the
opposite: to retain every peculiarity of the original, so far
as he is able, *with the greater care the more foreign it may
happen to be;'* so that it may 'never be forgotten that he is
imitating, and imitating in a different material.' The
translator's 'first duty,' says Mr. Newman, 'is a historical
one: to be *faithful.'* Probably both sides would agree that
the translator's 'first duty is to be faithful;' but the question at issue between them is, in what faithfulness
consists.[1]

Arnold, with the proviso that scholars of Greek be the
judges of how the original affected its natural hearers,[2] is in
favor of a translation which appears to be "something original
. . . from an English hand." To this end, Arnold seems to
advocate that translators use a contemporary diction:

> I advise him [the translator], again, not to trouble him-
> self with constructing a special vocabulary for his use in
> translation; with excluding a certain class of English
> words, and with confining himself to another class, in
> obedience to any theory about the peculiar qualities of
> Homer's style.[3]

He explains that, on the contrary,

> Mr. Newman says that 'the entire dialect of Homer being
> essentially archaic, that of a translator ought to be as
> much Saxo-Norman as possible, and owe as little as pos-
> sible to the elements thrown into our language by clas-
> sical learning.'[4]

According to Arnold, Newman went even further:

> Again; 'to translate Homer suitably,' says Mr. New-
> man, 'we need a diction sufficiently antiquated to obtain

pardon of the reader for its frequent homeliness. . . . I am concerned . . . with the artistic problem of attaining a plausible aspect of moderate antiquity, while remaining easily intelligible.'[5]

Both these theories of historical perspective in translation are powerful, and much can be said in favor of each. As Newman points out, many ancient works, such as the *Iliad* or *Beowulf,* are themsleves written in dictions which show varying levels of antiquity; there is a kind of fidelity in distinguishing between the newer and older dictions present. Further, to the modern observer, the conceptual underpinnings of the society which produced the poem vary in psychic distance: some concepts seeming modern and easily comprehensible, others, ancient and strange. On the other hand, to argue for Arnold, the older work, however much a repository of yet older tales, must have struck its first hearers as a new work; there is a kind of fidelity in restoring to a poem the freshness it once had. Further, one can be interested in the timeless aspect of a poem: those similarities in viewpoint and passions held in common which unite mankind across the centuries.

Unfortunately, neither Newman nor Arnold succeeded in producing a translation in line with his vision. Both men came to grief on the pseudo-archaic translation diction favored by most Victorian translators.

Victorian Practice: Diction

At any given time in the history of the English language, there are words which are in common use and others which are not. Within the diction of a time are subsets: the language used for a Parliamentary debate will differ from the language used for a friendly gossip, will differ from the language used in a gutter brawl. As the language changes, some words become obsolete, and these obsolete words, if used, seem to invoke the time of their common usage. A writer may employ an archaic diction from a given historical period to create a

poem which seems to be an artifact of that period. In contrast
a pseudo-archaic diction is not the language of a particular
period in English: it is the intentional placement of words
from many periods of English side by side, blurring the distinctions between periods, in an attempt to create an impression of "far away and long ago," or "once upon a time."

Newman's translation did not make the discriminations his
theory called for between levels of antiquity, because it was
written in a pseudo-archaic diction. The strange or obsolete
words in the following passage ("Eld," "in sooth," "liefly,"
"any-gait") are not used to stand out in contrast to a more
modern diction, nor are they from a specific period in the past:

> O gentle friend! if thou and I, from this encounter
>   'scaping
> Hereafter might forever be from Eld and Death
>   exempted
> As heavenly gods, not I in sooth would fight among the
>   foremost,
> Nor liefly thee would I advance to man-ennobling
>   battle.
> Now,—sith ten thousand shapes of Death do any-gait
>   pursue us
> Which never mortal may evade, though sly of foot and
>   nimble;—
> Onward! and glory let us earn, or glory yield to some
>   one.[6]

When we turn to Arnold, hoping to find a translation into
the language of his contemporaries, we discover Hector reply-
ing to Andromache's entreaties in the following manner:

> Woman, I too take thought for this; but then I bethink
>   me
> What the Trojan men and Trojan women might
>   murmur,
> If like a coward I skulked behind, apart from the battle.

Nor would my own heart let me; my heart, which has
    bid me be valiant.
Always, and always fighting among the first of the
    Trojans,
Busy for Priam's fame and my own, in spite of the
    future.
It will come, when sacred Troy shall go to destruction,
Troy, and warlike Priam too, and the people of Priam.
And yet not that grief, which then will be, of the
    Trojans,
Moves me so much—not Hecuba's grief, nor Piram my
    father's,
Nor my brethren's many and brave, who then will be
    lying
In the bloody dust, beneath the feet of their foemen—
As thy grief, when in tears, some brazen-coated
    Achaian
Shall transport thee away, and the day of thy freedom
    be ended.[7]

Admittedly, this diction does not attain to anything so cranky
as "any-gait,"* but Hector "bethinks him" and is "busy for
Priam's fame," while the Achaians are "brazen-coated." All of
these usages are archaic in Arnold's time. Arnold is also using
a special vocabulary, although he advised translators not to
construct one. Arnold tried to defend his diction, saying:

> . . . [There is a] poetical vocabulary, as distinguished
> from the vocabulary of common speech and modern
> prose: I mean, such expressions as *perchance* for *perhaps,*
> *spake* for *spoke, aye* for *ever, don* for *put on, charmèd* for
> *charm'd,* and thousand of others. . . . A diction that is
> antiquated for common speech and common prose, may

---

*However, the grammar of "And yet not that grief, which then will be, of the Tro-
jans / Moves me so much" is a masterpiece of unnecessary convolution.

very well not be antiquated for poetry or certain special
kinds of prose.[8]

Arnold, having capitulated to a special, "antiquated" vocabulary for poetry, joins his Victorian "brethren" in their inability to create a translation which would "lull the reader into
thinking he is reading an original;" and in their equal inability
to set a translation in a clearly defined period of history. J. M.
Cohen sums up the whole oeuvre of Victorian poetic translations with the tart comment:

> The theory of Victorian translation appears from our
> point of view to have been founded on a fundamental
> error. The aim was to convey the remoteness both in
> time and place of the original work by the use of a mock-
> antique language which was called by William Morris
> "Wardour Street English" after the fake-antique and the-
> atrical costumiers' shops which were to be found there.
> The theory [behind this diction] was set out by J. H. [*sic*]
> Newman. . . . [9]

There is, one may note, a discrepancy between the practice
ascribed to Newman's theory and the theory itself. Newman
had called for the honest transcription of the peculiarities of
the original, not the creation of Wardour Street English. Yet
both Newman and Arnold used this jargon. Arnold and Newman are read today for their theories. No one claims that they
are good translators. However, the kind of language they used
was the staple language of all Victorian translators of older
works.

Perhaps the best Victorian translators did not consciously
aim at remoteness of time and place. Their psuedo-archaic
vocabulary nonetheless resulted in it. The vocabulary at least
suggests an unconscious urge to view ancient poetry at a glam-
orous distance. Whether the Victorian translators were
seduced by the enjoyment of remoteness into the diction

which they used, or whether the diction which to them meant poetry engendered the remoteness, is a moot point. The fact remains, they chose to write in this style. Hugh Kenner, in *The Pound Era,* discusses at length the Victorian archaizing sensibility and its artifacts. He explains that the post-Romantic reader wanted

> " . . . to savor the romance of *time.*" [Whatever] anti-
> quarian passions . . . admired was set at a great dis-
> tance. . . . Such sentiments were not reserved for a few
> connoisseurs. People with 2/6 a month to spend could
> buy the *Morte d'Arthur* as the installments appeared, with
> Aubrey Beardsley designs modelled on Morris's to
> encumber it with a neurasthenic remoteness, thought
> "mediaeval." And Homer? *Very* remote; to represent the
> feel of his text . . . , his Victorian translators adduced Bib-
> lical obfuscations. . . .* And meaning gives way to
> glamour.[10]

J. M. Cohen believes that Victorian translation theory was founded on a fundamental error, but the case is rather that the pervasive Victorian diction for translation was frequently mis-applied. There are certain poems which *are* set "once upon a time." For them, Wardour Street English is a reasonable trans-lation diction. For instance, Dante Gabriel Rossetti (1828–1882), one of the most influential Victorian translators, used it successfully to translate "Dictes moi ou, n'en qu'el pays," by François Villon (1431–?). Rossetti's translation reads:

Ballad of Dead Ladies

Tell me now in what hidden way is
Lady Flora, the lovely Roman?
Where's Hipparchia, and where is Thais,

---

*Matthew Arnold is meant here. In *On Translating Homer* (1:165–66), he offered to the translator, whom he had advised "not to construct a special vocabulary," the King James Bible as an arbiter of acceptable words.

Neither of them the fairer woman?
Where is Echo, beheld of no man,
Only heard on river and mere,—
She whose beauty was more than human? . . .
But where are the snows of yester-year?

Where's Héloise, the learned nun,
For whose sake Abeillard, I ween,
Lost manhood and put priesthood on?
(From Love he won such dule and teen!)
And where, I pray you, is the Queen
Who willed that Buridan should steer
Sewed in a sack's mouth down the Seine? . . .
But where are the snows of yester-year?

White Queen Blanche, like a queen of lilies,
With a voice like any mermaiden,—
Bertha Broadfoot, Beatrice, Alice,
And Ermengarde the lady of Maine,—
And that good Joan whom Englishmen
At Rouen doomed and burned her there,—
Mother of God, where are they then? . . .
But where are the snows of yester-year?

Nay, never ask this week, fair lord,
Where they are gone, nor yet this year,
Save with this much for an overword,—
But where are the snows of yester-year?[11]
(*Rossetti's ellipses throughout*)

Rossetti's translation of this ballade succeeds because his language catches the mood of the Medieval French. Modern taste may jib at "dule and teen," but overall the sense of "once upon a time" is appropriate to an *ubi sunt* which places first-century Flora, twelfth-century Héloise, and fifteenth-century Joan of Arc on the same plane of pastness.

Thus, the problem is not that Wardour Street diction is never suitable, but that nearly all Victorian verse translation used it, whether suitable or not. (It is equally true that many modern American translations are put into a tough, contemporary idiom, whether it is suitable or not.) Rossetti had the discretion to translate only three of Villon's poems: "Dictes moi ou, n'en qu'el pays," "Morte, j'apelle de ta rigeur," and "Dame du ciel, regente terrienne."[12] All three poems lend themselves to Rossetti's preferred diction, and all three are atypical of the rest of Villon's Great Testament, which is primarily written in highly colloquial fifteenth-century Parisian French.

Lines 305–320 (Stanzas 39 and 40) of the Great Testament illustrate a side of Villon not amenable to Rossetti's diction:

> Je congnois que povres et riches,
> Sage et folz, prestres et lais,
> Nobles, villains, larges et chiches,
> Petiz et grans, et beaulx et laiz,
> Dames a rebrassez colletz,
> De quelconque condicion,
> Portans atours et bourreletz,
> Mort saisit san excepcion.
>
> Et meure Paris ou Helaine
> Quiconques meurt, meurt a douleur
> Telle qu'il pert vent et alaine;
> Son fiel se creve su son cuer,
> Puis sue, Dieu scet quelle sueur!
> Et n'est qui de ses maux l'alege:
> Car enfant n'a, frere ne seur,
> Qui lors voulsist estre son plege.[13]

(I know that poor and rich, wise and foolish, priests and laymen, noblemen, peasants, generous and stingy, short and tall, handsome and ugly, women in high-standing collars, whatever their station, wearing hennins or hoods,* Death seizes them without exception.

---

*Bonner (*Villon*, pp. 193–94) explains that high-standing collars were worn by noblewomen, but, judging by prohibitive ordinances, prostitutes copied the style. Hennins were also favored by noblewomen, while hoods were worn by bourgeoises.

Whether Paris dies or Helen, whoever dies dies in such
pain that he loses wind and breath, his spleen bursts on
his heart, then he sweats God knows what sweat, and no
one relieves his ills for there is no child, brother, or sister
who is willing to stand in for him.)

John Payne (1842–1916), whose translation of the works of
Villon first appeared in 1878, translates the above:

> I know full well that rich and poor,
>   Villein and noble, high and low,
> Laymen and clerks, gracious and dour,
>   Wise men and foolish, sweet of show
>   Or foul of favour, dames that go
> Ruffed and rebatoed, great or small,
>   High-tired or hooded, Death (I know)
> Without exception seizes all.
>
> Paris or Helen though one be,
>   Who dies, in pain and drearihead,
> For lack of breath and blood dies he,
>   His gall upon his heart is shed;
>   Then doth he sweat, God knows how dread
> A sweat, and none there is to allay
>   His ills, child, kinsman, in his stead,
> None will go bail for him that day.[14]

"Full well," "foul of favour," "drearihead," and "doth" all
come from the special Victorian vocabulary for translating
older poetry. Payne is not using it to show that Villon was
using a special archaic poetic jargon of Medieval French; Villon was not. Nor was Payne using a specific archaic diction to
place Villon's poem in a period of English history in some way
comparable to Villon's time. Payne was simply making sure
that Villon felt old to his Victorian readers.

When we turn to a Victorian translation of Horace, the
Roman poet of a time and ethos far from Villon's, we find the

same diction being used. The following translation of Horace's Ode 1. 11 is by Thomas Charles Baring (1831–1891):

Use Today, Forget Tomorrow

Ask not, 't is not right to know it,
What last end for thee and me
Heaven has set, nor Babylonian
Numbers try, Leuconöe.

Better, whate'er comes, to bear it;
Whether many winters more
We shall see, or this our last be,
Which along the Etruscan shore

Hurls the waves in spray to perish
On the shifting shingly beach.
If thou'rt wise thou'lt quaff, and quickly
Grasp the hopes within thy reach.

Even now, whilst we are talking,
Grudging time pursues his flight:
Use today, and trust as little
As thou mayst tomorrow's light.[15]

In these two translations, Villon and Horace are distinguishable from each other by the dissimilar content of the two poems. One would also expect a distinction to be made between the elegant language of the Roman and the earthier language of the Frenchman. Yet, Baring's Horace and Payne's Villon sound curiously alike. Worse, the distancing effect of Wardour Street diction dulls whatever urgency there is behind Horace's words and masks the starkness of Villon's vision. There is a false equation at work, namely: a great work is to be respected, and a respected work is to be translated into respectable language. J. M. Cohen complains that for many lesser Victorian translators

The more important the book in the cultural history of mankind, the more self-important the language in which it must be translated. Even "Don Quixote", which continually mocks at pomposities of verbiage and imagination, was subjected by its Victorian translators to a fatal process of verbal inflation.[16]

Humor is the first quality to fall victim to this disastrous form of respect. Jokes tend to evaporate in translation in any case, since they often rely on quirks of a particular language or on evanescent fashions and gossip. Creative translation can sometimes rescue linguistic and topical humor, but paraphrase robbed Victorians of that opportunity. The inflated language of poorer Victorian translators also felled a hardier type of humor: a sense of the ridiculous.

An example of such false respect can be found in the translations of Francis Hueffer (1845–1889). His book *The Troubadours* was a popular introduction to the themes and lyrics of the twelfth and thirteenth-century troubadours of Provence. Hueffer translates from a poem he incorrectly attributes to Folquet de Marseilles:

> Maybe I once was happy for a space,
> But joy and hope of love have passed away;
> No other good can make me blithe and gay,
> For all the world I hold in dire disdain.
> Of love the full truth let me now explain:
> I cannot leave it, nor yet on my way
> Pass back or forward, neither can I stay;
> Like one who mounts a tree mid-high, and fain
> Would mount still higher, or downward move apace,
> But fear and tremor bind him in his place.[17]

Hueffer comments:

> ... [The troubadours'] one almost incessant theme is love's disappointment. But this theme Folquet [sic] treats

like an artist. He avoids monotony by an ever new array of striking similes and allegories in which he clothes his longing. What, for instance, can indicate the hesitation of a timorous though passionate lover better than the image of a man who has reached the middle of a tree, and does not ascend further or regain the earth, for fear of losing his chance or his life? . . . [His poems] are full of sweetness.[18]

But surely the man is not so much in danger of losing his life as of breaking his leg? A lover treed like a kitten is *funny:*

> E s'ieu anc jorn fui gays ni amoros,
> Er non ai joy d'amor ni non l'esper;
> Ni autres bes nom pot al cor plazer,
> Ans mi semblan tug autre joy esmai.
> Pero d'amor lo ver vos en dirai:
> Nom lais del tot ni no m'en puesc mover
> Ni sus no vau, ni no puesc remaner;
> Aissi cum sel qu'en mieg de l'arbr'estai,
> Qu'es tan poiatz que non pot tornar jos
> Ni sus no vai, tan li par temeros.[19]

(If one day I was gay and love-filled, now I have neither joy of love nor hope: no other good things can please my heart, any other joy seems a bother. But about love I will tell you the truth: I don't leave off entirely, nor can I move away from it, nor go above, nor can I stay; thus, [I am] like a man who is stuck half-way up a tree, who has climbed so [high] that he can't back down and can't go up, both seem so scary.)

The poet does not "hold the world in dire disdain." He sees joy other than love as *esmai* 'a disturbance, a bother'. Hueffer shortchanges the unknown troubadour by a "process of verbal inflation," which takes *temeros* 'scary' and makes it over into "fear and tremor."

Pound, in his first attempt to reassess Provençal troubadours, assailed the pre-Raphaelites' diction, their historical
perspective, and their lack of humor. He bragged:

> . . . you will note that they [Pound's 1911 translations
> of Arnaut Daniel] are all free from what Morris and Ros-
> setti—and the smaragdite poets generally—have taught
> us to regard as mediaevalism. . . .
>   I do not mean to assail *plat ventre* the mediaevalism of
> the Victorian mediaevalists. Their mediaevalism was that
> . . . of magical ships and . . . Avalons . . . ; a very charm-
> ing mediaevalism if you like—I do more or less—but
> there is also the mediaevalism of mediaeval life as it was.
>   'Bona es vida
>   pos joia la mante,'
> brawls Arnaut in 'Can chai la fueilla.' 'Bully is living
> where joy can back it up.' This comes from a very real,
> very much alive young man who . . . will see no stags
> with crosses growing from their foreheads, he will not
> fly to an imprisoned lady in the form of a hawk; he will,
> I think, preserve through life a pleasing sense of humor.[20]

Unfortunately, the sort of translation on which Pound based
these claims reads:

> Only I know what over-anguish falls
> Upon the heart of love so over-borne,
> My over-longing that's so whole and strong
> Turns not from her, nay never since these eyes
> First saw her has the flame upon them quailed.
> And I, afar, speak to her words like flame,
> And near her, having much, there's nought for saying.[21]

Nay, the language of this over-longing heart has nought to
differentiate it from that of "the smaragdite poets generally."
Pound later confessed that in 1911 he had not begun to think
in any language other than Wardour Street.[22] The pull of this
language is so strong that many translators still write in it.

Pound did not work free of Wardour Street until the great translations of 1915–17. Most of the translations influenced by Pound's 1915–17 diction were not published until after 1950. By then, a new view of time, expressed by a new sort of diction, began to appear.

3

A New Vision of Time: Pound's Theory and Practice

Arnold Achieved:
The Past Seen from the Present

Pound's self-confessed failure in 1911, to present "medieval life as it really was," goaded him to search for a new translation diction and a new approach to historical perspective. The two major Victorian formulations held promise; their failure was only apparent, since neither had actually been tried.

Pound was attracted to both. On the one hand, Arnold's theory attracted him because he was eager to present the authors of the past as living men: "My job was to bring a dead man to life; to present a living figure,"[1] he wrote of his translation of Sextus Propertius. On the other hand, Newman's theories attracted the side of Pound which felt the gulf between modern and medieval sensibilities: " . . . the Provençal feeling is archaic, we are ages away from it."[2] These contradictory tendencies drove Pound in different directions at different times. Some of his translations favored Arnold's theory, some Newman's, and some were an amalgam of the two.

In 1914 Pound worked on a group of translations which he made into an almost pure realization of Arnold's theory. *Cathay,* published in 1915, contained fifteen translations from Chinese poetry, mostly of the eighth century A.D. Pound did not then know Chinese, although he later learned it. His translations were based on the notes of Ernest Fenellosa, an American who had studied Chinese poetry in Japan. Thus, Pound was working with a language whose sounds were unfamiliar to him, whose grammar had developed differently from that of Indo-European languages, and from which the extant body of translation was (and is) small. Perhaps for all these reasons, Pound was able to free himself of the almost conditioned response of psuedo-archaic diction for translation, which was until then as characteristic of him as of the rest of the Edwardian poets.[3] *Cathay*'s free verse is written in a restrained, unobstrusively modern English diction.

One of the most often cited poems in *Cathay,* "The River-Merchant's Wife: A Letter," illustrates the complete contrast between *Cathay* and Victorian or Edwardian translations:

While my hair was still cut straight across my forehead
I played about the front gate, pulling flowers.
You came by on bamboo stilts, playing horse,
You walked about my seat, playing with blue plums.
And we went on living in the village of Chōkan:
Two small people, without dislike or suspicion.

At fourteen I married My Lord you.
I never laughed, being bashful.
Lowering my head, I looked at the wall.
Called to, a thousand times, I never looked back.

At fifteen I stopped scowling,
I desired my dust to be mingled with yours
Forever and forever and forever.
Why should I climb the look out?

At sixteen you departed,
You went into far Ku-tō-en, by the river of swirling
    eddies,
And you have been gone five months.
The monkeys make sorrowful noise overhead.
You dragged your feet when you went out.

By the gate now, the moss is grown, the different
    mosses,
Too deep to clear them away!
The leaves fall early this autumn, in wind.
The paired butterflies are already yellow with August
Over the grass in the West garden;
They hurt me. I grow older.
If you are coming down through the narrows of the
    river Kiang,
Please let me know beforehand,
And I will come out to meet you
            As far as Chō-fū-Sa.

                    By Rihaku (Li T'ai Po)
                    8th Century A.D.[4]

While the diction is modern and English, the details are
ancient and Chinese. "While my hair was still cut straight
across my forehead," the poem opens, and gradually one infers
from the poem that this hairstyle is customary for young girl-
children in this society. There are bamboo stilts, foreign place
names, and monkeys. These details accumulate to limn a
Chinese setting. Pound also suggests subtly the antiquity of
the setting. Wai-Lim Yip notes:

One word . . . (妾) (literally, concubine, a humble term
used by women or wives when speaking of themselves)
and [a later word] . . . (君) (lord, you) reflect the two levels of formality in the forms of address between husbands
and wives that were commonly maintained at that time
(the eighth century). Pound, without overdoing it,
retains this flavor in the line . . .
    At fourteen I married My Lord you.[5]

The language of *Cathay* gets out of the reader's way. No
psuedo-archaic dialect intervenes with its own insistent
strangeness between reader and event. The reader is freed to
consider the foreign quality of the original in terms of con-

crete details. The past delineated is positioned firmly in a specific time and place. However, the modern diction of *Cathay*
also intentionally dates the era of English when the translation
was written. Victorian translations are, of course, labeled Victorian by their diction, but this is the judgment of a later time.
The intention of the Victorian translators was to set the whole
poem, language and content, in the far-off past. Pound's perspective in *Cathay* is of the past viewed from the present.

Poets searching for a corrective to Wardour Street English
found in *Cathay* the first sustained counterexample. Yet
Pound, having achieved this revolution, never used the diction
of *Cathay* in translation again. At heart, Pound was a convinced follower of Newman, imbued with a sense of the won-
drous otherness of the past. He said:

> We appear to have lost the radiant world where one
> thought cuts through another with clean edge, a world
> of moving energies . . . that border the visible, the matter
> of Dante's *paradiso*. . . .[6]

After *Cathay,* Pound translated in a number of dictions, all of
which, at least in part, owe their genesis to Newman's theory.

Newman Attempted:
The Poem as an Artifact of the Past

Pound's debt to Newman is revealed in his 1931 translation
of "Chi è questa che vien, ch'ogni uom la mira," Sonetto 7 of
Guido Cavalcanti (1250–1300). Pound deliberately used an
archaic dialect, saying:

> There is no question of giving Guido in an English
> contemporary to himself, the ultimate Britons were at
> the date unbreeched, painted in woad, and grunting in an
> idiom far more difficult for us to master than the Langue
> d'Oc of the Plantagenets or the Lingua di Si.

If, however, we reach back to pre-Elizabethan English,
. . . [we find] a period when the writers were still intent
on clarity and explicitness, still preferring them to mag-
niloquence and the thundering phrase. . . .[7]

Pound used "pre-Elizabethan English," that is, the archaic dialect of the Tudor poet Sir Thomas Wyatt, because he felt that
Wyatt's language faithfully represented the differences
between Cavalcanti's love ethic and the modern one. The
result reads:

> Who is she that comes, makyng turn every man's eye
> And makyng the air to tremble with a bright
>   clearenesse
> That leadeth with her Love, in such nearness
> No man may proffer of speech more than a sigh?
>
> Ah God, what she is like when her owne eye turneth, is
> Fit for Amor to speake, for I can not at all;
> Such is her modesty, I would call
> Every woman else but an useless uneasiness.
>
> No one could ever tell all of her pleasauntness
> In that every high noble vertu leaneth to herward,
> So Beauty sheweth her forth as her Godhede;
>
> Never before was our mind so high led,
> Nor have we so much of heal as will afford
> That our mind may take her immediate in its embrace.[8]

The lines are odd in precisely the way Newman called for,
drawing attention to the peculiarities of the original, and imitating the foreignness of Cavalcanti's notion. For instance, "So
Beauty sheweth her forth as her Godhede" draws attention to
the meaning of *E la beltate per sua Dea la mostra,* which to
Pound meant: "'Beauty displays her for her goddess.' That is
to say, as the spirit of God became incarnate in Christ, so is
the spirit of the eternal beauty made flesh amongst us in her."[9]

However, Pound noted:

> The objections to such a method are: the doubt as to
> whether one has the right to take a serious poem and turn
> it into a mere exercise in quaintness; the 'misrepresenta-
> tion' not of the poem's antiquity, but of the proportion-
> ate feel of that antiquity, by which I mean that Guido's
> thirteenth-century language is to twentieth-century Ital-
> ian sense much less archaic than any fourteenth-, fif-
> teenth-, or early sixteenth-century English is for us. . . .
> [Since] the fervour of the original . . . simply does not
> occur in English poetry in those centuries there is no
> ready-made verbal pigment for its objectification.[10]

The effect may be quaint, but it is not Victorian. Pound
knew what a Victorian translation of "Chi è questa che vien"
would sound like. He had made one himself twenty years
earlier:

> Who is she coming, drawing all men's gaze,
> Who makes the air one trembling clarity
> Till none can speak but each sighs piteously
> Where she leads Love adown her trodden ways? . . .[11]

Stuart Y. McDougal comments that the kind of archaism used
in the newer version, "while a little recherché," strikes the ear
freshly; the reader can "actively respond" to it, as he cannot
to the earlier pseudo-archaisms.[12]

Pound objected to more than the quaintness of "Who is she
that comes, makyng." If no one period of English possesses
the "verbal pigment" which exemplifies the Weltanschauung
of an original poem, all periods of English may be equally
unable to capture its viewpoint. In some ways, "Who is she
that comes, makyng" did not go far enough with Newman's
theories to suit Pound; it did not discriminate enough between
the various levels of antiquity in the poem.

Logopoeia: Newman Renewed

In order to distinguish between levels of antiquity and differences of culture Pound invented a new way of using English, which he called logopoeia. In a 1929 essay, "How to Read," Pound defined logopoeia as:

> . . . 'the dance of the intellect among words', that is to say it employs words not only for their direct meaning, but it takes count in a special way of habits of usage, of the context we *expect* to find with the word, its usual concomitants, of its known acceptances, and of ironical play. It holds the aesthetic content which is peculiarly the domain of verbal manifestation, and cannot possibly be contained in plastic or music. It is the latest come, and perhaps most tricky and undependable mode.[13]

Pound's definition has provoked a predictably large body of commentary. J. P. Sullivan gives a common view when he calls logopoeia

> . . . a refined mode of irony which shows itself in certain delicate linguistic ways, in a sensitivity to how language is used in other contexts, and in a deployment of these other uses for its own humorous or satiric or poetic aims, to produce an effect directly contrary to their effects in usual contexts. Thus magniloquence can be deployed *against* magniloquence, vulgarity *against* vulgarity, and poeticisms *against* poeticizing. *Logopoeia* is not simply parody, for it may be directed against the poet himself, but a very self-conscious use of words and tone which would be requisite for parody.[14]

However, if logopoeia were only a refined mode of irony, expressed by linguistic means, the existing terms parody, irony, and satire ought to suffice. A discussion limited to those elements of parody, satire, and irony which depend on linguistic manifestations might be of interest, but it would hardly

be revolutionary. Further on in "How to Read," Pound
remarked:

> Unless I am right in discovering *logopoeia* in Propertius
> . . . , we must almost say that Laforgue invented *logopoeia*
> observing that there had been a very limited range of
> *logopoeia* in all satire. . . .[15]

This suggests that Pound meant more by logopoeia than linguistic parody or irony or satire, none of which could be said
to be the property of Laforgue and Propertius alone. Pound's
comments imply that he had in mind the whole range of the
interplay of connotation and context. Pound's particular addition to the poetic repertoire was the deliberate manipulation
of the historical aspects of connotation. Pound discovered that
by juxtaposing words with different historical associations,
words from dictions of different times, or words closely associated with certain literary forms, he could summon to mind
their cultural contexts. He could also juxtapose literary forms
themselves to summon up their historical associations in the
same manner. Thus, for one poem, he could go to various
periods of English culture to pick out the associations he
wanted. Without making the denotations of his words
become historical footnotes to his translation, he could use the
connotations to imply the interrelations between the past and
present.

Both Donald Davie and Hugh Kenner have demonstrated
how Pound juxtaposes words and styles with different histories,[16] although neither of them has applied the term logopoeia
to their discoveries; Davie, in fact, rejects it.[17] But Davie's brilliant analysis of a poem in Pound's translation of the Confucian Odes[18] is an analysis of logopoeia in the sense defined
here.

The Odes in *The Classic Anthology as Defined by Confucius* are
translated from ancient Chinese. Although Pound did not
know Chinese when he translated *Cathay*, by the time he
translated *The Classic Anthology*, he had long been a student of
the language. Poem 246 in the Greater Odes section is titled

"Festal." Davie locates its source, or color, as coming from the English and Scottish folk-verse tradition; "The very first line, for instance, echoes a folk-composition reworked memorably by Burns."[19] Davie adds:

> Of the many traditional poems in English that this version depends upon our half-remembering, what may come to mind first is the famous "Back and side go bare, go bare":

> > I can not eate, but lytle meate
> >   my stomach is not good;
> > But sure I thinke, that I can drynke
> >   with him that weares a hood.
> > Thoughe I go bare, take ye no care,
> >   I am nothinge a cold:
> > I stuff my skyn so full within
> >   of ioly good Ale and olde
> >   Backe and syde go bare, go bare,
> >   booth foote and hand go colde;
> >   But Bellye god send the good ale inoughe,
> >   whether it be new or olde.[20]

Davie notes that four poems later, Pound is drawing on the rhythms and internal rhymes of Robert Browning's "Cavalier Tunes."[21] Pound, to make his points, is using the whole range of the English poetic tradition as bases of comparison for the Greater Odes.

"Festal" itself reads:

> Tough grow the rushes, oh!
> No passing kine break down
> their clumpy wads, and blades so glossy growin'.
> Our brothers will be here at call
> assembled as to rule
> wherefore lay down the mat, the mat
> and bring the old man his stool.

2

Put a soft straw mat on a bamboo mat
let lackeys bring in the stools,
toast against toast, wine against wine
observant of all the rules,
Then rinse the cups and bring catsups
with pickles, roast and grill,
trype and mince-meat and while drums beat
let singers show their skill.

3

The trusty bows are tough, my lads,
each arrow-point true to weight
and every shot hits plumb the spot
as our archer lines stand straight.
They shoot again and four points go in
as if they were planting trees,
For a tough wood bow and the archers row
attest the gentilities.

4

An heir to his line is lord of this wine
and the wine rich on the tongue.
But by the great peck-measure, pray in your leisure
that when you're no longer young
Your back retain strength to susteyne
and aid you kin and clan.
Luck to your age! and, by this presage,
joy in a long life-span.[22]

Davie shows how Pound, in his translation of "Festal," has
learned to indicate where the original Chinese poem is comparable to the English poetic traditions Pound is using to
translate it, and where it is different. He says that the point of
making the comparison of "Festal" to "Back and side go
bare,"

... and of the poet's inviting it, is not just that we may
see what tradition the poem is in, and what conventions

it observes; but also that we may see where it diverges from that tradition. For, in proportion as the traditional norm is established firmly, to just that extent do the departures from it stand out as intentional and significant.[23]

Davie points out that with details such as the spelling of "susteyne," Pound invites comparison of "Festal" with the poetry of sixteenth-century English poets.[24] Yet, at certain points, Pound challenges his own comparison. For instance, after the rhythm of "Back and side go bare" has been strongly set up in the reader's mind, Pound substitutes "each arrow-point true to weight" for the more expectable "each arrow-point weighs true."[25] This departure

> . . . jar[s] the reader into attending to what is said. For, if the traditional meter is established so insistently only to be rudely disrupted at crucial points, so the traditional sentiments are invoked only to throw into relief the places where the Chinese sentiments go beyond the tradition. . . . To look again at the sixteenth-century poem is to see very clearly where in the Chinese this stubborn novelty is. . . . it comes to a head in "attest the gentilities": what is novel and non-Western and therefore especially valuable about this drinking chorus is that in it drinking, and the rural sports which go with drinking, are seen in a peculiarly strict and insistent way as decorous, even ceremonial. "Assembled as to rule," "observant of all the rules"— . . . taken up in "attest the gentilities," . . . are then seen to be the backbone of the poem.[26]

Davie concludes that Pound's archaisms are thus not a simple matching of a certain English period with a certain Chinese period:

> . . . we seem required or invited to distinguish . . . precisely what period out of the long past of English history

is being alluded to—and this so as to suggest that in just
that period English approximated most nearly to such
and such a Chinese perception, or cluster of
perceptions.[27]

The Greater Odes section of *The Classic Anthology as Defined
by Confucius* (1954) attempts much more than did the 1931
"Chi è questa che vien." The Cavalcanti sonnet was translated
into a single archaic diction. "Festal" and the other poems in
the Greater Odes bring together many dictions: folk-ballads,
Robert Burns, Ben Jonson, Robert Browning, and many other
periods and voices.[28] These poems are written in what might
be called the archaic collage. Because each echo of a historical
genre or specific poem is made with a point in mind, the
poems in the Greater Odes do not degenerate into pseudo-dia-
lect. Instead, the translation both realizes Newman's expressed
goals and is modern, because these historical echoes could
have been assembled only at the time when the translation was
made. As Hugh Kenner reports:

> . . . if, as Wyndham Lewis once put it, whole landslides
> from other times and tongues are coming into his
> [Pound's] pages, it is into the twentieth century that they
> are sliding, at the bidding of a twentieth-century poet.[29]

A More Complex Vision of Time

Although the archaic collage went far towards realizing
Pound's ambition to distinguish differing shades of antiquity,
the technique did not allow him to express the entire complex
of motives which drove him to translate from older literatures.
Pound discussed these motives in 1918:

> My pawing over the ancients and semi-ancients has
> been one struggle to find out what has been done, once
> for all, better than it can ever be done again, and to find

out what remains for us to do, and plenty does remain, for if we still feel the same emotions as those which launched the thousand ships, it is quite certain that we come on these feelings differently. . . . No good poetry is ever written in a manner twenty years old, for to write in such a manner shows conclusively that the writer thinks from books, . . . and not from life, yet a man feeling the divorce of life and his art may naturally try to resurrect a forgotten mode if he finds in that mode . . . some element lacking in contemporary art which might unite that art again to its sustenance, life.[30]

Thus, Pound was also interested in the eternal verities of human emotion and in the curative effects the imitation of ancient literature could have on modern writing. Distinguishing the past from the present, however meticulously, will not in itself urge the relevance of the past. In order to express the relevance of a poem to modern concerns, while still respecting the gap between past and present, Pound was driven to create a synthesis of the two Victorian translation theories, and consequently a new historical perspective for translation.

Pound's friend, T. S. Eliot, was the first person to express the new theory. In an essay excoriating Gilbert Murray's translation of Euripides' *Medea,** Eliot called for a new kind of translator:

We need a digestion which can assimilate both Homer and Flaubert. . . . We need an eye which can see the past in its place with its definite differences from the present, and yet so lively that it shall be as present to us as the present.[31]

In some ways, this prescription of Eliot's is an application of a belief which Eliot had expressed in an earlier essay, "Tradition

---

*"As a poet, Mr. Murray is merely a very insignificant follower of the pre-Raphaelite movement," wrote Eliot in "Euripides and Professor Murray," *Selected Essays,* p. 40.

and the Individual Talent." There he said:

> . . . the historical sense involves a perception, not only of
> the pastness of the past, but of its presence: the historical
> sense compels a man to write not merely with his own
> generation in his bones, but with a feeling that the whole
> of the literature of Europe from Homer and within it the
> whole of the literature of his own country has a simul-
> taneous existence and composes a simultaneous order.[32]

These formulations have wide-ranging implications. Most
pertinent to the issue at hand are those regarding the relationship of the present to the past. According to Eliot, the present
has developed from the past, and not merely followed it. That
course of development can be studied, can become knowledge
in a mind. Through memory, the mind can view the past and
present simultaneously, can make its knowledge of the past a
force in its present: all time is simultaneous in thought.

Pound would add that development from past to present has
not been a linear progression from more ancient ideas to more
modern ones. In a letter commenting on his translations in
Quia Pauper Amavi of 1919, he wrote:

> . . . the Latin is really "modern." We are just getting
> back to a Roman state of civilization, or in reach of it;
> whereas the Provençal feeling is archaic, we are ages
> away from it.[33]

In this view, cultures are ancient or modern not as a consequence of their linear distance in time, but as a consequence
of their social organization and dominant ideas. Taking the
concept further, some aspects of a given culture may feel modern, or rather, compatible with a modern world view, while
other aspects of the same culture may feel archaic. This vision
of the shape of history might be represented, not by a straight
line, but by some sort of irregular, self-intersecting spiral.

Since past and present co-exist in the mind, it can be a legit-
imate poetic endeavor to present them simultaneously. This is
the notion behind the painting style of Cubism: the full face
and profile, the past and present pose co-exist on the canvas.[34]
However, the problem for the poet or translator is different
from the problem for the painter. Since a poem is itself read
over time, the poet cannot make a simultaneous or superim-
posed presentation, as the painter can. T. S. Eliot's own technique as a poet juxtaposed the events of the past and the present, allowing the mind of the reader to make the
superposition. This is the technique of *The Wasteland.* A translator, however, is bound to the events specified in the poem
he is translating. If he wishes to compare past and present
viewpoints, he may find himself in the awkward position of
embedding his translation within a discussion of the translation.* Pound used logopoeia to avoid this.

The Synthesis: Arnold Infused

The language of Pound's Confucian Odes is modern in the
sense that its collage of earlier styles is assembled from the
vantage point of the twentieth century; its language is not
modern in the sense of having been derived from the natural
language of twentieth-century speakers. The language Pound
used in his earlier translation of Sextus Propertius is modern
in the second sense. But, unlike the language of *Cathay,* the
modernity of diction in the *Homage to Sextus Propertius* is not
unobtrusive. In places it is highly coloquial, verging on slang.
In other places, it is insistently polysyllabic. There is also an
undercurrent of older strategies of language. The diction of
the *Homage,* modern as it is, performs the same logopoetic
functions as do the older dictions used to translate the Confucian Odes.

To elucidate, the following excerpt is from the first section

---

*In *The Cantos,* Pound often does offer scraps of translation surrounded by discussion.

of the *Homage:*

> Though my house is not propped up by Taenarian
>   columns
>   from Laconia (associated with Neptune and
>   Cerberus),
> Though it is not stretched upon gilded beams;
> My orchards do not lie level and wide
>   as the forests of Phaeacia
>   the luxurious and Ionian,
> Nor are my caverns stuffed stiff with a Marcian vintage,
> My cellar does not date from Numa Pompilius,
> Nor bristle with wine jars,
> Nor is it equipped with a frigidaire patent;
> Yet the companions of the Muses
>   will keep their collective nose in my books,
> And weary with historical data, they will turn to my
>   dance tune.[35]

In *The Pound Era,* Hugh Kenner analyzes the new historical perspective of the above passage:

> Something has happened. . . . There is no "point of view" that will relate these idioms: neither a modern voice ("bristle"; "frigidaire patent"; "collective nose") nor an ancient one ("Phaeacia"; "Marcian") can be assigned this long sentence; moreover "Laconia" has acquired what looks like a *sotto voce* footnote, while the modernisms ("frigidaire," "data") sound plausibly Latin. In transparent overlay, two times have become as one, and we are meant to be equally aware of both dictions (and yet they seem the same diction).[36]

Kenner is highlighting a triumph of logopoeia. *Homage to Sextus Propertius* is the synthesis of Newman's and Arnold's theories.

The great difference between Pound's historical perspective

and the Victorian can best be seen by directly comparing
Pound's translation of Propertius with a Victorian example.
Before Pound's translation, Propertius was not well known.[37]
The following translation by Sir Charles Elton (1778–1853),
of part of the opening of Elegy 2. 3, is typical of the little
available before the publication of Pound's *Homage:*

> 'Twas not her face, though fair, that caught my sight;
>   Less fair the lily's bell: as Scythian snows
> Should blend with Ebro's red their virgin white,
>   Or in pure cream as floats the scatter'd rose:
>
> Not tresses, that enring'd in crisped twine,
>   Flow loose with their accustom'd careless art
> Down her smooth marble neck; nor eyes that shine,
>   Torches of passion; load-stars of my heart:
>
> Not that through silken folds of Araby
>   The nymph's fine limbs with lucid motion gleam;
>   (For no ideal beauties heaves my sigh;
>   Nor airy nothings prompt my amorous dream:)
>
> Not so all charms, as when aside she lays
>   The mantling cup, and glides before my view;
> Graceful as Ariadne through the maze
>   Of choral dance with Bacchic revelers flew:
>
> Or when inspired by Aganippe's stream,
>   O'er Sappho's lyre with sportive touch she strays;
> And challenges Corinna's ancient theme
>   And coldly listens to Erinne's lays.[38]

Elton places Propertius in the distant past by means of several devices, two of which may simply be the result of translating by paraphrase. Elton uses polysyndeton, a grammatical
device favored in classical poetry, but generally used only spar-
ingly in English because certain grammatical relations which
remain clear in Latin become confused in English. Indeed, this
mishap overtakes Elton: his readers may fail to recognize "as
when" as the goal of that long chain of "nor's" and "not's."

Elton retains all of the proper names studding the elegy. His translation does not consider whether Corinna and Erinne are familiar to his audience nor whether they were familiar to Propertius's audience. These ladies, duly included in Elton's paraphrase, become undiscriminated classical decoration.

Finally, Elton takes plain statement in the Latin and elaborates on it until he feels it is suitably monumental; for instance, *de more comae per levia colla fluentes* 'as usual her hair flowing over her smooth neck' becomes "tresses that enring'd in crisped twine, / Flow loose with their accustomed careless art / Down her smooth marble neck." While the invincible humorlessness of some Victorian translators is not the topic here, I can not help remarking that it is a pity Elton turned *non sum de nihilo blandus amator* 'I am not a flattering lover for nothing' into "Nor airy nothings prompt my amorous dream."

Since Elton and Pound did not translate the same elegies, no direct comparison is possible. However, Pound translated Elegy 2. 1, in which Propertius had vowed to write the praises of Cynthia found in Elton's translation. Pound wrote:

> Yet you ask on what account I write so many love-
>   lyrics
> And whence this soft book comes into my mouth.
> Neither Calliope nor Apollo sung these things into my
>   ear,
>   My genius is no more than a girl.
>
> If she with ivory fingers drive a tune through the lyre,
>   We look at the process.
> How easy the moving fingers; if hair is mussed on her
>   forehead, . . .
> There are new jobs for the author,
> And if she plays with me with her shirt off,
>   We shall construct many Iliads.
> And whatever she does or says
>   We shall spin long yarns out of nothing.[39]

Elements in Propertius which Pound felt to be intractably Roman are represented in this translation. There is a grammatical apparatus of some formality, although nowhere approaching the convolution of Elton's. There are the Roman embellishments "soft book" and "ivory fingers," literally translated from the Latin. Also, there is the "we" of "we look at the process"—Pound's translation of *miramur arte.* "We" is a common substitute for "I" in Latin, but not in English, unless it is an editorial "we" expressing artistic judgment. Pound is invoking both these connotations, making this "we" expressive of both an ancient diction and a modern. In fact, what primarily strikes the reader who has turned from Elton's efforts to Pound's are the modern elements in the *Homage.* There are a number of colloquialisms, which verge on slang. Contemporary phrases are the most visibly modern elements in a poem because they are, by their nature, tagged current. Here Pound uses "new jobs," "mussed hair," and "spin yarns." "Shirts" should be added to the list of modernisms, not because they are colloquial, but because they are anachronisms in tunic and toga-wearing Rome. The free verse of the *Homage,* written at a time when free verse was still new and controversial, also creates an overall sensation of modernity.

Pound's translation from Sextus Propertius is written in two dictions; one modern, one ancient, which create a complex historical perspective by commenting on each other.

4

Pound's Influence on Historical Perspective

The main result of Pound's endeavors has been Arnold *redivivus,* not Newman. The current revolution in historical perspective stems mostly from *Cathay* and from the modern diction in the *Homage to Sextus Propertius.* With one important exception, translators influenced by Pound tend to be colloquial and up-to-date, ignoring Pound's frequent recourse to a ground bass of older dictions. They employ a variety of strategies to cope with the differences between past and present.

The Past Made Present

A substantial number of modern translators choose a historical perspective which downplays cultural differences. These poets have been influenced by Pound's ability to make the poetry of the past seem alive in the present, almost contemporary in nature.

A good example of this trend is Robert Fitzgerald's translation of Horace's Ode 1. 25. Fitzgerald shuns archaic and pseudo-archaic diction. He even makes a gesture toward the

colloquial: "Oh, Lydia, I'm dying for you!" Fitzgerald
translates:

> The young men come less often—isn't it so?
> To rap at midnight on your fastened window;
> Much less often. How do you sleep these days?
>
> There was a time when your door gave with
>   proficiency
> On easy hinges; now it seems apter at being shut.
> I do not think you hear many lovers moaning
>
> "Lydia, how can you sleep?
> "Lydia, the night is so long!
> "Oh, Lydia, I'm dying for you!"
>
> No. The time is coming when you will moan
> And cry to scornful men from an alley corner
> In the dark of the moon when the wind's in a passion,
>
> With lust that would drive a mare wild
> Raging in your ulcerous old viscera.
> You'll be alone and burning then
>
> To think how happy boys take their delight
> In the tender buds, the blush of myrtle
> Consigning dry leaves to the winter sea.[1]

The original ode reads:

> Parcius iunctas quatiunt fenestras
> iactibus crebris iuvenes protervi
> nec tibi somnos adimunt, amatque
>   ianua limen,
> quae prius multum facilis movebat
> cardines; audis minus et minus iam
> 'me tuo longas pereunte noctes,
>   Lydia, dormis?'
> invicem moechos anus arrogantis
> flebis in solo levis angiportu,

Thracio bacchante magis sub inter-
    lunia vento,
cum tibi flagrans amor et libido,
quae solet matres furiare equorum,
saeviet circa iecur ulcerosum,
    non sine questu,
laeta quod pubes hedera virenti
gaudeat pulla magis atque myrto,
aridas frondis hiemis sodali
    dedicet Euro.[2]

Fitzgerald's translation, except for a hint toward the end, almost makes the ode seem the production of a contemporary poet. The original poem abounds in Roman details which Fitzgerald has suppressed. *Thracio bacchante* 'the Thracian wind raging like a devotee of Bacchus', is not alluded to, but its function is explained by "when the wind's in a passion." *Sub interlunia* 'under the changes of the moon', with its hint of menopause, becomes "the dark of the moon." The cankered liver, *iecur ulcerosum*, the Roman seat of passions, becomes "ulcerous old viscera," and Eurus, the cold southeast wind from off the sea, is changed, by a process of association, to "the winter sea." Only in the last verse does Fitzgerald intentionally allow a Roman image to slip through: "the blush of myrtle." Myrtle, in contemporary usage, is not associated with youth or love, although the *Shorter Oxford English Dictionary* (1965) asserts that "myrtle was held sacred to Venus and is used as an emblem of love." Thus, while "the blush of myrtle" fits in well enough with the diction of the rest of the poem, the slight strangeness of the image brings with it a hint of an older heritage. Even so, the translation as a whole has been firmly transferred to the ambience of the translator's century, in a way almost never seen in Victorian translation.

John Warden is another poet whose translations tend to emphasize the contemporary affinities of his originals. His book *The Poems of Propertius* appeared in 1972. Warden's translation of the opening Elegy 2. 1 is convenient to compare with

Pound's translation of it quoted earlier. Warden writes:

> Question:
> where are they from, these songs that crowd my pages
>   and make their yielding way to the lips of men?
> I am the mouthpiece of no muse or god:
> SHE
> is the whole of my inspiration
> Dress her in shimmering silk and make her walk—
>   and that's the stuff of a whole volume;
> or say I see her with her hair down, tumbling all over
>   her brow:
>   I write a hymn to hair, and she's happy as a queen.
> If she strikes music from the lyre with delicate
>   fingertips,
>   I sing my wonder for her casual art;
> or when those eyes of hers droop at sleep's prompting,
>   why there's a thousand brand new themes for
>   poetry.
> Naked
>   (I've stripped her of her cloak)
>   and locked with me in
>   single combat
>   Oh whole epics were written for less.
> It doesn't matter what she does or what she says
>   each trivial incident begets
>   a mighty saga.[3]

Warden does not completely transfer the events into the twentieth century. Cynthia plays the lyre, not the guitar, and a muse and a god are lurking in the background. On the other hand, the muse and the god are not named. Not one Roman proper noun from the original is included in this passage: the *Iliad*, Calliope, Apollo, and the island of Cos are excised. Peculiarly Roman turns of phrase, "ivory fingers" and "soft book," have given way to "delicate fingers" and "songs that make their yielding way." Also, Warden's grammar is less formal than the Roman: he uses "there's" for "there are" and leaves totally unexpressed the connection between "naked" and "oh whole epics were written for less." Such informality of grammar is usually associated with the writing of this century. Not one archaic word or word order is to be found in this passage. The whole emphasis is on the similarities of lovers' raptures in any century. By toning down all the Roman phraseology and nomenclature, and by writing in a strictly modern style, Warden has greatly emphasized the modernity—or, possibly, the timelessness—of the poet's emotion.

John Frederick Nims, another translator whose emphasis is on the modern, does not abolish the names of the gods from Horace's Ode 2. 8. Rather, he tries to compare Horace's use of them to contemporary uses of the Deity's name. In this, he is following a hint from Pound, who once rendered *per magnum salva puella Jovem* as "Great Zeus, save the woman,"[4] which, hanging nicely between prayer-word and swear-word, has the unmistakable ring of "Good God!" Nims translates:

If for all the promises you regard so lightly
One, *one* penalty ever held, Varina,
Should one tooth darken, even a torn toenail
        Leave you less smooth, dear,
Yes, I'd trust you. But when you avow with
"God strike me dead!" and falsify it, Lord you're
Lovelier yet as you parade! The whole male
        Populace wants you.
You swear by your poor mother's corpse and
Right away two-time; swear by every sign, by
Heaven itself, and by the very gods, those
        Durable persons.
This, I assume, amuses even Venus,
Amuses nymphs (good simple souls) and hardened
Cupid, forever honing up hot steel on
        His bloody whetstone.
What's more, all the adolescents love you;
Droves of new callers come; their predecessors
Never stamp from the house of the proud lady
        Much as they vow to.

Mothers worry for their husky youngsters;
Dads for bank-accounts; nice girls at the altar
(Poor things!) brood, for fear they'll soon be groaning
  "Where is that husband?"[5]

Nims sets the tone with modern vocabulary containing elements of the colloquial: "two-time," "nice girls," "husky
youngsters"; "bank-accounts" is an amusing anachronism.
"God strike me dead!" and "Lord you're lovelier yet" are not
foreign to a monotheistic culture. Yet these phrases lead to the
polytheistic "swear by the gods, those / Durable persons." By
gentle degrees, Nims has led the reader from the Judaeo-
Christian tradition to the Roman pantheon. He shows how
the same casual attitude towards religion informs both "by
Apollo" and "cross my heart."
    "Durable persons" is a phrase only lightly suggested to
Nims by the Latin: *fallere . . . divos morte carentes*[6] 'to lie to the
deathless gods'. "Durable" humorously suggests that the dei-
ties have survived an excessive number of oaths. By calling the
simplices nymphae "good simple souls," Nims makes them into
more than the Roman-sounding decoration of a Victorian
translator. Nims intimates that the nymphs are not too bright,
but even they can see the joke. Finally, "hardened Cupid" for
ferus Cupido is an inspired epithet, because it at once summons
to mind the physical concomitants of sexual attraction and re-
invests Cupid with the semi-comic malevolence ascribed to
him by the Romans. Nims makes Horace's attitude towards
the gods seem comprehensible and modern.
    W. S. Merwin performs a similar office for the place names
studding Catullus 11. He translates:

Furius and Aurelius, bound to Catullus
Though he penetrate to the ends of the Indies
Where the eastern ocean crashing in echoes
    Pours up the shore,

Or into Hyrcania, soft Arabia,
Among the Tartars or the archers of Parthia,

Or where the Nile current, seven times the same,
    Colors the waters,

Or through the beetling Alps, by steep passes, should
  come
To look on the monuments of great Caesar,
Gaul, the Rhine, and at the world's bitter end
    The gruesome Britons,

Friends, both prepared to share with me all these
Or what else the will of heaven may send,
To my mistress take these few sentiments,
    Put none too nicely:

Let her spread for her lechers and get her pleasure,
Lying wide to three hundred in one heat,
Loving none truly, but leaving them every one
    Wrung out and dropping;

But as for my love, let her not count on it
As once she could: by her own fault it died
As a flower at the edge of a field, which the plow
    Roots out in passing.[7]

Catullus used all those place names, with their associations
of distant dangers, in order to make an ironic comparison to
the dangers of the actual service to be performed: delivery of
a poison-pen letter to Lesbia. The place names were not meant
to have specific associations for the Roman audience, but to
evoke faraway places with strange-sounding names. James
Cranstoun, a Victorian translator, saw only the strangeness.
His Furius and Aurelius would

    . . . cross the lofty Alpine fells, to view
        Great Caesar's trophied fields, the Gallic Rhine,
    The paint-smeared Briton race, grim-visaged crew,
        Placed by the earth's limit line. . . .[8]

Merwin sees the touches of irony: the *transaltas Alpes* are the
"beyond-being-tall Alps"; *septemgeminus Nilus* is something to
the effect of "Nile-fathered septuplets," or "the Nile in sep-

tuplicate"; and the *horribilesque ultimosque Britannos* are as much the "utterly frightful Britons" as they are "the most distant and fearsome." By a few well-chosen adjectives, Merwin makes it understood that all the distant place names are being used to an ironic purpose. His phrases "beetling Alps," "gruesome Britons," and "world's bitter end" build to the final irony of "take these few sentiments / Put none too nicely." Since Merwin has made it clear from the beginning that Catullus intended the place names to be strange to his Roman audience, the modern reader can accept the list in the same spirit as a modern equivalent, as if the poet had said "sail to Zanzibar, Tasmania, or the Kuril Isles." Yet, the same Roman names in the Victorian translation achieve Cranstoun's purpose of creating a perspective of the distant past.

Merwin's practice springs from Pound's but is different from it. Pound said that "my house is not propped up by Taenarian columns."[9] "Taenarian" and "propped up" clash, so that one is reminded that the *Homage* is the modern translation of an old poem. "The gruesome Britons" and "beetling Alps" do not set up contrasts in time, but seem to be from one contemporary diction into which "Hyrcania" and "soft Arabia" slide naturally.

The above four examples are representative of a new historical perspective, which has been employed in translations made subsequent to the 1919 publication of Pound's *Homage to Sextus Propertius*. Taking their tone mainly from the modern and colloquial elements in the Propertius translation, these translations emphasize the common ground of emotion on which we can meet these ancient authors. They enhance similarities and partially suppress differences, although they do not entirely ignore them. In this they differ from a smaller number of translations, which entirely do away with any differences in detail or viewpoint.

The Past Turned into the Present

When translating from older literatures, Ezra Pound usually preferred to use an archaic diction, or to blend older and newer dictions. Only one Roman poet, Catullus, tempted Pound to move his historical perspective entirely into the twentieth century. Pound translated Catullus 85 as:

> I hate and love. Why? You may ask but
> It beats me. I feel it done to me, and ache.[10]

This little trnaslation cannot be held to have influenced the translations of Catullus about to be discussed, because it was published after them in 1963. Rather, it is a testimonial to the impression of modernity which Catullus, of all the Roman poets, is most apt to inspire. The translators of Catullus who turn him into a modern-day poet culled their method from numerous hints in the *Homage to Sextus Propertius,* from phrases like

> I shall have doubtless, a *boom* after my funeral
>
> There will be a crowd of young women doing
>   homage to my *palaver*
>
> I *guzzle* with outstretched ears[11]
>   (*italics mine*)

Louis Zukofsky turned all of Catullus 8 into similar language:

> Miserable Catullus, stop being foolish
> And admit it's over,
> The sun shone on you in those days
> When your girl had you
> When you gave it to her
>   like nobody else ever will.
> Everywhere together then, always at it
> And you liked it and she can't say
>   she didn't.
> Yes, those days glowed.

Now she doesn't want it: why
   should you, washed out,
Want to? Don't trail her,
Don't eat yourself up alive,
Show some spunk, stand up
   and take it.
So long girl. Catullus
   can take it.
He won't bother you, he won't
   be bothered:
But you'll be, nights.
What do you want to live for?
Whom will you see?
Who'll say you're pretty?
Who'll give it to you now?
Whose name will you have?
Kiss what guy? bite whose
   lips?
Come on, Catullus, you can
   take it.[12]

Modern analyses of Catullus's language agree that Catullus often wrote a very colloquial Latin, meaning that Catullus presented the first written instance of the word *basium* 'kiss', and employed the then new overtones of *horribilis,* which corresponded somewhat to the modern "terrific." But Catullus was not using slave-class language, certainly not as Zukofsky in his translation relies on blue-collar language. On the other hand, Catullus's language, compared to the language of the other Julian poets, appeared very daring and low-brow, so perhaps Zukofsky does recreate the shock value.[13] In Zukofsky's translation, from "don't trail her" through "Catullus can take it," every single phrase is in the vulgar parlance; but the main purpose of the language is not to shock: the effect recreates Catullus's pain as if he were alive today.

Another recent translator of Catullus, Frank O. Copley, has compared the Roman poet to e. e. cummings.[14] Working from

this prescription, he has translated the entire Catullan oeuvre
in the style of cummings's *Tulips and Chimneys:*

Catullus 13

say Fabullus
you'll get a swell dinner at my house
a couple three days from now (if your luck holds out)
all you gotta do is bring the dinner
     and make it good and be sure there's plenty
Oh yes don't forget a girl (I like blondes)
and a bottle a wine maybe
     and any good jokes and stories you've heard
you just do that like I tell you ol' pal ol' pal
you'll get a swell dinner
   ?
   what,
        about,
            ME?

well;
    well here take a look in my wallet,
        yeah those're cobwebs
but here
    I'll give you something too
        I CAN'T GIVE YOU ANYTHING BUT
           LOVE BABY
no?
well here's something nicer and a little more cherce maybe
I got a perfume see
it was a gift to HER
    straight from VENUS and CUPID LTD.
when you get a whiff of that you'll pray the gods
to make you (yes you will, Fabullus)
   ALL
     NOSE[15]

Fabullus, Venus, and Cupid are mentioned, but the Roman connotations they have are entirely overwhelmed by "swell," "gotta," "pal," and "cherce." It is amazing that Warden can say "muse or god," and in the context of his translation this will underline the Roman milieu, while Copley can mention Fabullus, Venus, and Cupid, yet remain firmly in the twentieth century. The poem seems to take its date from "I Can't Give You Anything But Love, Baby," a popular song of the 1930s.

Pound, in the *Homage to Sextus Propertius,* had introduced slang as a means of producing a modern historical perspective. Louis Zukofsky and Frank O. Copley represent a small, but noticeable group of translators who sometimes translate their originals entirely into the twentieth century, overwhelming two thousand years with slang. Yet their historical perspective is related to the perspective of the group discussed in the previous section. For both groups, the thrust is towards making the emotions of the poets of the past seem vivid in the present by de-emphasizing the ancient background. A third and fourth group of translators, however, more fully share Pound's intention to recapture the intensity of past emotions but also to clarify differences in background.

Style and Content Contrasted

Up to this point, the discussion of Pound's influence has included only translations of the poets of Julian and Augustan Rome. This is no accident. The translators discussed above had in common a modernizing intent. Pound himself had judged imperial Rome, with its apartment houses, dole lines, sexual license, political unrest, and imperial wars, to be comparable to the conditions of modern civilization.[16] In contrast, Pound had felt that the social organization and value system of the medieval world was far removed from modern sensibility.[17]

Certain contemporary translators have made the same assessment of the Middle Ages, but they did not wish to express the differences by using archaic language. Burton Raffel, the leading exponent of this group of translators, believes that the translator of a dead language

> . . . must at one and the same time convey an alien spirit, expressed in alien ways, in the vehicle of his own modern tongue, and in the terms conditioned by the modern verse of that tongue.[18]

Raffel details the influences on his translations:

> . . . there was Arthur Waley. . . .
> There was also, perhaps even primarily, Ezra Pound. Together with Waley, I suspect, Pound is responsible for virtually all that is good in modern English and American verse translation. His Villonauds (not really translations) rocked my adolescent years. . . . And I weep still, reading Pound/Fenellosa's "The River-Merchant's Wife: A Letter". . . . How could such burning precision NOT profoundly affect a developing mind?[19]

Raffel, then, wishes to use the technique of *Cathay*, which creates its historical perspective by respecting the eighth-century content of the original poem, while treating it in the style of the twentieth century. To create this contrast, the language must be modern, but not colloquial; for, as we have seen, colloquialisms tend to bring the time of the translation into the present. In a modern, though uncolloquial, language, the translator will dwell on differences of detail: clothes, utensils, and customs.

Raffel uses the above method to create the historical perspective of his translation of *Sir Gawain and the Green Knight*, a fourteenth-century poem in Middle English. In the following lines, the contrast between present and past customs is great. Raffel is describing Gawain's reception at a castle where he has requested a night's lodging:

> . . . [The porter] bowed, went down the wall, and came back

In a moment, with men to greet Sir Gawain.
They dropped the drawbridge, came courteously out
And knelt in the snow, welcoming on their knees
That noble knight, honoring his rank;
They begged him to ride on that broad bridge
And he raised them with a hand and rode across.
They held his saddle and helped him down,
And ran to stable his horse. And squires
And knights swarmed from the castle, happy
To escort so excellent a soldier to their hall;
When he lifted his visor they hurried to take
His helmet from his hands, anxious to serve him;
And they took his sword, and his shield. And one
By one he greeted them all. . . .[20]

Medieval manners and customs are being carefully described.
The men have knelt ceremoniously in the snow. This is felt
to be right and proper. It is clear that by custom a night's lodging is Gawain's for the asking. Raffel then goes on to deal with
medieval furnishings and utensils. Gawain is given a bedchamber, lavishly described, and fresh clothing, lavishly
described, and a cloak, also lavishly described. Finally a meal
is brought to him.

And Gawain sat in that splendid place
And soon was warm, and his spirits rose.
A long table was laid on trestles,
And a white cloth hung on it, and across it
Another cloth, and silver spoons,
And a salt dish. He washed and went to his meat.
And men hurried to wait on him, brought him
Savory stews, and broths, seasoned
And hot, all double-sized portions, and fish
Of every kind—baked and breaded,
Grilled on charcoal, boiled, and in spiced
Soups—and sauces sweet to the tongue.
And Gawain called it a feast, graciously
Praised their table when they begged him to excuse it.

"This is food
And penance together, refuse it
If you will; tomorrow's will be better."
He laughed and was gay, and used
Their wine so well that he stuttered.[21]

The lavish detail has continued. The table is a trestle table, the common medieval arrangement. Gawain is given a spoon, but no fork, not yet in use in this society; and no knife, because he is expected to use his own. The spicy dishes are a late-medieval preference, as are the sweet sauces. In a further comment on the customs of the time, Raffel shows the extravagant hospitality with which Gawain is welcomed. His lines portray both what would have been considered proper manners and the eagerness for news characteristic of the folk in an isolated castle. Now that Gawain is well-wined, the castle personnel begin tactfully to pump him.[22] All these details create the ambience of the fourteenth century and no other time. In this, Raffel's practice is different from the practice of the translators previously discussed, since they frequently suppressed specifically Roman paraphernalia, or substituted modernisms.

So far, Raffel's method and his results closely resemble those of *Cathay*, but Raffel has larger aims. He believes, along with Pound and Eliot, that each age has its own way of structuring reality; like Pound, he was ambitious to explore the differences between these structures. Since Raffel had chosen not to use the archaic collage of *The Classic Anthology*, he had to find another means to convey his appreciation of the late Middle Ages' way of organizing reality. He decided that the answer lay in adhering to the principle by which the *Gawain*-poet organized descriptions. Raffel believes that the verbal descriptions of the *Gawain*-poet are structured differently from those of the twentieth century or the Renaissance. Raffel explains:

The *Gawain*-poet writes, sometimes, the way late-medieval artists paint, or tapestry-makers weave. . . . the principle of subordination, the trick of seeing things only in linear perspective, is not usual to the late-medieval sensibility. It is like the Duc de Berry's *Book of Hours:* the foreground is rich, vital, but though the background is clearly the background, though the basic laws of perspective are usually taken into account, the background is not . . . subordinated.[23]

Raffel points out that Renaissance painters not only obeyed the laws of perspective; they also made the distant background seem more faded and fuzzy. This is what Raffel means by subordination. "Their background," he comments, "is impossible to confuse with their foreground."[24] In contrast, background and foreground in the Duc de Berry's *Book of Hours* exhibit

neither confusion nor equivalence, but rather a kind of simultaneity, a kind of non-linear perception of two—or more—worlds at the same time. For beyond the background, there is usually another background, usually architectural rather than human—and beyond that second background there is a third, the decorative astrological work enscrolled across the top of the page. . . . The twentieth-century camera can see only the perspective, can see only the subordination, only the motion through time or through space. . . . But the *Gawain*-poet sees both the perspective and the stasis, the motion and the imperishable fixed things.[25]

Thus, without making recourse to an archaic collage, Raffel is able to imbue his translation with the late-medieval world view. He does so by understanding and conveying the principle of organization behind the medieval descriptions. It is this principle which allows Gawain to warm himself in the foreground of a description, while an equal particularity of detail is bestowed on the spoons and the tablecloth.

Raffel, then, has set his poem in the Middle Ages, as seen from the perspective of the twentieth century: using modern language and versification, he scrupulously describes antique artifacts and customs. Raffel's consciously medieval organization of the descriptions also helps confer a fourteenth-century aura on his translation.

The *Gawain*-poet, however, did not write a poem set only in the reality of the fourteenth century. He was an immensely accomplished writer, and he contrived to blend fairytale and reality in his poem.[26] *Sir Gawain and the Green Knight* begins once upon a time in the legendary past, and in the poem quasi-fairytale happenings shade into mundane reality with humorous ease.[27] Fortunately, Raffel is able to follow these shifts in tone. Where a Victorian probably would have used pseudo-archaisms for the fairytale portions, Raffel retains his modern diction. For example, Gawain has been journeying to keep his appointment with the Green Knight. It is extremely cold, and Gawain has been praying for a lodging, when he comes suddenly upon a castle

> With rows of battlements, and turrets, and beautiful
> Towers for sentries, and lovely loophole
> Windows, shuttered now—he'd never
> Seen a better fortress. And beyond
> The walls he could see a high-roofed hall,
> And pinnacled towers along it, fitted
> To the walls, carved and crafted by ingenious
> Hands. And high on those towers he saw
> A host of chalk-white chimneys, gleaming
> Bright in the sun—and everywhere the stone
> Painted and cut, bowmen's notches
> And watchmen's places scattered across
> The castle, so it seemed scissored out of paper.
> And resting on Gringolet, Gawain thought it
> A pleasant place to lodge in, while the holiday
> Ran—if ever he could manage to get
> > Inside.[28]

The pinnacled, turreted castle, bright in the sun, seems like something out of a fairytale to both the reader and Gawain; it looks unreal—"scissored out of paper." Yet, because the diction is modern, and not pseudo-archaic, Raffel is able to modulate, along with his author, to a very real and very tired Gawain, who wants to get inside.

Raffel has a knack of getting his readers to identify with the emotions of the fourteenth-century characters. Both the tired Gawain, in the lines above, and the fleering Green Knight, in the lines quoted below, seem all too human. Gawain had agreed to stand still under an ax-stroke from the Green Knight, but he has just, understandably, jerked back from the blow aimed at his neck. The Green Knight says:

"Gawain? You can't be Gawain, his name
Is too noble, he's never afraid, nowhere
On earth—and you, you flinch in advance!
I've heard nothing about Gawain the coward,
And I, did I flinch, fellow, when you swung
At my neck? I never spoke a word.
My head fell, and I never flinched.
And you, before it can happen your heart
Is quaking. Who doubts that I'm the better
                                    Man?"
        "I flinched," said Gawain,
"I won't again.
And this much is plain:
My head, if it falls, won't talk in my hands."[29]

Raffel makes the Green Knight's bragging seem very realistic and preadolescent. The choice of "flinch" for *fles* 'flee', *flaʒ* 'flew', and *schunt* 'flinch, twist aside', with its reminder of the game Flinch played by eight and nine-year olds, brings out all the grisly stupidity of this chicken-match.

To someone struggling with Middle English or reading a pseudo-archaic translation of this poem, it may not be apparent that the *Gawain*-poet intends on one level this encounter between Gawain and the Green Knight should seem stupid and childish, just as it seems to a modern reader. This, in fact, is the judgment of the other knights at Arthur's court.[30] On another level, the *Gawain*-poet does, of course, endorse the medieval view that the challenge is a valid test of Gawain's courage. Unfortunately, the level on which the contest has a serious meaning might be lost to a modern reader if he had to read it in an invented language which does not have the subtlety to convey the genial mockery also present. The reader, perhaps judging the contest silly according to his value system, and finding it taken in complete seriousness by a translator, might conclude the poem has no relevance to him. But when a recognizable point of view is presented to him along with an alien one, the reader has a better chance of appreciating the poem.

The Recapitulation of Philology: Logopoeia

In translations, as Pound demonstrated, the logopoeia which plays on the known history of words can be used to suggest the origins in place and time of the original poem. The bulk of recent translations eschew this device. Why? The reasons for this can only be guessed at: perhaps the furor surrounding Pound's politics has impeded recognition of Pound's innovations;[31] perhaps the historical logopoeia of *Homage to Sextus Propertius* escaped recognition until Hugh Kenner pointed it out in the 1950s;[32] perhaps the methods of *The Classic Anthology*, published in 1954, have not yet had time to enter the translator's repertoire; perhaps most translators, even good ones, are not capable of handling logopoeia; or perhaps they feel it requires archaic collage and they do not wish to use archaic language. Whatever the reasons, logopoeia has been slow to be taken up as a tool.

A first, limited use of it can be seen in Kenneth Rexroth's 1945 translation of "Rumor letalis," a medieval poem in Latin attributed to Peter Abelard (1079–1142). Rexroth uses logopoeia to suggest France as the poem's country of origin and the United States as the country of its translation. Rexroth's last two verses read in part:

> You were never the heroine
> Of dirty stories in the days
> When love bound us together.
> Now . . . filthy jokes about your
> Latest amour are the delight
> Of every cocktail table.
> Your boudoir is a brothel;
> Your salon a saloon;
> Even your sensibilities
> And your depraved innocence
> Are only special premiums,
> Rewards of a shameful commerce.
>
> O the heart-breaking memory
> Of days like flowers, and your
> Eyes that shone like Venus the star
> In our brief nights, and the soft bird
> Flight of your love about me;
> And now your eyes are as bitter
> As a rattlesnake's dead eyes,
> And your disdain as malignant.
> Those who give off the smell of coin
> You warm in bed; I who have
> Love to bring am not even
> Allowed to speak to you now.
> You receive only charlatans and fools;
> I have only the swindling
> Memory of poisoned honey.[33]

"Heroine of dirty stories" is the kind of logopoeia long known and used for satire: the connotation of "heroine" clashes with the denotation of "dirty stories." But Rexroth carries logopoeia further. "Amour," "boudoir," "salon," and "charlatan" are all words which have been adopted into English from French. All four have retained their foreign pronunciation. Rexroth has clustered the first three close together, reinforcing their foreign overtones. Each of those first three borrowed French words is matched to a British or American word: "amour" with "cocktail table," "boudoir" with "brothel," "salon" with "saloon." "Cocktail" and "saloon" are both of American origin and chiefly American usage, while "brothel" is of impeccably English origin, having developed in Middle English from Old English broðen 'ruined'. The last borrowed French word, "charlatan," occurs in the concluding verse, where it is balanced by "rattlesnake," a snake found only in the Americas.

The effect of pairing French words with American words is curious. The diction seems entirely modern: "boudoir" and "salon" are, after all, perfectly current words. The transformation would seem to be one of milieu, rather than time, despite the newer status of the American words. However, Rexroth has indicated that he is opposing time and time, as well as place and place, with one well-chosen word: "coin." A modern American tycoon would smell, presumably, of cash or banknotes, not coin. Rexroth, in the manner of Pound, is commenting on the process of translating a poem into a new language, the language of a new time and a new place. He has used the histories attached to the words of his translation to comment on the process of that translation. Pound did the same in *Homage to Sextus Propertius* when he set Roman *amphorae* 'wine jars' next to a frigidaire patent; and when he called Eleus, the vicinity of Olympia, "East Elis," making it sound like a London neighborhood.[34]

Rexroth's use of logopoeia for historical perspective in 1945 was an isolated event. Only one other translator was interested in using logopoeia: Paul Blackburn, who between 1950 and 1971 translated a great many poems of the Provençal troubadours. Blackburn had met Pound,[35] and was inspired to study Provençal by essays on and translations of the troubadours.[36]

Pound's own excursions into Provençal were many and varied. His translation experiments are interesting, but not entirely successful. The historical perspectives of his Provençal translations run the gamut from pseudo-archaic pre-Raphae-

litic to deliberately archaic. Davie, who approved of the
archaic collage in The Confucian Odes, says of Pound's
Arnaut Daniel translations:

> What first strikes the reader is the extraordinary indis-
> criminate diction of these versions: in order to get ono-
> matopoetic and rhyming words, Pound has had to let his
> diction veer crazily from colloquial slang to bizarre
> archaisms like "raik" and "wriblis". . . .[37]

These difficulties are apparent in Pound's translation of
Arnaut Daniel's "L'aura amara," which is sometimes marvel-
ous and sometimes maddeningly awful:

> The bitter air
> Strips panoply
> From trees
> When softer winds set leaves,
> And glad
> Beaks
> Now in brakes are coy,
> Scarce peep the wee
> Mates
> An un-mates.
>   What gaud's the work?
>   What good the glees?
> What curse
> I strive to shake!
> Me hath she cast from high,
> In fell disease
> I lie, and deathly fearing.
>
> So clear the flare
> That first lit me
> To seize
> Her whom my soul believes;
> If cad
> Sneaks,

Blabs, slanders, my joy
Counts little fee
Baits
And their hates.
    I scorn their perk
    And preen, at ease.
Disburse
Can she, and wake
Such firm delights, that I
Am hers, froth, lees
Bigod! from toe to earring.

Amor, look yare!
Know certainly the keys:
How she thy suit receives;
Nor add
Piques,
'Twere folly to annoy.
I'm true, so dree
Fates:
No debates
    Shake me, nor jerk.
    My verities
Turn terse,
And yet I ache;
Her lips, not snows that fly
Have potencies
To slake, to cool my searing.

After three more verses maintaining the same rhymes, Pound
ends:

Coda

At midnight mirk,
In secrecies
I nurse
My served make

> In heart; nor try
> My melodies
> At other's door nor mearing.[38]

Pound footnotes "make" as "mate, fere, companion," but gives no help with "mearing" (boundary marking?), nor does he rescue his ending from a certain midnight mirk. Arnaut's ending is also obscure, but his is the deliberate obscurity of veiled sensual musings. The translation is marred by pseudo-archaic excursions: "me hath she cast from high," "In fell disease / I lie," "Amor, look yare!" "I'm true, so dree / Fates."

Yet, despite its serious flaws, the translation has a gusto, a Donne-like blend of passion, intellect, and humor, that no translation of the troubadours into English before it had achieved.* "If cad / Sneaks, / Blabs, slanders, my joy / Counts little fee / Baits / And their hates" breaks into a consonantal bustle most like that found in John Donne's poem "The Sunne Rising":

> Busie old foole, unruly Sunne,
> Why dost thou thus,
> Through windowes, and through curtaines call on us?
> Must to thy motions lovers seasons run?
> Sawcy pedantique wretch, goe chide
> Late schoole boyes and sowre prentices,
> Goe tell Court-huntsmen, that the King will ride,
> Call countrey ants to harvest offices;
> Love, all alike, no season knowes, nor clyme,
> Nor houres, dayes, moneths, which are the rags of
> time.[39]

Also like Donne is the tone of self-awareness, at once ironic and joyful: the lines "Disburse / Can she, and wake / Such

---

*Besides Francis Hueffer, whose translations are represented in Chapter 2, only a handful of Victorian translators, including Ida Farnell, Louisa S. Costello, and Harriet Waters Preston had translated troubadour lyrics. All three translators are of the "palely loitering lover" school.

firm delights, that I / Am hers, froth, lees / Bigod! from toe
to earring" parallel the tone of Donne's "For Godsake hold
your tongue and let me love."[40] The comparison of Arnaut
Daniel, the champion of *trobar clus,* with a metaphysical poet
is a fruitful one. Both schools delight in difficult verse forms
and in an emphasis on passion and intellect combined.
Donne's love poetry plays with a wider range of intellectual
notions than does Arnaut's, but Arnaut had his fling with the
scholastics. Such words as *ententa* 'opinion' and *soma* 'conclu-
sion' in "L'aura amara" have overtones of the language of formal dispute. Both Donne and Daniel were damned by their
contemporaries and posterity as unconscionably difficult—not
without reason.

Pound, then, has made a semi-successful comparison of
Arnaut Daniel and John Donne, as he later compared Guido
Cavalcanti and Sir Thomas Wyatt. If Paul Blackburn had been
an unimaginative student of Pound, he might have proceeded
to compare the troubadours to various Elizabethan and Jaco-
bean authors. However, no writer, no matter how competent,
can work in the language of a past era and sound as if he is
tossing off the latest slang. As Christine Brooke-Rose points
out, "Amor, look yare!" is ludicrous as a translation of "the
truly colloquial *Amors, gara.*"[41] Blackburn realized that to
leave out a troubadour's sudden veer into the vernacular is to
miss much of the fun in Provençal poetry.

The Provençal troubadours wrote love lyrics which almost
never exceed sixty lines. In them, the lovers rarely deign to
notice more of external reality than a few ritual birds and
bushes. Since the references to twelfth-century clothes, food,
manners, and manors are so scanty, the translator cannot use
Burton Raffel's method to present both modern and medieval
perspectives. There are no leisurely passages, descriptive of
medieval life, to contrast with modern language. Instead, the
poems are almost all emotion. Translators have difficulties
finding room to explain that the objects of troubadour emotions are in some important ways different from their modern
equivalents. For instance, in troubadour love lyrics, convention has the poet express a passionate regard for a lady of rank

who is married, but not to the poet. A translator may feel the need to explain this and other differences between present-day and twelfth-century notions of romantic love, but he is faced with poems which casually omit to mention such medieval commonplaces.

Blackburn sought the solution in logopoeia, although not exactly the logopoeia of *Homage to Sextus Propertius* (which makes archaic dictions seem modern), nor yet the logopoeia of *The Classic Anthology* (which assembles different archaic dialects from a modern viewpoint). Sometimes Blackburn does combine ancient and modern dictions, but more often he develops a diction in which both modern colloquialisms and deliberate archaisms seem at home. Both the colloquial and the archaic call attention to themselves, and yet belong to his overall diction. Blackburn can allude to Chaucer ("All ways I have the semblance of a parfait knight")[42] or to William Carlos Williams ("Some mercy, beautiful thing")[43] with equal ease.

Blackburn creates his logopoeia in a number of different ways. When he wants to refer simultaneously to past and present viewpoints, he often will invent a verb. Since the verb is new, but odd, it has the effect of being the newest possible English, and at the same time draws attention to an alien quality in the original poem:

It is for your sake, . . .
That I *supple* and bend toward you

The charm of how you are gives me such joy
That my desire pleasures me every day.
Now totally and in full you *mistress* me.
How overmastered I am, I can scarce say

MORE THAN A BEGGAR I dare not
                          grumble,
More than a poor man who sleeps in a rich man's hall
                          who doesn't dare complain

> though his complaint be great, fearing
>   his lord take offense, I
> dare not *grate* against my mortal pain[44]
>   *(italics mine)*

"Mistress me" is a neat solution to the disconcerting troubadour habit of calmly referring to one's unrelenting mistress as
midons 'milord'. By reversing the conceit, Blackburn has managed to create an analogous sex-change in English. "Grate,"
which can still mean "to rub against with a grinding noise,"
has two obsolete meanings, which Blackburn here re-invents:
"to obtain by importunity," "to dwell querulously upon a subject."[45] The word seems to resonate in several directions,
towards "rate" (scold), and "ingrate," and the Scots "greet"
(weep). Like most of Blackburn's invented or slightly per-
verted verbs, it seems to reach both forward and backward in
time.

When Blackburn wishes to separate archaic from colloquial
speech, he does so. In the same poem are to be found the
archaisms:

> myself entire forgot
> my heart entire
> contemn
> puissance

and a modern note:

> But when he's exiled from home
>   it's hard
> it takes the fight out of him
> were I . . . to leave off loving[46]

The effect of this alternation of ancient and modern dictions
can best be demonstrated by analyzing an extended example
from Blackburn's translation of "Per fin' amor m'esjauzira,"

attributed to Cercamon:

> True love
> warms my heart
> no matter if he run hot or cold.
> My thoughts attract on her always,
> but can't know yet
> if I can finish the job, stay
> firm with joy, that is
> if she wants to keep me hers
> which my heart most desires. . . .
>
> I'd hardly have spoken out so soon
> if I'd known how hard she softened. No
> thing but does not humble itself toward Love—
>   her? She is fierce toward him!
> But a lady can have no valor, not
> by riches and not by power, if
> the joy of Love blow not within her. . . .
>
> The fairest woman ever used a mirror never
> saw anything soft and white as ermine,
>   as she is,
> fresher than a lily or rose—any flower!
> And nothing makes me despair more. God!
>   may I enjoy the hour
> when I can make love-play beside her!
> No. I, no. She does not turn towards me. . . .
>
>   And if she pleasure me next her,
>   if she let me lie next to her level
>   sure I would not die of this evil.[47]

The first three deceptively simple lines are a complicated
example of logopoeia. "True love / warms my heart" is modern in diction; "no matter if" is even breezily modern. Then
comes "he." *Amors* is masculine in Old Provençal, but not in
English: Love, personified, male, has antique connotations. "If
he run" contains the third person singular conditional, a form
little used in modern American English; it, too, has an old-

fashioned tone. Attached to it is "run hot or cold." The Provençal reads *Per fin' Amor m'esjauzira / Tant quant fai chaut ni
s'esfrezis* 'I rejoice in pure love whether it is hot or cold'.[48] *Fai
chaut* and *fai s'esfrezis* are idioms for the weather, similar to
modern French *il fait chaud* and *il fait froid.* But Blackburn
moves away from the weather. The modern associations to
running hot or cold are blood and tap water. Love's chills and
fevers belong to twelfth and twentieth century alike, but hot
and cold running water is by no means medieval. In thirteen
words, Blackburn has thoroughly compounded two different
times.

Later Blackburn contrasts times rather than intermingling
them. For example, "my thoughts attract on her," with its
irregular use of "attract" as an intransitive verb, is abruptly
challenged by the very colloquial phrase "if I can finish the
job." Then, twelfth and twentieth centuries are mingled
again, with a touch of the sixteenth for good measure. "If I'd
known how hard she softens," with its unusual grammar, is a
fairly literal translation of *'s'eu sabes cant greu s'afranquis,* and
displays the workings of a typical piece of troubadour wit.
However, the Provençal language has a penchant for meaning
a dozen things at once, and *cant greu s'afranquis* can also mean
"how slowly she sweetened," "with what difficulty she frees
herself," "how badly she repays," or even, "how harshly she
castrates." Blackburn has managed to retain a fair share of the
meanings, because "how hard she softened" is colored by the
sexual implications of "if I can finish the job, stay / firm with
joy." The next words are "No / thing but does not humble
itself toward Love," and the previous suggestions of a droop-
ing penis make it hard not to take the separation of "no" from
"thing" as intended to bring in an Elizabethan set of puns:
thing and no thing, which meant penis and vagina.*

The reader, with the help of phrases modern, Elizabethan,

---

*I have often wondered if troubadours made that pun. Could it be a possible inter-
pretation of *per qu'e.lh o retrai* in Bernard de Ventadorn's "Can vai la lauzeta"? Some
troubadours mention algebra and so they were likely to have been familiar with the
Arabic symbol for zero, 0. At any rate, the letter o pictures a hole, and that certainly
signified a vagina in Bernard's period.

and seemingly Provençal, is now oriented towards a bawdy approach to sex he can readily understand. Blackburn then proceeds to shatter any illusion that modern and Provençal conceptions of sexual passion are the same. They may overlap, but they are not the same. Blackburn writes, "But a lady can have no valor . . . if the joy of Love blow not within her." Female valor gained through love is a common enough conception in troubadour poetry, but curiously Blackburn is culling it from *domna no pot ren valer,* which is more likely to mean "a lady can be worth nothing" if the joy of love does not inspire her. Similarly, Blackburn's "No. I, no," sounds as if the translator has played a clever game with one of those sighing lovers' interjections so intractable to modern translation, *las!* or *ai!* But Cercamon actually did write *eu non,* which can be translated by a perfectly colloquial "not me." Blackburn has chosen to bring in archaic overtones in places where they are not necessarily forced on him by the Provençal. His point is that underlying the lyric there is both an attitude towards sex easy for us to understand and another, less familiar attitude, which seriously considers that the pains of the unrequited lover ennoble him, and which assigns value and valor to his noble-hearted mistress.

Blackburn appreciated his debt to Pound and paid him homage in the course of his translations. In Blackburn's lines are deliberate echoes of Pound's Provençal translations:

Blackburn: and the birds all chirm and twitter

Pound: By auzels who . . . / Chirm each to each

Blackburn: My thoughts attract on her

Pound: . . . even as you and I / Pipe towards
            those girls on whom our thoughts attract

Blackburn: The cold and drizzle clink against
            the gentle season to arrest it.
            From the hedges and from thickets
            I hear the lancing song contest it.

Pound: So press the words to arrest it . . .
                Arnaut cares lyt who praise or who contest
                  it.[49]

Blackburn's verbal echoes leave no doubt that he looked upon Pound as the source of his interest in and guide to the translation of Provençal lyrics. For him, as for the other poet-translators discussed in this chapter, Pound was the leader in demonstrating a new historical perspective for translation, in which the past is a time deliberately viewed from the present, and the discrepancies between past and present are an issue to be considered in the translation.

Part Two
The Creative
Translation
as Criticism

5

Victorian Criticism by Translation

Victorian Theory

In general, when Victorians discussed the translation of poetry into poetry, they had paraphrase in mind. Creative translation was unacceptable. Documentation supporting this statement is hard to find, because Englishmen of the nineteenth century believed so strongly in the necessity of fidelity to the text that they felt argument against creative translation superfluous. Perhaps the rooted nineteenth-century attachment to paraphrase and aversion from creative translation can be inferred from the angry reception accorded to Ezra Pound's creative translation of Sextus Propertius in 1919.

The Victorian argument raged between strict literalists and slightly less strict literalists. For instance, Robert Browning (1812–1888) wrote in the Foreword to his translation of *Agamemnon* that it is the translator's duty "to be literal at every cost save that of absolute violence to our language. . . ."[1] But when Sir Thomas Herbert Warren replied in 1895 that a "good translation should be not so much exact as faithful,"[2] he made it clear that fidelity, to him, meant adherence to a narrow interpretation of Dryden's definition of paraphrase.[3] After all, it is to the nineteenth-century English and German passion for exactitude in historical studies that we owe the modern foundations of the sciences of archeology and philol-

ogy. Perhaps the genuine fear Victorians felt for creative trans-
lation can best be expressed by quoting the only reference
Matthew Arnold made to it in all of *On Translating Homer.*
During the course of a long argument in favor of using
English hexameters to translate Homer, Arnold admitted that
Homer might be rendered into

> . . . a blank verse of which perhaps the best specimens are
> to be found in some of the most rapid passages of Shake-
> speare's plays. . . . But the translator who determines to
> use it, must not conceal from himself that in order to
> pour Homer into the mould of this metre, he will have
> entirely to break him up and melt him down, with the
> hope of then successfully composing him afresh; and this
> is a process which is full of risks. It may, no doubt, be
> the real Homer that issues new from it; it is not certain
> beforehand that it cannot be the real Homer . . . ; still,
> the chances of disappointment are great.[4]

And with that, Arnold returns to his argument in favor of hexameters, which he feels are less likely to lead the translator
into the dangerous fields of creative translation.

The most famous, and perhaps only, example of creative
translation in the nineteenth century is Edward Fitzgerald's
rendering of the *Rubáiyát of Omar Khayyám.* According to G.
Heron-Allen, some of Fitzgerald's stanzas are composites of
two or more of Khayyám's, some refer to no specific stanza,
but are reflections of the whole spirit of the original *Rubáiyát,*
and some derive not from the *Rubáiyát* at all, but from other
Iranian poetry of the same era.[5] However, Fitzgerald's translation did not touch off an uproar over the issue of infidelity,
most probably because Persian, then, as now, was not a language known to an appreciable number of English speakers.
A. J. Arberry points out that "Fitzgerald is often very far
indeed from the actual wording of Omar, to an extent that
would be condemned as impermissible in any version of a
European poet."[6] Since Fitzgerald's readers were unable to

ascertain his method of translation by comparison with the text, the *Rubáiyát* had no appreciable influence on other Victorian translators.

The major Victorian controversy, then, did not center on creative translation versus paraphrase. Paraphrase had won the day. However, the Victorians did discuss the question of how and in what ways a paraphrase is a criticism of the original poem.

The Written Rules

In 1934, Pound commented that, in addition to criticism by discussion, there are such categories of criticism as "criticism by new composition" and "criticism by translation."[7] He added:

> Criticism so far as I have discovered has two functions:
> 1. Theoretically it tries to forerun composition, to serve as gunsight, though . . . I believe . . . the man who formulates any forward reach of co-ordinating principle is the man who produces the demonstration. . . .
> 2. Excernment. The general ordering and weeding out of what has actually been performed. The elimination of repetitions. The work analogous to that which a good hanging committee or a curator would perform in a National Gallery or in a biological museum;
> The ordering of knowledge so that the next man (or generation) can most readily find the live part of it, and waste the least possible time among obsolete issues.[8]

On the surface, Pound and the Victorians are agreed on these definitions. Matthew Arnold, and John Dryden before him, believed that translation should perform the critical function Pound called "excernment." Most of Dryden's Preface to *Sylvae* (1685) is concerned with explaining the particular excellences by which Dryden was attracted to translate Vergil, Lucretius, Theocritus, and Horace. Arnold's *On Translating*

Homer presupposes that Homer should be translated because he is a great poet. Thus, neither gentlemen would have been shocked to encounter Pound's pronouncement that translation is a form of criticism. However, in practice there are fundamental differences between Pound's outlook on translation as criticism and the Victorian position.

Victorians believed in three criteria for criticism by translation. First, since a translation of poetry into poetry should be a paraphrase, criticism by translation may not entail deviating from the sense of the original. Second, translation makes its criticism by reproducing the individuating traits an author employs in his poetry. Third, a translation should reproduce the overall effect of the original poem.

These principles are drawn from Sir Thomas Herbert Warren's essay of 1895, "The Art of Translation." His essay is an excellent source for learning the simplified version of Dryden and Arnold which became the received Victorian and Edwardian opinion.

Regarding paraphrase, Warren says:

> Translation has already been defined as the expression, in another set of words . . . of the thoughts of one man already expressed in one set of words.[9]

He immediately follows this rather broad definition by quoting Dryden on paraphrase.

Warren expresses the second criterion:

> . . . the most important matter of all in translation [is] the reproduction of the *essential and differentiating character* of the original author.[10]

This line of reasoning runs through translation theory from Roman antiquity[11] to Dryden and later Arnold, in an unbroken line. Matthew Arnold urged his hypothetical translator to steep himself in the individuating characteristics of Homer: " . . . the translator of Homer should above all be penetrated by a sense of four qualities of his author,"[12] which Arnold described:

> Homer is rapid in his movement, Homer is plain in his words and style, Homer is simple in his ideas, Homer is noble in his manner.[13]

Arnold condemned translators who failed to reproduce all four of Homer's characteristics.[14] Even the much-criticized Francis W. Newman agreed with his fellow-Victorian that a translator should reproduce all of Homer's distinguishing characteristics; he merely disagreed as to what they were. According to him:

> Homer's style is direct, popular, forcible, quaint, flowing, garrulous. . . . Homer rises and sinks with his subject, is prosaic when it is tame, is low when it is mean.[15]

Thus, the two major Victorian theorists were agreed that a translation should make its criticism by reproducing every single one of the original author's individuating traits, be it added, both good and bad. To quote from Dryden, on whose theories the Victorians heavily relied:[16]

> If the Fancy of *Ovid* be luxuriant, 'tis his Character to be so, and if I retrench it, he is no longer *Ovid*. It will be replyed that he receives advantage by this lopping of his superfluous branches, but I rejoyn that a Translator has no such Right. . . .[17]

The above canon seems based on the proposition that the whole is equal to the sum of its parts. Yet, many Victorian critics also believed in an "organic whole" theory, which holds that the whole is greater than the sum of its parts. If Arnold had thought that the scrupulous reproduction of all an author's traits would create the desired translation, he would not have needed to include the third Victorian desideratum.

Sir Thomas Warren again supplies an excellent statement of
the theory received from Arnold:

> There is one proposition on which all translators seem
> practically and naturally agreed. *The aim of a translation
> should be to produce an impression similar, or as nearly as may
> be similar, to that produced by the original.* . . . [or] in the case
> of the ancient classics . . . *an impression similar to that pro-
> duced by the original on its original hearers.*[18]

Arnold was aware that no translator can hope to know the
effect of an ancient work on its original audience. He warned
his hypothetical translator that "No one can tell him how
Homer affected the Greeks;"[19] "the Greeks are dead."[20] He
advised the translator to turn for advice to scholars

> . . . who possess, at the same time with a knowledge of
> Greek, adequate poetic taste and feeling. No translation
> will seem to them of much worth compared with the
> original; but they alone can say whether the translation
> produces more or less the same effect on them as the
> original. They are the only competent tribunal in this
> matter. . . . Let not the translator, then, trust to his
> notions of what the ancient Greeks would have thought
> of him. . . . Let him not trust his own judgment of his
> own work. . . .[21]

This counsel of despair exposes the weakness in Arnold's
argument. The translator-critic, while distrusting his own
judgment, is to attempt somehow to recreate the original,
even though he cannot, for "no translation will seem . . . of
much worth compared to the original."

The Unwritten Rules

In actuality, Victorian translators found themselves unable
to abide by their expressed concerns as fully as they wished,

because their translations were governed by additional considerations, which they themselves did not always recognize.
Most Victorian translators seem to have felt that reproducing
the individuating traits of the original required, above all,
reproducing the original meter and rhyme scheme, whether
congenial to the English language or not. For instance,
although Matthew Arnold admits the possibility of completely forgetting Homer's meter and translating him in a different form, the whole thrust of his argument is against this
course.

The metrical systems of most Latin languages are based on
quantity or syllable count, rather than stress. English versifiers
customarily substituted stressed syllables for long quantities
and unstressed syllables for short; to render syllable-count
verse, they usually substituted a stressed meter with the same
number of syllables: for example, iambic tetrameter was commonly used to render octosyllabic verse. These approxima-
tions, with their fixed accent patterns, often forced a rigid regularity on verses noted for their flexibility.

The Victorians themselves were aware of the problem,[22] but
only one English critic, James Spedding, suggested a more
flexible approach to stress. Spedding's argument was embodied
in his review of On Translating Homer for Fraser's Magazine:

> . . . a new English metre may be invented resting upon
> six regularly recurring accents as the ground, and made
> musical by some variation played upon it with quantity;
> just as Latin takes quantity for its ground, and obtains its
> variations through the management of the accent.[23]

Spedding believed that quantity is "distinguishable in English
through all its degrees, by any ear that will attend to it."[24] He
offered an example of his proposed hexameter:*

---

*Spedding claims to be imitating Vergilian hexameters, not Homeric, but he suggests
that the resultant meter can be used for translating Homer.

Verses so modulate, so tuned, so varied in accent,
Rich with unexpected changes, smooth, stately,
   sonorous,
Rolling ever forward, tidelike, with thunder, in endless
Procession, complex melodies—pause, quantity, accent,
After Virgilian precedent and practice, in order
Distributed—could these gratify th' Etonian ear-
   drum?[25]

The Oxonian eardrum was not gratified. Matthew Arnold reacted harshly to Spedding's essay:

> I think prudent criticism must certainly recognise, [that] in the current English hexameter, . . . the English ear, [and] the genius of the English language, have, in their own way adopted, have *translated* for themselves the Homeric hexameter; and that a rhythm . . . which is thus, in a manner, the production of nature, has in its general type something necessary and inevitable, . . . which precludes change that is sweeping and essential. I think, therefore, the prudent critic will regard Mr. Spedding's proposed revolution as simply impractical.[26]

While a twentieth-century listener usually prefers Spedding's hexameters to Arnold's, Victorians seem to have sided with Arnold. At least, no original poems or translations appeared in Spedding's meter. In a footnote, Arnold explains that he disliked Spedding's hexameter because "it is . . . an attempt to make a wholly new English hexameter by habitually altering the position of four of [the accents]. . . ."[27] This indicates that Arnold wished to retain the regularity of scansion by feet, and did not think that variable positions for stressed accents were acceptable to English ears. Arnold not only felt that English, stress-based hexameters were a reasonable equivalent to Greek, quantity-based hexameters, but also that imitating those hexameters was essential to a criticism of

Homer:

> Applied to Homer, this metre affords to the translator the
> immense support of keeping him more nearly than any
> other metre to Homer's movement; and, since a poet's
> movement makes so large a part of his general effect . . .
> it is a great thing to have this part of your model's gen-
> eral effect already given you in your metre, instead of
> having to get it entirely for yourself.[28]

Arnold had begun by demanding a translation which would
convey Homer's rapidity of movement, plainness of words and
style, simplicity of ideas, and nobility of manner. These criticisms do not logically imply that Homer must be translated
into hexameters, yet Arnold can not rid himself of the desire
for them.

When we turn to the supposed opposition, the camp which
objected that hexameters had never been a native English
meter, we find F. W. Newman transforming Homer's hexameters into ballad meter-plus-a-syllable, a strict convention
which results in a basically fifteen-syllable line, approximating
the syllable count of the majority of the Greek lines. The principle governing Newman's choice of meter is, after all, not so
very different from Arnold's, whose hexameters also averaged
fifteen syllables per line.

Evidently, Victorians wanted to find a set of rules to govern
the imitation of a meter. Yet, correspondences between the
rhythms of two different languages are usually too inexact to
allow the formulation of a neat set of rules for capturing the
feel of one in the other: freedom and intuition are called for.

Another unwritten rule seems to have governed Victorian
criticism by translation. Criticisms of the original were to be
made "locally," that is, effects of the original poem were to be
reproduced at the line or stanza where they occurred in the
original poem, or not be reproduced at all. For example, if a
pun in the original proved unreproducible in English, the
translator was not to try to make a similar pun earlier or later.
Not only was the translator to eschew any meaning not clearly

justifiable by the original, he was also enjoined from altering the order of events in the original. Victorians translated line by line where possible, and stanza by stanza where not.

In obeying such unwritten riders, Victorians found it difficult to follow their written criteria. Once they had followed the order of events and the form of the original, few translators found any slack left for examining individuating characteristics and overall effect.* The difficulties put in the way of

(text continues at right)

---

*It could be done, occasionally. Pound made an excellent verbal paraphrase and formal reproduction of Bertran de Born's *planh,* "Si tut li dol elh plor elh marrimen" ("Planh for the Young English King," *Personae,* pp. 36–37).

Sirventes in Praise of War

Bem platz lo gais temps de pascor
Que fai folhas e flors venir,
E platz mi quant aug la baudor
Dels auzels que fan retentir
5   Lor chan per lo boschatge,
E platz mi quan vei per los pratz
Tendas e pabalhos fermatz,
    E ai grant alegratge
Quan vei per champanha renjatz
10 Chavaliers e chavaus armatz.

E platz mi quan li coredor
Fan las gens e l'aver fugir,
E platz mi quan vei après lor
Granré d'armatz ensems venir,
15 E platz mi en mon coratge
Quan vei fortz chastels assetjatz
Els barris rotz e esfondratz
    E vei l'ost el ribatge
Qu'es tot entorn claus de fossatz

Victorian translation by these unwritten rules can best be judged by seeing the effect.

Victorian Practice

It is convenient to look at translations of "Bem platz lo gais temps de pascor," known as the Sirventes in Praise of War, attributed to the Provençal poet, Bertran de Born (c. 1146–c. 1214). Both a Victorian and an Edwardian paraphrase of it exist, and Pound has made a creative translation of it. The text and a literal translation of the poem are given below so that the near-literality of the paraphrases and their attempts to follow the meter and rhyme of the original may be appreciated.

===

Literal Translation

> I am well pleased with the happy Easter-season
> which makes leaves and flowers come;
> and it pleases me, when I hear the impudence
> of the birds, who make ring
> 5   through the woods their song;
> and it pleases me, when I see over the fields
> tents and pavillions planted;
> and I get great joy
> when I see throughout the field ranged
> 10   knights and armored horses.
>
> And it pleases me, when the skirmishers
> make the people and their baggage flee;
> and it pleases me, when I see after them
> a great gathered mass of armed men coming;
> 15   and it pleases me in my core
> when I see strong castles assailed
> and the barricades overturned and caving in
> and I see the host by the riverbank,
> which is enclosed on all sides by ditches,

Sirventes (continued)

20   Ab lissas de fortz pals seratz.

E altresim platz de senhor
Quant es premiers a l'envazir
En chaval armatz, sens temor,
Qu'aissi fai los seus enardir
25   Ab valen vassalatge,
E pois que l'estorns es mesclatz,
Chascus deu esser acesmatz
        E segrel d'agradatge,
Que nuls om non es re prezatz
30   Tro qu'a maintz colps pres e donatz.

Massas e brans elms de color
E scutz trauchar e desgarnir
Veirem a l'intrar de l'estor
E maintz vassals ensems ferir,
35   Dont anaran aratge
Chaval dels mortz e dels nafratz;
E quant er en l'estorn entratz
        Chascus om de paratge,
No pens mas d'asclar chaps e bratz,
40   Que mais val mortz que vius sobratz.

Eus dic que tan no m'a sabor
Manjar ni beure ni dormir
Com a quant aug cridar: *A lor!*
D'ambas las partz, e aug ennir
45   Chavaus voitz per l'ombratge,
E aug cridar: *Aidatz! Aidatz!*
E vei chazer per los fossatz
        Paucs e grans per l'erbatge,
E vei los mortz que pels costatz
50   An los tronzos ab los sendatz.

Baro, metetz en gatge
Chastels e vilas e ciutatz
Enanz qu'usquecs nous guerrejatz.

Translation (*continued*)

20   barred by palisades of strong stakes.

And also I'm pleased with a lord
when he is first in the attacking,
armed, on a horse, without fear,
so that there he puts courage in his men
25   for valiant vassal-service,
and when, after the melee is being disputed,
each man must be ardent
and follow it with pleasure,
as no man is worth anything
30   until he has taken and given many blows.

Maces and swords and colored helms,
shields pierced and stripped,
we shall see at the beginning of the fighting,
and many vassals fight together,
35   so that running here and there
are the horses of the dead and wounded
and when now in the battle are entered
each man of high birth,
there is no thought but of splitting heads and arms,
40   and that it is better to be dead than alive and conquered.

I tell you that there is no such savor for me
in eating, drinking, or sleeping,
as there is when I hear crying: *At them!*
on both sides and I hear neighing
45   horses' voices through the shadow,
and I hear crying: *Help! Help!*
and I see fallen in the ditches,
in the weeds, the lowly and great,
and I see the dead who through their ribs
50   have stumps with flag-silks.

Barons, pawn
castles and towns and cities
before you don't wage war among yourselves.

Sirventes (concluded)

Papiols, d'agradatge
55 Ad Oc-e-No t'en vai viatz
E dijas li que trop estai en patz.[29]

The Sirventes in Praise of War is admired today for the zest with which it presents its bloodthirsty position,[30] and for its realism.[31] Victorians either admired its exhortations to courage,[32] or condemned its bloodymindedness.[33] The poem is remarkable for the way it uses the repetition of the *tz* (pronounced like English *ts*) and *ch* (pronounced like English *ch*) to bray its call to war. The pair of sounds mimic the clash of sword on sword and the splintering of spear on shield. During the first three verses, six lines begin with some variant of *platz mi* 'it pleases me'. The entire poem employs only four end-rhymes: two of them, *-atge* and *-atz* (pronounced AH-cheh and ahts), take up the last six rhymes in each ten-line verse. *Tz* is a common ending in Provençal, but in this poem it recurs too frequently to be dismissed as an accident of grammar: there is an *-atz, -ortz, -otz, -aintz,* or *-etz* at every turn. These repeated *ts* and *ch* sounds impart to the *sirventes* its driving ferocity.

Yet, when we look at a Victorian translation of "Bem platz lo gais temps," the major effort of the translator is not directed at reproducing these sounds. In John F. Rowbotham's book *The Troubadours and Courts of Love* (1895), the translation carefully preserves the form, reproducing the masculine and feminine endings, the rhyme scheme, and the syllable count of the lines.

Rowbotham translates only four of the verses. He worked directly from manuscripts in the French Bibliothèque Nationale,[34] and he does not give a transcription of the text used, so it is impossible to know whether or not he intentionally deleted the last stanza and the *tornadas*. Indeed, only one of the manuscripts extant today contains the second *tornada*. Since Rowbotham elsewhere gives complete translations or explains that he is presenting only one verse, it is probable that he

Translation (concluded)

> Papiols, please,
> 55 be off with you to Yea-and-Nay
> and tell him that he stays too long at peace.

---

thought he was translating the entire *sirventes,* and that he was not making a critical judgment by curtailing the poem.

He translates:

[I]

Well do I love the lusty spring,
When leaves and flow'rets peep to light!
I love to hear the song birds sing
Among the leafage in delight
    Which forms their airy dwelling.
And when on tented fields I spy
Tall tents and proud pavilions high,
    My breast with joy is swelling;
Or when I see in legions lie
Squadrons of armoured chivalry.

[II]

What joy when scouts are skirmishing,
And scatter craven knaves in flight!
What joy to hear the fighters fling
High words and cries about the fight!
    What bliss is in me welling,
When castle walls that flout the sky
Stagger to their foundations nigh!
    What joys are me impelling,
When gallant troops a city try,
With trenches fenced impregnably!

[IV]

Swords, spears, and helmets glittering,
Shields shivered, and in sorry plight—
Such sights and sounds does battle bring;
With crowds of vassals left and right

Their master's foemen felling,
And horses mad, with rolling eye,
Who frenzied through the battle fly.
The man of race excelling
Thinks but of blood and butchery
And yearns for death or victory.[35]

Rowbotham has followed the sense of the poem in a close to line-by-line version. The one diversion from the sense ("What joy to hear the fighters fling / High words and cries about the fight" for *E platz mi quan vei après lor / Granré d'armatz ensems venir*) is demanded neither by Rowbotham's rhyme scheme nor by his general interpretation, so most probably he was following a different reading of the manuscript from the one now commonly accepted. He uses a minor amount of padding ("which forms their airy dwelling," "of rich rewards them telling" to get all his feminine rhymes, but he has in general left little out and added little.

Rowbotham does make some attempt at the sounds of the poem. He does not translate *e platz mi* as "and it pleaseth me." That particular Edwardian lisp was Pound's in 1910.[36] Rather, Rowbotham uses, when possible, "What joy," which at least approaches the sound of *-atge,* although somehow the burden is wrong. He does well with mimicking Bertran's initial alliteration: "tall tents," "proud pavilions," "scouts" "skirmishing" "scatter," and "shields shiver." He even manages to find a rhyme word with a good strong meaning: "butchery." Nevertheless, it is the choice of rhymes which brings Rowbotham to ruin. Bertran de Born rhymes twenty-four times on *-atz* and twelve times on *-atge.* Rowbotham is not going to find a rhyme in English of a harshness comparable to *-atz* on which he can rhyme sixteen times. He makes do with *-ing, -ight, -elling,* and *-igh.* *-Elling* and *-igh* take the positions of *-atge* and *-atz* respectively. They are much too liquid. For all his skill, Rowbotham's rhyme scheme deprives him of the voracious enjoyment deployed through all the lines by Bertran's *e platz mi,* which phrase is the technical heart of the poem.

Barbara Smythe translated the same poem in 1911. She worked from the text in Stimming,[37] and her version includes all five verses and both *tornadas*. Smythe, like Rowbotham, follows the meter and rhyme scheme of the *sirventes*, although she does not attempt to keep the same rhymes from verse to verse:

The Joys of War

[I]

I love the spring-tide of the year
When leaves and blossoms do abound,
And well it pleases me to hear
The birds that make the woods resound
With their exulting voices.
And very well it pleases me
Tents and pavilions pitched to see,
And oh, my heart rejoices
To see armed knights in panoply
Of war on meadow and on lea.

[II]

I like to see men put to flight
By scouts throughout the countryside,
I like to see, armed for the fight
A host of men together ride;
And my delight's unbounded
When castles strong I see assailed,
And outworks smashed, whose strength has failed,
And near the walls, surrounded
By moats, and by strong stakes enrailed,
The host that has the ramparts scaled.

[IV]

Axes and swords and spears and darts,
Shields battered in with many a blow
We'll see when first the battle starts,
And clash of arms as foe meet foe;
The steeds of dead and dying

Wildly will rush throughout the field
And all who wish to be revealed
As brave will e'er be trying
How best their axes they may wield,
For they would rather die than yield.

[VI]
Barons, without delaying,
Pawn every city, castle, hall,
And never cease to fight and brawl.

[VII]
Papiol, make no staying,
Lord Yea-and-Nay go rouse and call,
Tell him this peace on me doth pall.[38]

Evidently, to Barbara Smythe, rhyme is the most important quality of the Provençal. She preserves it even at the expense of rampant inversions, a host "enrailed," supernumerary "darts," and an unnecessary intensive in "on me doth pall," her last words and a suitable epitaph for her translation. The literal sense of Bertran de Born's poem is carefully followed in her version; the meter and rhyme scheme are faithfully copied, and nothing else of the poem is attempted.

"The Joys of War" could be much better written within the boundaries of its own conventions, as Rowbotham's translation shows. Smythe could simply be dismissed as a bad versifier, if she had not been printed in 1911, reprinted in 1929, and printed again in 1966. Her book can easily be found in libraries; her translations are reprinted in several anthologies of medieval verse.[39] A number of publishers and editors seem to have agreed with her that following the literal sense and the formal scheme of a poem is sufficient effort for the translator.

6

Pound's Criticisms
by Translation

Pound's Practice

"Sestina: Altaforte," Pound's translation* of the Sirventes in
Praise of War, embodies a rejection of every Victorian tenet
of translation except one: a translator should strive to reproduce the overall impression of the original poem. To begin
with, Pound's translation of 1909 is a sestina; while the sestina
is a strict form, it bears no direct or simple correspondence to
Bertran's rhymed ten-line stanzas. In a 1913 interview, Pound
explained why he chose the sestina form:

> I had had de Born on my mind. I had found him untrans-
> latable. Then it occurred to me that I might present him
> in this manner. I wanted the curious involution and
> recurrence of the Sestina.[1]

This statement of Pound's tells us that "Sestina: Altaforte"
was intended to criticize the Sirventes in Praise of War by

---

*I have called "Sestina: Altaforte" a creative translation, although there are good argu-
ments in favor of calling it an imitation. It is one of the works in which Pound mingled his modes. However, since in my definition a poem is a creative translation insofar as the changes it makes in the sense of the original are criticisms of the original,
the conclusions I draw from Pound's critical practice in "Sestina: Altaforte" are relevant to my argument regardless of the category to which the translation is assigned.

showing involution and repetition to be its salient characteristics. Of necessity, once he had chosen the sestina form,
Pound had rejected paraphrase, because the repetition of six
end words necessarily involved many changes in literal
meaning.

Here is Pound's version:

Sestina: Altaforte

Loquitur: *En* Bertrans de Born.
    Dante Alighieri put this man in hell for that he was
    a stirrer up of strife.
    Eccovi!
    Judge ye!
    Have I dug him up again?
The scene is at his castle, Altaforte. "Papiols" is his
jongleur. "The Leopard," the *device* of Richard Coeur
de Lion.

I

Damn it all! all this our South stinks peace.
You whoreson dog, Papiols, come! Let's to music!
I have no life save when the swords clash.
But ah! when I see the standards gold, vair, purple,
    opposing
And the broad fields beneath them turn crimson,
Then howl I my heart nigh mad with rejoicing.

II

In hot summer have I great rejoicing
When the tempests kill the earth's foul peace,
And the lightnings from black heav'n flash crimson,
And the fierce thunders roar me their music
And the winds shriek through the clouds mad,
    opposing,
And through all the riven skies God's swords clash.

III

Hell grant soon we hear again the swords clash!
And the shrill neighs of destriers in battle rejoicing,
Spiked breast to spiked breast opposing!
Better one hour's stour than a year's peace
With fat boards, bawds, wine and frail music!
Bah! there's no wine like the blood's crimson!

IV

And I love to see the sun rise blood-crimson.
And I watch his spears through the dark clash
And it fills all my heart with rejoicing
And pries wide my mouth with fast music
When I see him so scorn and defy peace,
His lone might 'gainst all darkness opposing.

V

The man who fears war and squats opposing
My words for stour, hath no blood of crimson
But is fit only to rot in womanish peace
Far from where worth's won and the swords clash
For the death of such sluts I go rejoicing;
Yea, I fill all the air with my music.

VI

Papiols, Papiols, to the music!
There's no sound like to swords swords opposing,
No cry like the battle's rejoicing
When our elbows and swords drip the crimson
And our charges 'gainst "The Leopard's" rush clash.
May God damn for ever all who cry "Peace!"

VII

And let the music of the swords make them crimson!
Hell grant soon we hear again the swords clash!
Hell blot black for alway the thought "Peace"![2]

The most cursory reading reveals that Pound has made a great many changes in the sense and order of the *sirventes:*

some details of the poem are omitted, others added, and the order of events is rearranged. For instance, Papiols the *jongleur* is addressed at the beginning of the poem, rather than at the end; the armored horses are moved from the first verse to the third; the season is no longer spring, but hot summer; we have a thunderstorm and a sunrise nowhere to be found in the original; the vignette of the bodies tumbled in the weeds is omitted. These are wholesale changes.

True, Barbara Smythe adds anticlimactic darts and Rowbotham adds "rich rewards" in order to rhyme, but neither approaches the kind and number of changes to be found in Pound's version. In addition, both Smythe and Rowbotham adhered to the unwritten nineteenth-century rule that a translation follow closely the formal arrangement of its original. Pound judged the elements of involution and repetition in Bertran's poem to be so important that he willingly sacrificed strict formal mimicry to them.

The Praise of War is involuted in the sense that it revolves around one theme only: the sensory impressions of war. As for repetition, the Praise of War uses some variant of *e platz mi* seven times; the *ts* and *ch* sounds continually recur.

Pound's version makes non-local equivalents for these qualities. That is, Pound does not use the formula "it pleases me" or mimic the *ts* and *ch* exactly where they occur, but instead uses equivalents where English permits. The form of the sestina itself engenders the repetition of six end words. To this formal requirement Pound has added the repetition of many internal words, as an equivalent of Bertran's repeated internal rhyme of *platz* with the line-ending *-atz*. In order to capture the sword clash of the *ch* and *ts* sounds, Pound has crashed consonant clusters together against the barriers of the spondees. There are "swòrds swórds opposing" and "spìked bréast to spìked bréast opposing," "stìnks péace," "wínds shríek," and "rúsh clásh." "Swords clash" itself appears five times. English *ds*, pronounced *dz*, is, be it noted, the voiced counterpart of *ts*. Pound harps on the *ds*: fields, winds, clouds, boards, bawds, and everywhere, swords. Pound has used a Germanic tendency of English, its ability to heap up consonants, as an equivalent to the sound qualities in the Provençal. The spondees also imitate the rhythm of phrases like *Ĕ plátz mĭ quánt áug* or *Ĕ plátz mĭ quán véi áprĕs lór / Gránré d'ărmátz* or *Quĕ núls óm nón ĕs ré prĕzátz.*

The success of Pound's criticism by creative translation can best be judged by comparison with the endeavors of translators by paraphrase. In paraphrase, some variant of the *platz mi* formula must be repeated seven times, but English offers no equivalent meaning which has an equivalent sound. Here is a list of attempts to paraphrase it:

It pleaseth me	(Pound)
I love to see *plus* what joy to	(Rowbotham)
I like it when	(Wilhelm)
I love seeing	(Bonner)[3]

None of the above improves upon a seven-times closer acquaintance.

Although Pound has forgone Bertran's rhyme scheme, he has not totally ignored its effects. In a short poem with so much repetition, the mind can carry irregularly spaced internal rhymes from verse to verse. Pound has created several rhyming series: one is "kill" "shrill" "fill"; another is "nigh" "pry" "cry"; another is "skies" "rise" "pries" (these last two series bear the same close aural relationship to each other that -*atz* and -*atge* have); and for good measure there is "flash" "crash."

While Pound's non-local formal equivalents indicate many qualities of the original, Pound has undeniably sacrificed some qualities. In so doing, he defies the Victorians' express injunction to reproduce every essential and individuating characteristic. The action in the *sirventes* becomes more fierce in each stanza, climaxing in the vignette of the dead bodies, ribs pierced with splintered lances. Pound's translation can reach no such climax, but must, as a sestina, obsessively circle its theme.[4] Pound also lost an element of paradox. The *sirventes* opens with *pascor* 'Easter, spring' and closes with *patz* 'peace'. *Pascor,* the time of spiritual and vegetative rebirth, opened the

twelfth century's annual war season. Bertran summons up
spring and the birds and the budding trees only to plant his
fields with tents. By framing his war cry with *pascor* and *patz*,
Bertran suggests that religion and nature are at odds with war.
Furthermore, *patz* is an *-atz* rhyme. By deferring so expectable
a rhyme, Bertran made the absence of peace be loud in every
stanza. In Pound's poem, war is the state of nature and
approved by God. "Sestina: Altaforte" occurs in "hot summer," when "tempests kill the earth's foul peace" and
"through all the riven skies God's swords clash." The rising
sun throws spears and Bertran is made to pray: "May God
damn forever all who cry 'Peace!'" These choices are criticisms not necessitated by the sestina form. Pound probably
sacrificed the paradox to make the praise of war more intense.
Or perhaps he simply failed to see the paradox. However,
Pound's choice of "peace" as a repeated end word shows at
once the strength and weakness of the choice of a sestina.
"Peace" is justified by its unspoken presence throughout the
sirventes, but this choice forfeits the wit of its verbal absence.

For all its lacks, "Sestina: Altaforte" does "present" Bertran
de Born's Praise of War better than any of its Victorian predecessors. In this, one of his earliest published translations,
Pound brought into question all the means by which Victorians intended to arrive at the desired goal: a translation which
reproduces an overall impression similar to that of the
original.

Pound's Theory

Expression of the theories behind Pound's translation practice lies scattered throughout his essays and letters. His com-
mitment to creative translation is stated almost as a side issue
in his defense of non-local criticism. While considering the
problems of translating logopoeia, Pound remarked:

Logopoeia does not translate; though the attitude of
mind it expresses may pass through a paraphrase. Or one

might say, you can *not* translate it 'locally', but having determined the original author's state of mind, you may or may not be able to find a derivative or an equivalent.[5]

Pound here takes for granted that the translator is interested, not in translating the sense of the original, but in finding an "equivalent" for the original author's "state of mind." This formula moves the translator definitively away from paraphrase. Paraphrase is resigned to losing the original author's verbal mastery, rather than ever saying something he did not say, while imitation, as Dryden explained, permits one to add "new Beauties to the piece, thereby to recompense the loss which it sustains by change of Language. . . ."[6] Pound restricted liberty in "adding new Beauties to the piece" to those which are a "derivative" or an "equivalent" of something in the original poem. Thus, he was describing creative translation, not imitation.

Most of Pound's reasons for rejecting the Victorian compulsion to copy form can be found in his essay on Cavalcanti. For instance, in it he takes up metrical equivalence. He says that to substitute iambic pentameter for Italian hendecasyllables "thoroughly falsifies the movement of the Italian. . . ."[7] He equally rejected a syllable-for-syllable equivalent, complaining that it turned Dante's *Nel mezzo del cammin di nostra vita* into "If you fall off the roof you'll break your ankle." However, he added, those who hear "the inner form of the line . . . find the movement repeated in—'Eyes, dreams, lips and the night goes,'" a free-verse equivalent.[8] As for copying Italian rhymes:

> . . . it is not that there aren't rhymes in English; or enough rhymes or even enough two-syllable rhymes, but that the English two-syllable rhymes are of the wrong timbre and weight. They have extra consonants at the end, as in *flowing* and *going;* or they go squashy; or they fluff up as in *snowy* and *goeth*. . . . Against which we have our concealed rhymes and our semi-submerged alliteration. . . .

It is not that one language cannot be made to do what another has done, but that it is not always expeditious to approach the same goal by the same alley.[9]

In consequence, Pound translated a sonnet by Guido Orlando, not into the hendecasyllables of its Italian original, not into the iambic pentameter of the traditional English imitation, but into four-stress or even three-stress lines. His translation begins:

> Say what is Love, whence doth he start?
> Through what be his courses bent?
> Memory, substance, accident?
> A chance of eye or will of heart?[10]

Pound explained:

> . . . I have given a *verbal* weight about equal to that of the original, and arrived at this equality by dropping a couple of syllables per line.[11]

Pound's most radical departure from Victorian theory was his refusal to reproduce all the individuating traits of the original, both good and bad. He repeatedly stated his belief that a translation is necessarily a partial criticism of the original poem and that a translator may therefore intentionally sacrifice certain traits the better to indicate others. He said of his 1920 translations of Arnaut Daniel:

> . . . [The troubadour's] triumph is, as I have said, in an art somewhere between literature and music; if I have succeeded in indicating some of the properties of the latter, I have also let the former go by the board.[12]

Pound's comment of 1931, regarding his translation of Cavalcanti, makes the same point:

> I have not given an English 'equivalent' for the *Donna mi Prega;* at the utmost I have provided the reader, unfa-

miliar with old Italian, an instrument that may assist him in gauging *some* of the qualities of the original.

As to the atrocities of my translation, all that can be said in excuse is that they are, I hope, for the most part intentional, and committed with the aim of driving the reader's perception further into the original than it would without them have penetrated.[13]

Further, Pound felt that the inevitable losses in translation were not always to be regretted:

Even though I know the overwhelming importance of technique, technicalities in a foreign tongue cannot have for me the importance they have to a man writing in that tongue; almost the only technique perceptible to a foreigner is the presentation of content as free as possible from the clutteration of dead technicalities, . . . and from timidities of workmanship. This is perhaps the only technique that ever matters, the only *maestria*.[14]

Therefore, Pound cheerfully lopped off superfluous branches, Dryden and the Victorians notwithstanding. J. P. Sullivan is especially illuminating regarding Pound's negative criticism of Propertius:

Not the least important aspect of the *Homage* is the criticism it offers of Propertius. This criticism is both negative and positive. Like all good criticism, it judges its subject and illuminates it; it brings out what has been ignored or overlooked, and condemns what has been overpraised.[15]

[Pound] has felt free to omit the unassimilated mythological allusions. . . . And where Pound does make use of the mythological allusions, his compressions do more for the poetry than the carefully worked out and often frigid parallels that Propertius deploys.[16]

In the section of "Cavalcanti" titled "Guido's Relations," Pound seems to envision an original poem surrounded by a family of translations, each differing markedly from the others, yet all equally valid, since each expresses a separate vision of the original poem. This vision can only arise when the older Platonic view of translation has given way to a relativistic viewpoint. As J. P. Sullivan expresses it:

> It is partly due to Pound with his insistence on "making it new," that we have freed ourselves from the inert Arnoldian conception of a classic, the belief that there is *one* Homer whose qualities are objectively there and merely require the right choice of meter and diction for their reproduction in English.[17]

Pound's innovations have freed modern translators from slavish adherence to sense for sense, rhyme for rhyme, and meter for meter. Instead, they turn a battery of *ad hoc* strategies (often strategies suggested by Pound) on the original poem in an attempt to give critical insight into why the original poem has importance for them.

7

Pound's Influence: Intentional Sacrifice

Sound against Sense

Pound's decisions to break with paraphrase and reproduction of all traits set up a situation in which the translator could ask himself whether to sacrifice sound to sense or sense to sound. The Victorians had attempted to keep both, a laudable goal, but one which in practice often vitiated each to the point of keeping neither. Granted, Pound's notion of reproducing sound was not the Victorian notion either, but the issue here is the intentional sacrifice of one to the other. Pound's admirer Paul Blackburn can calmly stand Victorian theory on its head:

> If the meaning is irrelevant by comparison with the musical values of the piece, translate, as best possible, what Pound calls "the *cantabile* values." But choose, so you know WHAT it is you're doing.[1]

Two "Seafarers"

Probably the best known and most influential of Pound's deliberate sacrifices is contained in his translation of "The Seafarer." In it, Pound ignores the meaning of many lines in order to imitate the sound of Anglo-Saxon poetry. Just how greatly literal sense was sacrificed to sound can be demonstrated by citing lines 80b–89. The Old English is shown below with Pound's version interlineated.

> Dagas sind gewitene,
> Days little durable,

ealle onmedlan   eorþan rices;
And all arrogance of earthen riches,

næron nu cyningas   ne caseras
There come now no kings nor Caesars

ne goldgiefan   swylce iu wæron,
Nor gold-giving lords like those gone.

þonne hi mæst mid him   mærþa gefremedon
Howe'er in mirth most magnified,

ond on dryhtlicestum   dome lifdon.
Whoe'er lived in life most lordliest,

Gedroren is þeos duguð eal,   dreamas sind gewitene,
Drear all this excellence, delights undurable!

wuniað þa wacran   ond þas woruld healdaþ,
Waneth the watch, but the world holdeth.

brucað þurh bisgo.   Blæd is gehnæged,
Tomb hideth trouble. The blade is layed low.

eorþan indryhto   ealdað ond searað. . . .
Earthly glory ageth and seareth.[2]

Although Pound has kept to the meaning in a very general way, he has changed individual meanings with abandon, always in the interest of sound. Consider

> wuniað þa wacran   ond þas woruld healdaþ,
> Waneth the watch, but the world holdeth.

The Anglo-Saxon line actually means, "Weaker folk live on and possess the earth." Similarly, Hugh Kenner points out that

. . . Pound's splendid phrase, 'The blade is layed low,' derives from a phrase ('Blæd is gehnæged') which sounds as if it ought to treat of blades, but according to the lexicon means 'glory is humbled'.[3]

"And all arrogance of earthen riches," translates a line meaning "all pomp of an earthly kingdom." "Arrogance," a close enough meaning, has been chosen for alliteration; "earthen" to copy the sound of *eorþan;* and "riches," to keep the sound of *rices* (pronounced REE-chess). The meaning has been shifted, but the sound, singing on the low, back vowels—the vowels of f<u>a</u>ll, f<u>a</u>t, and f<u>oa</u>l—keeps to vowels more predominant in Old English. In Modern English, the mid and front vowels—the vowels of b<u>u</u>t, b<u>e</u>t, and b<u>ai</u>t—are more frequent. Kenner explains Pound's intent:

> It is clear from the reduplications of his sense that developing the sense is the least of the Seafarer-bard's concerns; the meanings of the words fit in somehow, vessels into which to discharge his longing, as the structure of sound is built up, prolonged, modulated. And 'The Seafarer' being the kind of poem it is, Pound has made a similar English poem. . . . He is interested neither in Anglo-Saxon lexicography, nor in the rules for its versification (which he commences to flout in the second line); but in how the bard's throat shapes air. . . .[4]

Kenner shows what is excellent and exciting about Pound's criticism, but he does not go into the lacks of Pound's translation, or discuss the sacrifices Pound's decision entailed, beyond those of literal sense.

Burton Raffel, who translated "The Seafarer" in the fifties, admires Pound's version, but complains:

> . . . [it] is curiously stilted in places, blatantly inaccurate in others (*mæg ic* means "I can", not "May I")—but I think the reader. . .begins to feel something of the power and loveliness of the original poem. . . .

But I think our standard must be higher. . . . it seems
to me, for example, that "abided" for *gebiden hæbbe,*
rather than the modern equivalents, "endured" or "expe-
rienced", makes little sense. I also think this approach
makes for inferior music: a good translation must constantly refer more forward than back, must keep the
receiving language even more in mind than the original
one.[5]

Raffel says that in his version of "The Seafarer":

The syntax and rhythms of the original have been
bluntly discarded. . . . The images have been handled
with considerable freedom—though no more, actually,
than Pound allows himself. . . . But the freedom is (or
attempts to be) the right and the duty to re-create, not to
imitate, not to make Anglo-Saxon verse sound in modern
English as it sounded in the year 850 A.D. (an impossibility, surely). . . .[6]

Raffel's translation concentrates on complexities of meaning
and emotion. His lines about the old seaman's feelings towards
the ocean achieve a complexity of tone probably precluded by
the archaic diction and sound of Pound's version:

And who could believe, knowing but
The passion of cities, swelled proud with wine
And no taste of misfortune, how often, how wearily,
I put myself back on the paths of the sea.
Night would blacken; it would snow from the north;
Frost bound the earth and hail would fall,
The coldest seeds. And how my heart
Would begin to beat, knowing once more
The salt waves tossing and the towering sea! . . .
But there isn't a man on earth so proud,
So born to greatness, so bold with his youth,
Grown so brave, or so graced by God,

That he feels no fear as the sails unfurl,
Wondering what Fate has willed and will do.
No harps ring in his heart, no rewards,
No passion for women, no worldly pleasures,
Nothing, only the ocean's heave. . . .
    And yet my heart wanders away,
My soul roams with the sea, the whales'
Home, wandering to the widest corners
Of the world, returning ravenous with desire,
Flying solitary, screaming, exciting me
To the open ocean, breaking oaths
On the curve of a wave.[7]

Where Pound's criticism by translation showed how the Old English sound contributed to an elegiac tone, Raffel's explicates the complicated Old English symbolism. In "The Seafarer," the ocean is simultaneously the real ocean, frightening, fascinating; and also a symbol of some ambiguity: both a lure and a penance.

Pound catches nothing of this. Where Raffel has "my soul roams . . . returning ravenous with desire . . . breaking oaths / On the curve of a wave," Pound is less exciting:

So that but now my heart burst from my breastlock
My mood 'mid the mere-flood,
Over the whale's acre, would wander wide.
On earth's shelter cometh oft to me,
Eager and ready, the crying lone-flyer,
Whets for the whale-path the heart irresistibly,
O'er tracks of ocean. . . .[8]

On the other hand, where Pound has "Days little durable, / And all arrogance of earthen riches," Raffel is flatter:

        The days are gone
When the kingdoms of earth flourished in glory;
Now there are no rulers, no emperors,

No givers of gold, as once there were,
When wonderful things were worked among them
And they lived in lordly magnificence.[9]

Each of these translations is good in its way; each chooses to
emphasize certain aspects of the Old English poem at the
expense of others in direct defiance of Victorian precept.

Two "Gawains"

Raffel applied the principles developed for his Old English
translations to his later translation of *Sir Gawain and the Green
Knight.* He believed that:

> No one can produce, in modern English, exact sound
> equivalents of the *Gawain*-poet's rugged Northern
> speech. . . . The modern English is inevitably more
> effete: we have lost one kind of music and learned
> another. One does what one can.[10]

Therefore, although Raffel chose a four-stress line reminiscent
of the original form, he did not attempt to imitate the sound
of northern Middle English. Instead, he attempted to convey
the main thrust of the poem, its "ambiguity" and its
"balance."[11]

Conversely, John Gardner, another modern translator of
Gawain (and a novelist of some repute), was intrigued by those
effects of the *Gawain*-poet which depend on sound. He claims
that his translation "offer[s] what is so far the closest approx-
imation of the poet's rhythm and tone,"[12]* although to do so
he has "consistently narrowed the connotations of some of the
poet's words."[13] Gardner concentrates on imitating the chatter
and rush of the *Gawain*-poet's speech.

We have earlier seen Raffel's success in conveying the com-

---

*Gardner follows a theory which considers the *Gawain*-poet to have written five-
stress lines (Gardner, p. 87).

plexities, ironies, and ambiguities of *Gawain*. His translation usually surpasses Gardner's in these areas. However, when the *Gawain*-poet primarily uses rhythm and alliteration to convey his effects, Gardner excels. For instance, in Part 3 of the poem, Gawain is resting at a lord's castle. Every day, while Gawain lies abed, his host goes out hunting and the lady of the castle comes seeking Gawain, who, consequently, experiences a purely medieval quandary. He cannot make love to the lady, because that would be a sin. But, odd as it seems to a present-day reader, he cannot simply tell the lady, "Go away!" because *that* would offend against the code of courtly love, and make him discourteous and unknightly. The dilemma is not modern and cannot be explained in modern terms. In this section, Gardner's imitation of the *Gawain*-poet's style lends a medieval tinge to his verse. The resultant blend of times helps demonstrate that Gawain's point of view is not modern; nonetheless his dilemma is real and comic.

First Gardner catches the alliterative yowling, yelping, yelling, boasting, bugling breathlessness of the boar hunt:

> Soon by the side of a quagmire the hounds hit a scent;
> The hunting-lord cheered on the hounds that had hit it
>   first,
> Shouted out wild words with a wonderful noise;
> And when those hounds heard him shout they hurried
>   forward
> And fell on the trail in a flash, some forty at once,
> And then such a howl and yowl of singing hounds
> Rose up that the rocks all around rang out like bells;
> Hunters cheered them on with their horns and their
>   voices;
> Then, all in a group, they surged together
> Between a pool in those woods and a rugged crag,
> The dogs in a scrambling heap—. . . .
> Many were the bugle notes of the men and the dogs
> Who bounded after that boar with boasts and noise
>   for the kill;

Again and again, at bay,
He rushes the hounds pell-mell
And hurls them high, and they,
They yowp and yowl and yell.[14]

Then Gardner modulates to the bedroom scene, the *Gawain*-poet's alliteration his satirical weapon:

Thus they drove away the day with their hunting;
And meanwhile our handsome hero lies in his bed,
Lies at his ease at home. . . .[15]

"And meanwhile our handsome hero lies in his bed" strikes exactly the right tone. It translates *Whyle oure luflych lede lys in his bedde*[16] 'while our gracious knight lies in his bed'. "Our lovely laddy" would have been too sarcastic. "Our handsome hero" perfectly pinpoints the friendly irony of the original.

Now, in strong contrast to the boisterous boar hunt comes the quiet patter of courtly-love formulae:

"Sir, if you're really Sir Gawain, it's surely most
    strange—
A man whose every act is the apex of virtue
And yet who has no idea how to act in company;
And if someone teaches you manners they slip your
    mind;
All I taught you yesterday you've forgotten already,
Or so it seems to me, by some very sure signs."
"What's that?" said the knight. "I swear, I'm still in
    the dark.
If things really stand as you say, I'm sadly at fault."
"I taught you, sir, of kissing." . . .
"I didn't dare ask a kiss for fear you'd deny it.
If I asked and you refused I'd be most embarrassed."
"Well mercy!" said the merry wife, "how *could* I refuse
    you?
You're a great strong knight; you could take what you

wished, if you wanted—
If a woman were so churlish as to refuse you."
"True, by God," said Gawain, "your reasoning's good;
But where I come from force is not much
        favored. . . ."[17]

The bedchamber rhythm is slow and caressing, its alliteration soft and lisping. *S* predominates: "sir," "strange," "someone," "slip," "seems," "signs." The contrast between venery in the courtyard and venery in the bedroom is presented by the *Gawain*-poet's own contrasts of rhythm and alliteration. The reader also begins to get a feel for the longish, rather talkative line of the *Gawain*-poet.

Raffel, committed to a pared, more modern line, is less successful. Although the hunt yells lustily enough

And men and dogs lifted their voices
And ran behind him [the boar], noisily racing
                                    To a kill
            And often he spun about,
            And stood, and sliced with his
                    snout,
            And ripped a yelping,
            Leaping dog, and routed
The rest . . .[18]

the contrasting scene in the bedchamber does not come alive:

                "Ah sir,
Can you really be Gawain? Your soul reaches
Up for Goodness and Holiness, nothing
Else. Polite manners escape you;
Taught the truth you carefully forget it. . . .
"You're far too strong to accept a 'no'—
If anyone were boorish enough to deny you."
"You're right!" Gawain exclaimed. "Except that
Force and threats are indecent, with friends. . . ."[19]

Gardner's "But where I come from force is not much favored" is a much more literal and much funnier translation of *Bot þrete is vnþryuande in þede þer I lende*[20] 'But force is [considered] ignoble [the word has overtones of "unhealthy"] in the place where I live'. Gawain comes from Arthur's court, the cynosure of courtliness. In this passage, the witty courtly play on alliteration, comparable in spirit to the punning games at the court of Queen Elizabeth I, helps the reader understand, more than do Raffel's capital letters, that there are non-modern conventions at work which make courtly love-talk a question of "good manners" and scholiast "reasoning."

Raffel and Gardner each consciously chose whether to favor sound or sense. Influenced by Pound, they felt free to imitate "some qualities of the original"[21] and to let others "go by the board."[22] They have discarded the Victorian view of translation as a failed substitute for the original poem. Instead, as D. S. Carne-Ross puts it, they see translation as a critical commentary on the original poem,[23] a commentary which may legitimately aim at partial exposition.

8

Pound's Influence:
Formal Freedom

Loose Imitation of Form

For the Victorians, the notion of poetry itself was inextricably bound up with the notion of meter scannable by fixed rules. Although they believed that they owed attention to all aspects of the original poem, in reality Victorians paid most attention to finding a strict form which would be a suitable criticism of the form of the original. They either sought to substitute stress for quantity directly, syllable for syllable, or to make a line-by-line substitution of an English meter for the meter of the original.

Even when a modern translator chooses to mimic the formal qualities of his original, he usually does not attempt to render them in the Victorian manner. Instead, he may diverge from and return to a recognizable pattern, and the pattern itself may not be a clear one-for-one equivalent of the original's.

John Gardner gives the following account of his decision not to follow Victorian practice when translating *Sir Gawain and the Green Knight:*

> When I began, my general principle was to follow the poet's own rules of alliterative versification exactly . . . ;

in the end I found it necessary to abandon that principle about as often as I followed it, for it betrayed me into writing self-conscious verse.[1]

Anglo-Saxon Stressed Verse:
A Question of Burden

The loose imitation of form Gardner is espousing was first demonstrated in Pound's "Seafarer," which neither follows the Old English rules of versification nor substitutes an exact set of rules of its own. As the critic John Hollander comments:

> ... Pound's translation points up some of the basic devices of Anglo-Saxon verse and carries them over into modern English, if not tit for tat at each occurrence, then often one for another, and always with sufficient regularity to make them understood as conventions.[2]

In contrast, the earliest nineteenth-century versions of Old English poetry used ballad meter; the later ones tried to copy the rules of Old English versification exactly.[3]

To give an extremely simplified version of the Anglo-Saxon rules,[4] an Anglo-Saxon line is composed of two half-lines, which are separated by a caesura (symbolized by ‖). Each half-line has two stressed syllables and an elastic number of unstressed syllables in three basic patterns: / × / ×, × / × /, and × / / ×, where × stands for one *or more* unstressed syllables and / stands for one stressed syllable. Other allowable patterns are achieved by combining a secondary stress, \, with the primary stresses and the unstressed syllables. Among the allowable patterns are / × \ / and / / × \. Thus, a half-line must have a minimum number of four syllables. Among the few forbidden patterns for a half-line is × × / /. The two half-lines are bound together by alliteration.

Charles W. Kennedy, whose translation of "The Seafarer" was published in 1960, follows the Victorian translation mode by keeping to a strict metrical copy. A comparison of Pound

and Kennedy will show how much metrical freedom Pound
took. Kennedy wrote:

> A song I sing ‖ of my sea-adventure,
>
> The strain of peril, ‖ the stress of toil,
>
> Which oft I endured ‖ in anguish of spirit
>
> Through weary hours ‖ of aching woe.
>
> My bark was swept ‖ by the breaking seas;
>
> Bitter the watch from ‖ the bow by night
>
> As my ship drove on ‖ within sound of the
>
> rocks.
>
> My feet were numb ‖ with the nipping
>
> cold. . . .[5]

This translates:

> Mæg ic be me sylfum   soðgied wrecan,
> siþas secgan,   hu ic geswincdagum
> earfoðhwile   oft þrowade,
> bitre breostceare   gebiden hæbbe,
> gecunnad in ceole   cearselda fela,
> atol yþa gewealc,   þær mec oft bigeat
> nearo nihtwaco   æt nacan stefnan,
> þonne he be clifum cnossað.   Calde geþrungen
> wæron mine fet. . . .[6]

Kennedy's version makes it obvious how much English has
changed in sound. The Anglo-Saxon is slower, weightier; its
syllables open the mouth wider. Adhering to the rules of the

original form produces, not a similar sound, but a quicker, lighter sound pattern.

Pound's version of "The Seafarer" seeks to overcome the change in the language by reducing the number of unstressed syllables, thus increasing the weight of the lines. To do so, Pound wrote half-lines with fewer than four syllables and half-lines in the pattern x x / /.[7] Pound's opening is scanned below; underlines indicate some of the forbidden half-lines:

> x / x   x /   \   /   \   / x
> May I for my own self ‖ song's truth reckon
>
> / x / x   x / x /   \
> Journey's jargon, ‖ how I in harsh days
>
> /   \   x / /
> <u>Hardship ‖ endured oft.</u>
>
> / x /   \   x / x / x
> Bitter breast-cares ‖ have I abided,
>
> /   x   x /   \ x x /   /
> Known on my keel ‖ <u>many a care's hold</u>
>
> x /   \ /   x   \ x /   /
> And dire sea-surge, ‖ <u>and there I oft spent</u>
>
> / x /   \   x   x /   /
> Narrow nightwatch ‖ <u>nigh the ship's head</u>
>
> x   x /   \ x /   / x
> While she tossed close to cliffs. ‖ Coldly
>
> x / x
> afflicted,
>
> x /   x x /   x /
> My feet were by frost ‖ <u>benumbed.</u>[8]

Despite the fact that it breaks the rules, Pound's effort sounds more like the Old English than Kennedy's, which follows them.

Michael Alexander, who in 1966 dedicated his book *The Earliest English Poetry* to Ezra Pound, writes that he "was fired by the example of Ezra Pound's version of *The Seafarer* (which gives far and away the most concentrated impression of Anglo-Saxon poetry)."[9] Alexander states that he worked by "extending Pound's translation-method," although he chose to drop certain archaisms.[10] Regarding metrical practices, Alexander says:

> I am aware that reproducing the metre and keeping to the 'rules' of the original do not necessarily deliver the goods. But in Anglo-Saxon verse the form is of the essence . . . [for] it is a form which reinforces the meaning: the stresses fall on the four most important words in the line. . . .
>
> My aim, therefore, has been to keep to the original metre as far as possible. . . . Local departures from the strict classical form have been made for reasons that seemed good to me at the time.[11]

Upon examination, Michael Alexander's idea of keeping "to the original metre" is very different from the Victorian idea. He breaks the rules, just as Pound did, by increasing the proportion of stressed syllables. His version (with most forbidden half-lines underlined) opens:

$$\times \quad / \quad \times \quad / \qquad\qquad \times \quad \times \quad / \qquad \times \quad / \quad \times$$
The tale I frame ‖ shall be found to tally:

$$\times \quad / \quad \times \times \times \quad \times \qquad \times \quad /$$
the history is of myself. ‖

$$/ \quad \times \qquad \backslash \quad /$$
Sitting day-long

$$\times \quad \times \quad / \qquad / \qquad\qquad / \qquad \times \quad \times \qquad \backslash \quad \times \qquad / \quad \times$$
at an oar's end ‖ clenched against clinging sorrow,

$$/ \qquad \backslash \qquad \times \quad \times \qquad / \qquad\qquad \times \qquad / \quad \times \quad \times \quad /$$
breast-drought I have borne, ‖ and bitternesses too.
$$\times \quad \times \qquad / \qquad \times \quad / \qquad\qquad \times \qquad / \qquad \backslash \qquad \times \quad \backslash$$
I have coursed my keel ‖ through care-halls without

$$/$$
    end

$$\times \quad \times \qquad / \qquad\qquad / \qquad\qquad \times \quad / \quad \times \quad \times \qquad \times \quad /$$
over furled foam, ‖ I forward in the bows

$$\times \qquad\qquad \times \quad / \quad \times \quad \times \qquad\qquad / \qquad\qquad / \qquad / \quad \times$$
through the narrowing night, ‖ numb, watching

$$\times \qquad \times \quad / \qquad \times \quad / \qquad \times \quad \backslash$$
for the cliffs we beat along. ‖

$$\acute{C}\text{old th}\grave{e}n$$

$$\overset{/}{\text{nailed}}\ \overset{\times}{\text{my}}\ \overset{/}{\text{feet,}}\ \|\ \overset{/}{\text{frost}}\ \overset{/}{\text{shrank}}\ \overset{\backslash}{\text{on}}$$

$$\overset{\times}{\text{its}}\ \overset{/}{\text{chill}}\ \overset{/}{\text{clamps,}}\ \|\ \overset{/}{\text{cares}}\ \overset{/}{\text{sighed}}$$

$$\overset{/}{\text{hot}}\ \overset{\times}{\text{about}}\ \overset{\times}{}\ \overset{/}{\text{heart.}}\ \dots\ ^{12}$$

For the mathematically minded, the ratio of primary plus secondary stresses to unstressed syllables in the passages quoted is 1.33 in Pound, 1.00 in Alexander, and 0.81 in Kennedy. The ratio in the Old English is 0.90. Since in Old English the stressed syllables carry more burden than do their modern English counterparts, a translation with a ratio of 0.90 would still sound lighter. Kennedy, following the rules, has not even achieved this ratio, because he has fewer secondary stresses than the original does. Pound and Alexander, with their higher ratios, actually come closer to the burden of the original.

Villon's Rhymed Octosyllables: Rhyme on the Strong Word

The modern poet Robert Lowell's translations from François Villon read as if he had Pound's strictures in mind. Pound said Villon's "poems are gaunt,"[13] and "Translation of Villon is difficult because he rhymes on the exact word, on a word meaning sausages, for instance."[14]

Victorian handling of Villon's form is ably exemplified by Charles Algernon Swinburne's 1878 translation of Stanzas 40 and 41 (lines 313–28) of the Great Testament:

> And Paris be it or Helen dying,
>   Who dies soever, dies with pain.
> He that lacks breath and wind for sighing,
>   His gall bursts on his heart; and then
>   He sweats, God knows what sweat!—again,

No man may ease him of his grief;
   Child, brother, sister, none were fain
To bail him thence for his relief.

Death makes him shudder, swoon, wax pale,
   Nose bend, veins stretch, and breath surrender,
Neck swell, flesh soften, joints that fail
   Crack their strained nerves and arteries slender.
   O woman's body found so tender,
Smooth, sweet, so precious in men's eyes,
   Must thou too bear such count to render?
Yes; or pass quick into the skies.[15]

Swinburne's translation retains Villon's rhyme scheme of
ababbcbc exactly. Four-foot English lines replace the French
octosyllabic lines. Unlike his contemporary Payne, whose *Villon* is quoted earlier, Swinburne has solved his rhyme problem.
Villon's rhymes, as Pound noted, are on strong words: *doleur*
'grief', *alaine* 'breath', *cuer* 'heart', *sueur* 'sweat', *alege* 'relief',
pallir 'grow pale'. Swinburne manages to rhyme on many of
these in English translation: "grief," "relief," "pale."
Although "then" and "again" are hardly strong rhymes,
Swinburne draws attention away from them to the inner assonances and half-rhymes of "breath" "sweat" and "burst"
"heart."

His problems with meter are less well resolved. Villon
wastes no words; each detail fills in the clinical picture:

     La mort le fait fremir, pallir,
     Le nez courber, les vaines tendre,
     Le col enfler, la chair mollir,
     Joinctes et nerfs croistre et estendre.[16]

     (Death makes him shiver, grow pale,
     his nose curve, his veins grow taut,
     his neck swell, his flesh grow flabby,
     his joints and nerves enlarge and stretch.)

Where Villon has two nouns and two verbs per line, Swinburne finds himself using three pairs or padding with adjectives. The result, although it keeps to the visual realism of the original, seems less "gaunt."

Robert Lowell is concerned to keep Villon's spare quality. In fact, he comments that his "Villon has been somewhat stripped. . . ."[17] In his translation of Stanzas 40 and 41, Lowell uses irregular end rhyme, both full and partial, and echoes Pound's use of irregular inner rhyme in "Sestina: Altaforte." Lowell translates:

40
Helen has paid this debt—
no one who dies dies well:
breath goes, and your eyes too,
your spleen bursts through your life,
then sweat . . . God knows . . . you sweat!
No mother, child or wife
wishes to die for you,
and suffer your last hell.

41
Who cares then to die shriven?
Feet cramp, the nostrils curve,
eyes stare, the stretched veins hiss
and ache through joint and nerve—
Oh woman's body, poor,
supple, tender—is this
what you were waiting for?
Yes, or ascend to heaven.[18]

(ellipses Lowell's)

By freely varying the positions of his rhyme words and by liberal use of off-rhyme, Lowell, like Swinburne, succeeds in rhyming where rhymes intensify meaning: "debt" "sweat"; "no one dies well" "hell"; "shriven" "heaven." Even a rhyme on "this" is not a throwaway, because in context it is a heavily accented word. He has strong internal rhymes on "dies" "eyes" and "care" "stare."

Lowell's meter works better than Swinburne's. Lowell has substituted six and seven-syllable lines for the octosyllables of the French. In this, he may have taken a tip from Pound, who once commented on a translation from Italian:

> . . . I have given a *verbal* weight about equal to that of the original, and arrived at this equality by dropping a couple of syllables per line.[19]

Thus, in Stanza 41, Lowell can pair nouns and verbs, paring away the adjectives, just as Villon did.

Both Michael Alexander and Robert Lowell, following Pound's practice, are able to bring critical attention to bear on salient qualities of the original form. When a freer verse form binds itself into patterns, the patterns are all the more noticeable; the critical comments draw all the more attention.

Abandoning the Original Form

Roman Elegiac Couplets: A Positive Criticism

Under Pound's theory of intentional sacrifice, a translator may choose to abandon the form of the original entirely. In his *Homage to Sextus Propertius,* Pound made no effort to indicate the original verse form. Propertius's elegiac verse alternates dactylic hexameters with "pentameters" (so named by the Victorians), "pentameters" actually being hexameters with shortened third and sixth feet. Propertius's couplets can be symbolized by

where ___ stands for a long syllable, ‿ for a short syllable, ‿̄ means either one long or one short syllable is allowable, and ‿‿ means either one long or two short syllables are allowable. The primary or secondary stress of a word may fall anywhere in the line on either a ‿ or ___.

In Pound's translation, the lines are of many and varying lengths, as analysis of a brief passage demonstrates:

Stresses

Was Vénus exacérbated by the exístence of a

    cómparable équal?   5

    Is the órnamental góddess full of énvy?   3

Have you contémpted Júno's Pelásgian témples,   4

    Have you deníed Pállas góod eyes?   3

Or is it my tóngue that wróngs you

      with perpétual ascríption of gráces?   5

There cómes, it séems, and at ány rate   3

    through périls, (so mány) and of a véxed life,   3

The géntler hóur of an últimate dáy.[20]   4

J. P. Sullivan believes that

> A more profitable way of looking at the *vers libre* that Pound adopts as a substitute for the elegiac couplets of his original is to consider it in terms of *sense units*. The Latin elegiac couplet tends to be complete in sense, and complete in grammar. Each two-line unit is a closed system, and even this system often falls into two units, the second line frequently illustrating or summarizing the

first. It can and does lead to pleonasm and padding . . . , vices which Pound is often concerned to eliminate. This militates against making a proper generalization about Pound's verse tactics. . . . But where such vices are not in question . . . , we find [in Pound's translation] a tendency toward a long line followed by a shorter line (occasionally two shorter lines); this is not dictated by the Latin verse pattern but by the *sense pattern*.[21]

Pound, by concentrating on sense units, has sacrificed the Latin form and has instead evolved a suitable rhythm in his own language.

Yet, Pound's abandonment of Propertius's meter may paradoxically have been a positive criticism of the elegiac couplet. Pound may have intended to demonstrate by the use of free verse that Propertius used his meter in a much more interesting and flexible way than rigid, stress-counting renditions indicate.

Pound associated free verse with Latin and Greek quantitative meters. He said:

I think the desire for vers libre is due to the sense of quantity reasserting itself after years of starvation. But I doubt if we can take over, for English, the rules of quantity laid down for Greek and Latin, mostly by Latin grammarians.[22]

Two recent versions of Propertius follow Pound's example of abandoning the form of the original. J. P. McCulloch tends, like Pound, to translate in sense units; John Warden uses a variety of free and structured forms.

Below is an excerpt from McCulloch's translation. Cynthia's ghost is speaking:

"Do you forget our intrigues
    in the watching Roman night,
do you forget my window
    polished by our midnight meetings,

> when I came down a rope
> hand over hand, landing in your arms?
> Oftentimes the two of us & love mingled at the
>   crossroads,
>   heartbeat to heartbeat,
>   the road hot beneath our cloaks.
> The southerly squalls sweep deaf to our silent love pact,
>   those lies whipped off with the wind."[23]

For the most part, each of McCulloch's lines is a sense unit complete in itself, although there is enjambment across "window/polished." McCulloch is intent on tone, and uses the devices of his own language to get it, not the devices suggested by the Latin. For instance, alliteration is heavily used, although there is very little alliteration in the Latin passage. McCulloch catches up "hand over hand" with "heartbeat to heartbeat" and "the road hot." His winds are signalled by *s* and *w*: "Southerly squalls sweep," "lies whipped off with the wind." The lines, predominatly two and three-stress, can sweep out to five stresses. McCulloch creates the intense aura of sex and intrigue to be found in Propertius, but all in verse patterns newly created. He makes no gesture towards Propertius's verse form.

John Warden translates the poems of Sextus Propertius into a variety of verse forms; sometimes free verse, sometimes rhymed couplets, sometimes tercets, and sometimes more complex forms like:

> Leave me alone, you've sucked me dry
> the one you torture is not I
>   but just an empty shell
> go find yourself a virgin heart
> that has not felt your poison dart
>   a better place to dwell.[24]

The mere fact that such a variety of forms is used shows that formal equivalence is not Warden's primary interest, because Propertius used only elegiac couplets. Warden is willing on occasion to suggest the elegiac couplet in the Victorian manner by alternating lines of six and five stresses.[25]

Unlike McCulloch and Pound, in his free verse Warden works away from matching Latin sense units with English sense units. Sometimes he dismembers his lines into short phrases, using the pause at the line end to slow the pace and bring attention to bear on each of his words. The opening of Elegy 3. 17 is a good example of this:

> Bacchus YOU
> yours is the altar I crouch at now
> breathe gentle father
> gentle on my sails
> you with the power to still
> love's frantic gusting
> with wine the painkiller
> coupler disuniter YOU
> sluice this folly from my soul
> this thing (you know what I mean
> Ariadne on lynx-back
> has written your record in the stars)
> stoking the fires in my bones
> has two antidotes
> death
>   & wine
> night alone undrunk
> racks a man tosses his heart
> hoping and fearing all over the bed
> soak my blazing temples with your
>   benison
> serving a summons on sleep
> to enter my bones
> and vines I'll plant you
>   whole rows of them
>   terraced hills of them
>   (up all night keeping off predators)
> till the must is thick on the vats
> and my feet stained purple

To you Bacchus horns and all
I dedicate my life[26]

These sentences, broken up at places which strain against the
sense, concentrate on the aching torments of love:

night alone undrunk
racks a man tosses his heart
hoping and fearing all over the bed

In comparison to Warden, the Victorian James Cranstoun
dogtrots from couplet to couplet:

To Bacchus

Humbly to thine altars now I hasten,
    Fill my sails, and waft me o'er the brine;
Bacchus! thou canst haughty Venus chasten,
    And dispel the cares of love with wine. . . .

In my bones the old flames ever-burning
    Death or wine shall doom to disappear;
Sober nights keep lonely lovers turning
    On their couch, distraught by hope and fear.

But if thou this fever fierce dispellest,
    Wooing o'er my weary soul to sleep,
I thy vines will plant, train trimly-trellised,
    And secure from prowling wild beast keep—

Foam my vats with purple must, and tender
    Grapes ne'er fail my treading feet to stain!
And to thee, O hornèd god! I'll render
    Homage all my days that yet remain.[27]

Latin elegy was an elastic form into which such different
authors as Tibullus, Propertius, and Ovid poured their longer
poems; just as epic writers employed dactylic hexameter; and
just as, for several centuries, English poets employed blank
heroic verse. The essence of such meters is malleability. To

this extent, Pound, and Warden following him, by abandoning the original form are making positive criticisms of Propertius's use of meter.

Formal Freedom: Pro and Con

License to forgo imitation of form has freed poets to concentrate on other aspects of the original if they wish. It has also opened translation to a wider range of rhythms. After two centuries in which translation seemed to center around a norm of rhymed iambic pentameter couplets, free verse, with its great variety of line and stress patterns, comes as a welcome relief.

However, if conventionally scanned verse runs the danger of devolving into monotony, free verse runs the danger of becoming a formless sprawl. Robert Lowell warns:

> Strict metrical translators still exist. They seem to live in a pure world untouched by contemporary poetry. Their difficulties are bold and honest, but they are taxidermists, not poets, and their poems are likely to be stuffed birds. A better strategy would seem to be the now fashionable translations into free or irregular verse. Yet this method commonly turns out a sprawl of language. . . . I believe that poetic translation—I would call it an imitation—must be expert and inspired, and needs at least as much technique, luck and rightness of hand as an original poem.[28]

Unfortunately, many modern translations do sprawl. A great number of minor translators have adopted the method of making line-for-line, unrhymed free verse translations in a modern diction, and calling the result poetry. Maurice Valency takes the involved rhymes and deliberately obscure meanings of Raimbaut d'Aurenga, and turns them into:

> Full well I know how to speak of love
> For the good of other lovers,

But for my own good, which means more to me,
I can find no word to say.
For neither presents nor praise,
Nor curses nor hard words avail me,
Yet I am true to love,
Sincere and frank and loyal,

So I shall teach the art of love
To other good lovers of women,
And if they follow my instructions,
I shall make them conquer in a trice
As many hearts as they desire—
And let him go hang or burn
Who believes not what I say,
For all honor shall come to those
Who hold the key to this art.[29]

Anthony Bonner, a knowledgeable critic in prose, produces
Bertran de Born's "Sirventes cui motz no falh," and it sounds
little different from Valency's Raimbaut:

> I've made a *sirventes* without a line
> missing, and it cost me nothing.
> I'm the sort of man that if I have
> a brother, cousin or relation, I'll share
>   my last egg or farthing with him,
> but if he then wants my part too,
>   out he goes without a thing.[30]

And Bonner's Villon does not sound much different from his
Bertran:

> For if when young he was amusing,
> now nothing he says is pleasant:
> old monkeys always are offensive,
> and their grimaces displeasing.
> If, to please, he doesn't say

a word, people think he's senile;
if he speaks, he's told to shut
his mouth and stop his driveling.[31]

Galway Kinnell's free-verse version of Villon is considerably
better:

For if he was amusing once
Now nothing he says gets a laugh
An old monkey is always unpleasant
And every face it makes is ugly
If trying to please he keeps quiet
Everybody thinks he's senile,
If he speaks they tell him "Pipe down
That plum didn't grow on your tree."[32]

Most readers would probably prefer the Villon of Rossetti
or Swinburne to that of Bonner, and a number would still prefer Rossetti over Kinnell. On the other hand, most modern
readers would probably prefer Bonner's version to John
Payne's:

For if in youth men spoke them fair,
    Now do they nothing that is right;
(Old apes, alas! ne'er pleasing were;
    No trick of theirs but brings despite.)
    If they are dumb, for fear of slight,
Folk them for worn-out dotards hold;
    Speak they, their silence folk invite,
Saying they pay with others' gold.[33]

The great translators transcend the fashion of their times; the
minor ones merely manipulate it. Thus, the translations of
Valency, Bonner, and Payne show clearly the fashions of their
times and demonstrate how these have changed: the Victorian
compulsion to copy form is no longer with us.

9

Pound's Influence:
Deletion and Exaggeration

Pound's belief that a translation is a critical commentary led
to his practices of deletion and exaggeration. Pound included
judgments on quality and interpretation within his translations. Therefore, his deletions served two opposed critical
functions. Some were simply negative criticisms of the excised
matter. Others were positive criticisms, intended to rescue a
good poem whose literary allusions had lost their point.

Pound used exaggeration to help explain meanings muted
in an original, but clear to its contemporary audience, such as
a cautiously expressed political criticism. Such exaggerations
simply clarify an intention of the original. However, at times
Pound exaggerated themes in the original beyond what its
author could have intended. Pound did this when he was seeking to offer a new reading which challenged an entrenched
critical position.

Deletion and exaggeration were naturally forbidden by Victorian theory, which enjoined the translator to seek the one
true reflection of the original, but in a view which holds each
translation to be an idiosyncratic critical commentary, deletion
and exaggeration become acceptable ways of making critical
points.

Deletion

"The Seafarer" was Pound's first published negative criticism by deletion. He disliked the end of the poem, but, instead of straightforwardly omitting it, he argued that it was not really part of the poem, but a later, inferior, addition:

> It seems most likely that a fragment of the original poem, clear through about the first thirty lines and thereafter increasingly illegible, fell into the hands of a monk with literary ambitions, who filled in the gaps with his own guesses and "improvements". . . . I have rejected half of line 76 [*deofle togeanes* 'against the devil'], read "Angles" for angels in line 78, and stopped translating before the passage about the soul and the longer lines beginning "Mickle is the fear of the Almighty," and ending in a dignified but platitudinous address to the Deity. . . .[1]

This argument did have the support of Old English scholars.[2]
    Eight years later, Pound published his *Homage to Sextus Propertius* without apologizing for, or rationalizing, his deletions of historical and mythological material. J. P. Sullivan comments:

> Where . . . [Propertius's] mythological mania is most obvious, Pound has not used the poem. But even when he has chosen a poem to translate, he has felt free to omit the unassimilated mythological allusions. . . .[3]

Pound took Elegies 2. 30A and 2. 32, halved them, and combined them into Part 11 of the *Homage,* which ends:

> "Your glory is not outblotted by venom,
> Phoebus our witness, your hands are unspotted."
> A foreign lover brought down Helen's kingdom
>   and she was led back, living, home;
> The Cytherean brought low by Mars' lechery
>   reigns in respectable heavens, . . .

Oh, oh, and enough of this,
        by dew-spread caverns,
The Muses clinging to the mossy ridges;
        to the ledge of the rocks;
Zeus' clever rapes, in the old days,
        combusted Semele's, of Io strayed.
Oh how the bird flew from Trojan rafters,
    Ida has lain with a shepherd, she has slept between
    sheep. . . .
All things are forgiven for one night of your games . . .
Though you walk in the Via Sacra, with a peacock's tail
    for a fan.

The ellipses after "heavens" and "games" are Pound's. "Oh, oh, and enough of this" seems to express Pound's feeling that Propertius has sufficiently enumerated the amours of the gods, and thereafter Pound omits references to Minerva's distaste for Panpipes, Caliope's alleged liaison with Oeagrus, Saturn's seductions, Pasiphae's bull, Danae's shower, and a band of Hamadryad Peeping-Thomasinas.

The modern poet Kenneth Rexroth uses deletion to make a negative criticism of a poem by Sulpicius Lupercus Servasius Iunior, a poet of the fourth century. L. R. Lind notes that "the translator condenses, and translates only the second and third stanzas of the poem."[4] Servasius opens:

Omne quod Natura parens creauit,
quamlibet firmum uideas, labascit:
tempore ac longo fragile et caducum
    soluitur usu.
amnis insueta solet ire ualle.[5]

(All that Mother Nature has created, however indestructible you may think it, is perishable: fragile and fleeting, it is dissolved by time and long use. The old torrent makes a new valley.)

Rexroth cuts straight to:

> Rivers level granite mountains,
> Rains wash the figures from the sundial,
> The plowshare wears thin in the furrow;
> And on the fingers of the mighty,
> The gold of authority is bright
> With the glitter of attrition.[6]

Evidently, Rexroth likes the images of attrition, but feels that the generalized clichés of the opening lessen their power. Like Pound, he has used deletion to criticize what he dislikes while presenting what he values.

Conversely, Pound used deletion to make positive criticisms of Propertius. J. P. Sullivan points out that Propertius often used mythology well:

> Propertius frequently manages to use mythological situations symbolically, a fairly rare distinction which he shares with Horace and Virgil. . . . Not infrequently he succeeds in fusing erotic mythology with his own situation and thus effectively adds a third dimension to his affair with Cynthia. . . . Mythology is used to idealize her. . . .[7]

Sullivan explains that "Propertius could, by a mere name, bring a whole story before his reader's mind. . . ." However, the modern reader, unfamiliar with the mythology, finds it "a stumbling block."[8] Pound, therefore, in order to rescue the poetry from an undeserved aura of obscurity, deletes part of Elegy 2. 13A.

In this elegy, Propertius imagines his own funeral. The end of Pound's translation reads:

> Nor at my funeral either will there be any long trail,
>   bearing ancestral lares and images;

No trumpets filled with my emptiness, . . .
A small plebeian procession. . . .

You will follow the bare scarified breast
Nor will you be weary of calling my name, nor too
        weary
        To place the last kiss on my lips
When the Syrian onyx is broken.

"HE WHO IS NOW VACANT DUST WAS ONCE THE SLAVE OF ONE PASSION":

Give that much inscription
        "Death why tardily come?"
You, sometimes, will lament a lost friend,
        For it is a custom:
This care for past men,

Since Adonis was gored in Idalia, and the Cytherean
Ran crying with out-spread hair,
        In vain, you call back the shade,
In vain, Cynthia. Vain call to unanswering shadow,
        Small talk comes from small bones.[9]

Pound renders Propertius's affected humility: "A small plebeian procession"; he captures the adolescent bathos: "Nor
will you be . . . too weary / To place the last kiss on my lips";
he achieves the shift to a more ironic adult perspective: "For
it is a custom: / This care for past men. . . ." Then, via the
vivid image of grief-stricken Cytherea (Venus), the poem suddenly moves away from various shades of self-pity to a serious
confrontation with the meaning of death: "Vain call to unanswering shadow, / Small talk comes from small bones."

The shifts in tone are in the original, but Propertius relied
on excised mythological references to achieve them. First,
Propertius writes his poetic epitaph and compares his resultant

fame to the Phthian hero:

> et duo sint versus: QVI NVNC IACET HORRIDA
> PVLVIS
>   VNIVS HIC QVONDAM SERVVS AMORIS
>   ERAT.
> nec minus haec nostri notescet fama sepulchri,
>   quam fuerant Phthii busta cruenta viri.

> (Let there be [on my tombstone] two lines of verse: Who
> now lies here rude dust once served one love alone. This
> [will make the] fame of my sepulchre be no less known
> than was the gory tomb of the Phthian hero.)

The Phthian hero is Achilles, the comparison intentionally
ludicrous. Next, Propertius wishes he had died in the cradle.
His mind still on the Trojan War, he remarks that if Nestor
had not lived so long:

> non ille Antilochi vidisset corpus humari
>   diceret aut "O mors, cur mihi sera venis?"

> (he would not have had to see Antilochus [his son] bur-
> ied, nor have said, "Death, why do you come so late for
> me?")

Propertius seems to be implying, among other things, that if
Nestor had died young, Roman students would have escaped
having to memorize the tag; now that Propertius has lived so
long, students will be mouthing his *duo versus.* The boast is
half serious, half comic. Finally, after shifting again to irony:
"You will weep at least sometimes" *(non numquam flebis)*, Propertius composes a serious address to Venus, in which "Thou,
Venus" is purposely confused with "Thou, Cynthia."

Pound evidently judged that Propertius can no longer evoke
laughter at the mere thought of comparing himself to Achilles
and Nestor; nor would the modern audience understand that

Propertius was mock-claiming the status of a classic for his two lines of verse. Pound shifted the burden of the humor to nonallusive irony. "Death why tardily come?" is in quotes for those who can recognize the source, but can stand on its own as an instance of maudlin self-pity. By judicious deletion, Pound has managed to reproduce the emotional gamut of the original passage, and even, with the image of Venus grieving, to suggest some of Propertius's skill at mythological allusion.

John Warden evidently learned from Pound. Warden understands the limits of contemporary acquaintance with mythology, yet, by using deletion, he conveys Propertius's facility with allusion. Warden translates from Elegy 2.3:

> Woman-proof, eh?
> Proud words but just look at you.
> Barely a month's rest
> and another shameful volume
> ready for writing.
>
> It was an experiment
> to find out whether fishes
> could live on the dry land
> or the savage boar
> change his natural habitat
> in favour of the ocean
> or Propertius
> take to serious study
> and work nights.
>
> But you can't get away from love
> he breaks you down
> in his own good time.
> It wasn't so much her beauty (Oh, her beauty—
> skin whiter than lilies
> Spanish vermilion set against snows of Tauris
> rose petals floating on milk)
> or her hair flowing modishly
> over her delicate shoulders

or her eyes burning like torches
twin stars of my firmament;
and any girl can glow
with the sheen of Arabian silk
(I'm not the sort
to fall for things like that)
But the way she dances
    (when dinner's over and the wine is served)
       graceful as Ariadne queen among maenads
and plays the lyre with the skill of the muse herself
and writes like a second Corinna
Oh my darling
on the day that you were born
    shining love
       sneezed loud and clear
and all the other gods heaped on you
presents from heaven
       (not as you may think
your mother's womb; gifts like yours
are the products of no human parturition
nine months is far too short)[10]

When the above translation is compared to Sir Charles Elton's, given earlier, the difference between modern and Victorian treatment of Roman allusions is striking. Elton has retained Ariadne, Bacchus, Sappho, Scythia, Ebro, Aganippe, Corinna, and Erinne. In Elton's time and ours the ancient names studding his verses lend dignity to his statements, so that his meaning seems to run, "It is not only Cynthia's great beauty which attracts me, but also her skill in dancing and composing poetry." However, in Propertius's day, some of the names and places were common property and some were obscure. These nuances escape Elton. Consequently, in his translation, Propertius's overlong paean has lost its comic point. Warden, by deleting many of these references, casts off the mantle of dignity, and is able to distinguish the different levels of familiarity. Ariadne and the muse are well known. The place names, modernized (Spain, the Taurus Mountains

of Turkey), are places we have heard of. Then comes that suddenly obscure reference to Corinna. Warden's translation
makes it clear that Corinna was obscure in Augustan times,[11]
that Propertius, howevermuch impressed with Cynthia's
dancing, intends his compliment to her poetry to be less than
fulsome. In Warden's hands, as in Pound's, deletion can serve
as a positive criticism.

Exaggeration

Pound intentionally exaggerated certain tones and meanings in the poetry of Sextus Propertius, because he felt that
otherwise his radical new reading might go unnoticed. He was
explicit about his intent to challenge the accepted reading:

> The philologists have so succeeded in stripping the
> classics of interest that I have already had more than one
> reader who has asked me, 'Who was Propertius?' As for
> my service to classical scholarship, presumably nil, I shall
> be quite content if I induce a few Latinists really to look
> at the text of Propertius instead of swallowing an official
> 'position' and then finding what the textbooks tell them
> to look for.[12]

He also remarked:

> MacKail* (accepted as "right" opinion on the Latin
> poets) hasn't, apparently, *any* inkling of the *way* in which
> Propertius is using Latin. Doesn't see that S. P. is tying
> blue ribbon in the tails of Virgil and Horace.[13]

According to the view expressed in 1895 by the so stigma-
tized John W. Mackail, a Latin scholar, Propertius was the

---

*Pound may here be referring to William Gardner Hale, whose name he frequently
confounded with Mackail's, but he is most probably referring (correctly) to John W.
Mackail, author of the then authoritative *Latin Literature* (New York: Charles Scribner's Sons, 1904 [1st printing, 1895]).

embodiment of "abandonment to sensibility," "absorption in self-pity and the sentiment of passion," and "self-absorption."[14] This was the tune sawed by the band of Latin literature surveys. R. Y. Tyrrell in 1893 praised Propertius's "ardent sincerity in the expression of the passion of love."[15] J. Wight Duff, in his 1909 literary history of Rome, found Propertius a man of "desperate sincerity," a man whose character was the embodiment of a "pre-eminently Italian intensity of warm, luxurious passion."*[16] Propertius the sincere and self-pitying was the poet made familiar to Victorian readers by Victorian translators.

J. P. Sullivan, whose major field is the classics, argues that Pound's reading is an important critical re-evaluation. Sullivan says that "Propertius' private themes, the center of his art, are in modern eyes love, passion, and his mistress Cynthia."[17] But, Sullivan explains, Pound was not so much interested in the love-poetry as in pointing out themes in Propertius which had been misunderstood or ignored.[18] He argues that Propertius did put forth some cautious criticism of Horace's and Vergil's poetic support of Augustus,[19] and believes that Pound's shift in emphasis brings "to the fore an important and neglected aspect of Propertius' work. . . ."[20]

Pound shifts emphases in the *Homage* by means of selection and arrangement and by outright exaggeration of meaning. In Propertius, at least three-fourths of the poems are concerned with love; in the *Homage,* about half the translated selections deal with the art of poetry or the pressures to write propaganda. Pound opens the *Homage,* not with a love poem from Book 1, but with the beginning of Book 3:

> Shades of Callimachus, Coan ghosts of Philetas,
> It is in your grove I would walk,
> I who come first from the clear font

---

*To which one can only reply with the ridicule of W. S. Gilbert: "MAD MARGARET: He gave me an Italian glance—thus *(business)*—and made me his" (*Ruddigore* [1887], *The Complete Plays of Gilbert and Sullivan,* The Modern Library [New York: Random House, n.d.], p. 424).

Bringing the Grecian orgies into Italy,
                    and the dance into Italy.
Who hath taught you so subtle a measure,
            in what hall have you heard it;
What foot beat out your time-bar,
            what water has mellowed your whistles?

Out-weariers of Apollo will, as we know,
    continue their
            Martian generalities,
        We have kept our erasers in order.[21]

To open with the above elegy puts emphasis on Propertius's artistic credo. Propertius's Book 1 opens with love songs to Cynthia, whereas in this elegy Propertius declares formal allegiance to the Alexandrian school of poetry founded by Philetas of Cos (fl. 290 B.C.) and continued by the poet-critic Callimachus of Cyrene (fl. 260 B.C.).[22] This particular elegy also emphasizes Propertius's antipathy to writing pro-war and Empire propaganda: Propertius declares: *a valeat, Phoebum quicumque moratur in armis! / exactus tenui pumice versus eat*[23] 'Goodbye to whoever delays Appolo with weapons! Let the verse be made precise with a finicky pumice-stone [*i.e.,* eraser]'.

However, the exaggeration goes beyond that of selection and placement. Pound has also deliberately exaggerated the anti-imperial trend of Propertius's words. Later in this same elegy Propertius writes:

multi, Roma, tuas laudes annalibus addent,
        qui finem imperii Bactra futura canent.
    sed, quod pace legas. . . .[24]

(Rome, many add to your praises, who sing that Bactra is about to become the boundary of the empire. But what will you read in peace?)

Pound translates the lines as a defiant rejection of imperial propaganda:

Annalists will continue to record Roman reputations,
Celebrities from the Trans-Caucasus will belaud Roman
    celebrities
And expound the distensions of Empire,
But for something to read in normal circumstances?[25]

J. P. Sullivan explains that the second of the above lines "is achieved by taking *Roma, laudes, imperii, Bactra,* ignoring their actual meaning in the context and producing a plausible and amusing line."[26] But "distensions of Empire" and "normal circumstances" are not merely plausible and amusing phrases. They exaggerate what the Latin merely hints: the tense of *futura* seems to imply that Propertius did not approve of the semiperpetual state of war. So also does the line *sed, quod pace legas* 'But what will you read in peace?' Under the lenient censorship of Augustus, Propertius was allowed to go so far, but there were limits on what he could say. Pound has gone far beyond what was allowed Propertius. By so exaggerating, Pound has brought out for the modern audience what was probably quite clear to the Roman reader, yet had been ignored by Victorian and Edwardian critics.

More than one recent translation has used exaggeration as a method of criticism. James J. Wilhelm, a scholar and translator in the field of Provençal poetry, does so in his translation of our much-discussed *sirventes,* Bertran de Born's Praise of War. Wilhelm begins with the accustomed meaning:

How I like the gay time of spring
That makes leaves and flowers grow,
And how I like the piercing ring
Of birds, as their songs go
Echoing among the woods.
I like it when I see the yield

Of tents and pavilions in fields,
And O, it makes me feel good
To see arrayed on battlefields
Horses and horsemen with shields.[27]

But when he gets to the two *tornadas,* Wilhelm rejects one, which appears in only one of fifteen extant manuscripts,[28] and translates the other:

Barons, put up as pawns
Those castles, cities, and villas well-stored
Before bringing each other war![29]

The perplexed reader is likely to turn to the original *tornada,* only to find that it says:

Baros, metetz en gatge
Chastels e vilas e ciutatz
Enans qu'usquecs nous guerrejatz.

(Barons, pawn castles and towns and cities before you don't wage war among yourselves.)

Wilhelm has changed the meaning because he feels that, taking the poem as a whole, "the tornada really serve[s] the opposite purpose from what most people think. . . ."[30] Wilhelm says that the poem

is about as realistic a literary portrait as we have anywhere of the brutality of war. . . . The Provensal word for spring, *pascor,* which descends from Late Latin *Pascha,* meaning Easter, seems double travestied. . . . Instead of inviting war, as one expects a warmonger to do, does Bertran not in fact actually discourage combat by portraying it in all of its starkest colors?[31]

It appears that Wilhelm, disagreeing with the usual interpretation of the poem, has exaggerated a meaning he believes to be present. His reading does not entirely convince me, just as I am not entirely convinced that Propertius was as vehemently anti-empire as Pound paints him. Still, Wilhelm's translation first drew my attention to the spring harvest of tents and the Easter ceremony of war. Like Pound, Wilhelm has made exaggeration a corrective to an entrenched critical position.

Frank O. Copley uses exaggeration in translating Catullus. He said of Catullus's style:

> . . . his poems for the most part have all the ease and simplicity, the clarity and the subtlety of a conversation between good friends. But he also understood the poetry of slang and obscenity; he knew that even the polite formula and the dull cliché have their poetic uses.[32]

In order to demonstrate the range and quality of Catulus's language, Copley has translated him into the idiom of e. e. cummings.[33] John Frederick Nims, a poet and translator, has objected that this falsifies Catullus.[34] However, Copley is trying to make a critical point, and to make it against several centuries of translation written as if Catullus had never used any slang and had never used a dirty word.

Copley wrote his translation of Catullus 13 (earlier quoted in full) against such products as the following, written by James Cranstoun in 1867:

An Invitation to Dinner

If the gods will, Fabullus mine,
With me right heartily you'll dine.
Bring but good cheer—that chance is thine
      Some days hereafter;
Mind, a fair girl too, wit, and wine,
      And merry laughter.

Bring these—you'll feast on kingly fare;
But bring them—for my purse—I swear

The spiders have been weaving there;
    But thee I'll favor
With a pure love, or what's more rare,
    More sweet of savor,

An unguent I'll before you lay
The Loves and Graces t'other day
Gave to my girl—smell it—you'll pray
    The gods, Fabullus,
To make you turn all nose, straightway.
    Yours aye, Catullus.[35]

Cranstoun has portrayed the conversational tone discussed by
Copley, but not the slang.

Copley's version uses slang throughout, although the slang
in Catullus is limited to only a few lines of the original. When
Catullus writes *uenuste noster / . . . accipies meros amores / seu
quid suauius elegantiusue est: / nam unguentum dabo*[36] 'My dear,
take a pure love, or something more suave and more elegant:
I will give you perfume', he is writing in the language of the
Roman smart set.[37] *Venuste, elegantiusue,* and *suauius,* words
special to Catullus's circle,[38] produce a tone which could fairly
be translated: "DAHLING, take my utterly pure love, or
something too, too suave and elegant—a scent." Against these
lines is set perfectly ordinary language. *Cenabis bene, mi
Fabulle, apud me / paucis . . . diebus* 'Fabullus my friend, you
will dine well at my place in a few days' is plain, unaffected
conversational Latin. Therefore when Copley begins

> say, Fabullus
> you'll get a swell dinner at my house
> a couple three days from now[39]

and carries this tone throughout the entire poem, he is exaggerating the amount of slang in Catullus. Further, the slang
chosen by Copley is not exactly the slang indicated by Catullus: *suauius* and "cherce" are poles apart. Copley may have felt
that doing the poem in the "DAHLING" idiom would turn

the undertone of homosexuality conveyed by the proximity of *uenuste noster* and *accipies meros amores* into a trumpet blast. He chose instead a diction with more virile connotations for his American audience, and reduced the homosexual implications to their proper proportions:

> you just do that like I tell you ol' pal ol' pal
> you'll get a swell dinner
>   ?
>   what,
>   about,
>   ME? . . .
>   I CAN'T GIVE YOU ANYTHING BUT
>   LOVE BABY
> no?[40]

By exaggerating the amount of slang in Catullus, and by changing its type, Copley is able to present his thesis that it is there at all.

Copley and Wilhelm exaggerate in order to overcome an entrenched position. They force the reader to notice what is new in their readings, and the critics to re-examine the original poem, if only to make a rebuttal.

If a translation of a work were somehow to be the only comment ever made on it, then Rexroth, Warden, Copley, and Wilhelm's deletions and exaggerations would be irresponsible. However, considering that literal translations, paraphrases, and critical commentaries galore exist for the poems they so handle, deletion and exaggeration are acceptable critical tools.

10

Pound's Influence: Criticism by Analogy

Local and Non-Local Derivatives and Equivalents

Victorian translators not only translated by paraphrase, but by and large tended toward the literal pole of the range permitted by paraphrase. Similarly, while many modern translators make creative translations, in general they tend more toward paraphrase than toward imitation. Translators usually shy away from altering an original as radically as "Sestina: Altaforte" alters the Sirventes in Praise of War. But translators have wholeheartedly accepted Pound's strategy of criticism by analogy. When an original poem depends for its effects on a lost cultural background, or on subtleties peculiar to the capabilities of its own language, modern translators abandon paraphrase. They search for an allusion known to their audience, or create a play on the English language. These analogous effects may be achieved at the same point in the poem or they may be introduced elsewhere, as the structure of English permits. This is what Pound urged when he commented, "*Logopoeia* does not translate. . . . Or one might say you can *not* translate it 'locally', but . . . you may . . . be able to find a derivative or an equivalent."[1]

Victorians, in addition to shunning analogy, also tended to exclude all meanings not present in the original poem. Thus, translation was necessarily a process of loss with no compensatory gains. Victorian translators were often reduced to pointing out the jokes they could not reproduce in footnotes, which at least acknowledged the humor they could not copy.[2] Hugh Kenner suggests that Victorian difficulties partly inhered in "the cult of the dictionary, an eighteenth-century invention which came to inhibit everyone by suggesting that languages were systems of equivalences."[3]

Pound did not see languages as systems of equivalences, but as shaped energies, as he attempted to explain in a youthful and cumbersome simile:

> Let us imagine that words are like great hollow cones of steel of different dullness and acuteness; I say great because I want them not too easy to move; they must be of different sizes. Let us imagine them . . . radiating a force from their apexes—some radiating, some sucking in. . . . Some of these kinds of forces neutralize each other, some augment. . . . This peculiar energy which fills the cones is the power of tradition, of centuries of race consciousness, of agreement, of association; and the control of it . . . nothing short of genius understands.[4]

Wai-Lim Yip rightly connects the cones to logopoeia, which "takes count of habits of usage," and which, "having determined the original author's state of mind," one may be able to translate by "a derivative or an equivalent."[5] Yip concludes that the state of mind of the original author is compounded of the "power of tradition, of centuries of race consciousness, of agreement, of association." He then remarks that the translator's

> role as a "bridgemaker" lies *not* where he can annotate . . . in terms of the "tradition, race consciousness, agreement and association" in the original language, but where he can improvise . . . to obtain corresponding effects . . . in the "tradition, race consciousness, agreement and association" of his *own* language.[6]

Such thinking caused Pound to translate the Greek word
krēdemnon as "bikini": " 'My bikini is worth yr/ raft'. Said
Leucothoe."[7] A *krēdemnon,* according to the Greek scholars
Liddel and Scott, " . . . seems to have been a sort of *veil* or
mantilla with lappets passing over the head and hanging down
on each side, so that at pleasure it might be drawn over the
face."[8] Hugh Kenner, in his essay, "Leucothea's Bikini,"
points out the numerous considerations which induced Pound
to turn an Argive article of female headwear into a bikini. For
one thing, Ulysses is supposed to look funny wearing a
female's bonnet. For another:

> With tiller and yardarm gone, the raft a shuttlecock for
> wind gods, Poseidon Earthshaker rearing up great black
> waves, are we to pause for an archaeological footnote
> about the costumes of Greek ladies? Or to wonder why
> a sea nymph's costume includes something to put on her
> head? Something, moreover, with strings to tie it shut
> across her face? A miraculous garment is what the story
> requires, a miraculous garment wearable at sea.[9]

Similarly, Pound translated *a valeat, Phoebum quicumque moratur in armis* as "Out-weariers of Apollo will, as we know, continue their / Martian generalities. . . ."[10] Since the associations
of English allow a pun at this point, Pound takes the opportunity to make a non-local equivalent of the puns in
Propertius.

Following Pound's lead, many modern translators are
replacing footnote with analogy. Since 1940, translators and
translation theorists have written extensively on the need to
consider the resources of the language into which the translation is being made. John Peale Bishop, a poet and a translator, credits Pound as the initiator and adds:

> . . . Pound's aim thirty years ago was what I think must
> be our aim—to make available to readers in English what
> would be otherwise inaccessible to them and to write
> nothing which will cause the translator to sound as

though it were English that to him was the alien speech.[11]

Modern theorists feel strongly about the desirability of translations that are good English poetry. One, D. S. Carne-Ross, went so far as to commission poets who did not know Greek to translate from the *Iliad* for a BBC radio project. He explained:

> Translators were chosen for the excellence of their English, rather than the excellence of their Greek, and several, some of the most successful, in fact, knew no Greek at all. Some people, I know, regard this as little short of immoral: all I can say is that it works. If a man is a poet, and the right kind of poet for the job in hand, he can *guess* what the original is like from a crib. . . .[12]

Poets have gone to Pound's work for practical examples of how to make criticism by analogy. In particular, the *Homage to Sextus Propertius* demonstrated how the strengths peculiar to English could be used to compensate for untranslatable effects dependent on the serendipities of other languages.

Imitating the Devices of the Original

Topical Allusions
In the *Homage,* Pound often used modern allusions to explain Roman topical references. For instance, he wrote, " . . . my house . . . is not stretched upon gilded beams; / . . . Nor is it equipped with a frigidaire patent. . . ."[13] Elsewhere he commented, "Go on, to Ascraeus' prescription, the ancient, / respected, Wordsworthian. . . ."[14] The frigidaire patent explains the gilded beams. Propertius was proclaiming his lack of the latest in home furnishings. The reference to Wordsworth characterizes Propertius's view of "Ascraeus." Pound may have decided not to identify Ascraeus as Hesiod specifically to avoid a stock response to the name of Hesiod. Then

the anachronistic analogy could summon a response parallel to the one Pound felt in Propertius. Such analogies can never be exact parallels, but they can help the reader relate Roman culture to his own.

Pound's influence can be seen in the anachronistic analogies favored by Dudley Fitts in his translations of Martial's epigrams. Fitts explains that he has chosen to use analogy because

> Nothing is more inert than a witticism that has to be explained. Topicality, the recondite allusion, special jargon—these are matters that can not be handled . . . in a . . . footnote without inviting the embrace of death.[15]

Therefore, when Fitts comes to Martial's excuse for being late, he writes:

> Pete, I admit I was late. It took me ten hours
> to cover a mile.
>   It was not my fault, but yours:
> Why did you lend me your car?[16]

"Car" replaces "mules" for the same reasons that frigidaire is added to Propertius: to make Martial's point clear in modern terms.

In another poem, Fitts finds an extended analogy for a down-home Roman girl affecting to be a Greek hetaera:

Local Products Preferred

> Abigail, you don't hail from La Ville
> Lumière, or Martinique, or even Québec, P.
> Q., but from plain old Essex County;
> Cape Ann, believe me, for ten
> generations.
>   Accordingly, when
> you gallicize your transports, such as they are,
> and invoke me as *mon joujou!, petit*

trésor!, vit de ma vie!, I grow
restive.
        It's only bed-talk, I know,
but not the kind of bed-talk you
were designed for, darling.
                Let's you and me
go native. Damn your Berlitz. Please,
woman, you're an Abigail,
             not a *pièce exquise.*[17]

Instead of Martial's three Greek-speaking cities, listed in order
of increasingly impure accent, Fitts produces three analogous
French-speaking cities. For the common Roman name *Laelia,*
Fitts substitutes "Abigail." Martial says that *Laelia* is not a *Lais,*
evidently a name common among Greek courtesans; Fitts substitutes the French phrase *pièce exquise.*

    Fitts's practice is a complete turnabout form the Victorian
practice of dutifully reproducing each proper name in Martial,
no matter that its point has long been lost. James Cranstoun,
for instance, begins one translation:

> To boast, Charmenion, is your practice
> That you're from Corinth—now, the fact is
> Disputed not by one or other—
> But why, for heaven's sake, call me Brother—
> Me, born in Celteberia's land,
> A citizen from Tagus' strand?[18]

Cranstoun makes it clear that Corinth was far from Celteberia,
but not that Celteberia was in Spain; nor does he give any hint
of the Roman stereotypes of Greek and Spaniard underlying
Martial's question. Greeks were supposed to be overcivilized
and ineffective; Spaniards, aggressively masculine and ener-
getic administrators.
    The difference between Cranstoun and Fitts is the differ-
ence between Victorian paraphrase and modern creative translation. The Victorian translates literally the place names and

objects in the name of fidelity. Fitts, following Pound, tries to parallel tone, rather than the literal sense.

Homophones

Puns on homophones can also be imitated either locally or non-locally. Pound evidently felt that if an author punned frequently, a faithful translator should pun too, even at the expense of additional or shifted meanings.

> If she goes in a gleam of Cos, in a slither of dyed stuff,
> There is a volume in the matter. . . .[19]

translates:

> sive illam Cois fulgentem incedere coccis,[20]
>   hoc totum e Coa veste volumen erit. . . .[21]

(Say that shimmering she walks in scarlet Coan [silk]; the entire book will be of Coan clothing.)

Volumen usually meant "book," but books were scrolls, and *volumen*, in poetic usage, also meant "swirl" or "fold."[22] Pound has shifted the pun from the folds of cloth to the body within, and in the process retained Propertius's wit.

A number of recent translators follow Pound's example. J. P. McCulloch unashamedly turns a Propertian reference to Socrates into "What good do your Platonic platitudes / do you now?"[23]

Horace, too, puns occasionally, as in the opening of Satire 1. 8: *Olim truncus eram,* says the wooden Priapus: "Once I was a log" or "Once I was a blockhead." Translator Smith Palmer Bovie consequently puns when he can, dubbing Cicuta the Moneylender (whose name means hemlock), "the Shylock named Hemlock."[24] Bovie adds a bilingual pun in legal jargon to some joshing about the personal quirks of Trebatius, the lawyer:

Treb[atius]:
    To one in default of sleep, I decree as follows:
Rub well with oil the party of the first part, then swim
(Transnatate) the Tiber thrice, then habeas your corpus
Well soaked with wine at night.[25]

Dudley Fitts demonstrates Martial's dapper wit by supplying puns on both "shy" and "two":

Madrigal for Two Voices

'Q's in love with Lily.'
               'Lily who?'
'Shy-an-eye-Lily.'
               'Q's shy two.'[26]

Elsewhere, Fitts recreates a pun locally:

On Chloe, a Widow Too Frequent

On each of the seven tombs of her seven husbands
you will find this plain inscription:
ERECTED BY CHLOE.[27]

This translates:

Inscripsit tumulis septem scelerata uirorum
se FECISSE Chloe. Quid pote simplicius?[28]

(On the tombs of seven husbands poisonous Chloe has inscribed that she built them [*or*, she did it]. What could be plainer?)

Fitt's Chloe seems to have employed a different murder weapon, but the joke is made.

The intricate double and triple meanings in Provençal poetry are indicated in Paul Blackburn's translations. His facility rescues a pun in Peire Vidal's "A per pauc de chantar no.m lais." Vidal is complaining that the Spanish kings fight each other, instead of their common enemy, the Moors:

> Dels reis d'Espanha.m tenh a fais,
> Quar tan volon guerra mest lor. . . .[29]

(It troubles me about the kings of Spain, because they so desire war among themselves.)

The phrase *me tenh a fais* combines several idioms. Joseph Anglade takes it to mean "it troubles me."[30] However, *fais* alone means "burden, weight, bundle," and *a fais* means "together, as one." *Faire fais* means "to trouble, to make sick," and *tener a* means "to take for, to understand as."[31] Peire Vidal seems to have scrambled several idioms in order to say all at the same time that the kings of Spain, "taken as a group," "burden me" and "make me sick," but "I understand the lot of them." Blackburn neatly renders the passage:

> The kings of Spain
> give me a general pain.[32]

Most of Vidal's meanings are there, plus an apposite slur on the Spanish kings' military leadership.

The return of the pun marks a great change in translation style. Victorian translators seem never to pun in their Provençal translations, although Provençal was a language in which it was almost impossible to avoid punning. They punned rarely in their Latin translations, even when the poet translated, such as Propertius or Martial, often punned. The puns in recent translations, despite their shifts in meaning, are given as criticisms of the original poem, as Pound taught translators to do.

Meaning Spread

Pound's innovation of criticism by analogy, both local and non-local, has even affected poet-translators who do not like Pound's poetry. Allen Tate's translation of "Pervigilium Veneris"[33] demonstrates non-local imitation of the most sophisticated order. Tate imitates the Latin device of meaning spread: a word with disparate meanings is used, with both meanings simultaneously intended.

"Pervigilium Veneris," a Late Latin poem, was written for the ancient festival in honor of Venus.[34] It celebrates vegetal, animal, and human sexuality and fertility. The ninety-three line poem uses the spread of meanings commonly found in Latin words to create an overpowering aura of sexuality. Words used to name the parts of flowers frequently have other meanings referring to parts of the human body: the poem does not mention leaves without also meaning hair, or mention buds without also meaning breasts. When, near the beginning of the poem, Venus causes the roses to flower, the anonymous author repeatedly used the words *nodi* 'clusters', *papillae* 'buds', and *gemmae* 'buds.' However, *nodi* also means "sashes," and *papillae,* "breasts." *Gemmae* usually means "jewels."

Pound was interested in the poem, devoting part of an essay, "The Phantom Dawn,"[35] to it. He remarked elsewhere on its use of meaning spread in the word *comae* 'leaves' or 'hair'.[36]

Tate wrote in his Introduction to "The Vigil of Venus" of "doctoring the material in the eighteenth-century manner,"[37] thus acknowledging a reversion to pre-Victorian methods of translation. However, Tate stays fairly close to the Latin, making a creative translation, not a full-scale imitation.

As Tate describes the activities of Venus:

IV

She shines the tarnished year with glowing buds
That, wakening, head up to the western wind
In eager clusters. Goddess! You deign to scatter
Lucent night-drip of dew; for you are kind.

Tomorrow may loveless, may lover tomorrow
make love.

V
The heavy teardrops stretch, ready to fall,
Then falls each glistening bead to the earth beneath:
The moisture that the serene stars sent down
Loosens the virgin bud from the sliding sheath.

 Tomorrow may loveless, may lover tomorrow
  make love.

VI
Look, the high crimsons have revealed their shame.
The burning rose turns in her secret bed,
The goddess has bidden the girdle to loose its folds
That the rose at dawn may give her maidenhead.

 Tomorrow may loveless, may lover tomorrow
  make love.

VII
The blood of Venus enters her blood, Love's kiss
Has made the drowsy virgin modestly bold;
Tomorrow the bride is not ashamed to take
The burning taper from its hidden fold.

 Tomorrow may loveless, may lover tomorrow
  make love.[38]

In a comparatively simple use of non-local analogy, Stanza 6 contains "The burning rose turns in her secret bed." No bed occurs in the Latin, but since the English meanings of bed include both gardens and couches, Tate has taken this opportunity to imitate the device of meaning spread.

A far more complicated imitation takes place in Stanza 5. Tate translates *virgines papillas solvit umenti peplo* 'unfolds the virgin buds from their dewy blouse' as "Loosens the virgin bud from the sliding sheath." Tate could not suggest, as could the Latin author, that the wet, unopened buds were breasts. Tate instead turned to the garment, the blouse, and made it a sheath, which in English is both a tight-fitting dress and the bud cover. Further, by the addition of the adjective "sliding" before sheath, Tate achieves yet more meaning spread. The budsheath, if characterized as sliding, becomes simultaneously clothing and foreskin. This addition is a criticism, both of method and meaning, because it is a non-local equivalent to the suggestions of the Latin Stanza 7:

> cras ruborem qui latebat veste tectus ignea
> uvido marita nodo non pudebit solvere.[39]

(Tomorrow the married woman will not be ashamed to release from the dewy knot [or sash] the redness which was hiding, covered with a glowing garment.)

Roses have both male and female organs, and here the Latin is deliberately unclear as to whether the *rubor* 'redness, blush, cause-for-shame' belongs to the male or the female. Tate, by a brilliant invention, has transferred this hermaphroditic ambiguity to Stanza 5. Then, in Stanza 7, Tate drops the female imagery, and concentrates on the usually undiscerned male imagery:

> Tomorrow the bride is not ashamed to take
> The burning taper from its hidden fold.

There is no taper in the Latin. Tate takes the image from J. W. Mackail's intriguing prose translation.[40] Elsewhere close to literal, Mackail translates the above two lines:

> . . . tomorrow the bride unashamed will unfold from the wet cluster the crimson that lurked hid in its taper sheath.[41]

Mackail, perhaps hoping to keep some of the male references in English, invents taper, but holds it to the status of an adjective. Tate, seeing its possibilities, has made it into a burning noun.

Tate's ability to imitate Latin devices is not limited to mean-

ing spread. The opening of Stanza 4 shows how he can shift
meaning slightly to re-create metaphors in the Latin manner.
The Latin imagery deals with jewelry: *ipsa gemmis purpurantem
pingit annum floridis* 'she herself paints (*or* adorns) the crimson-
ing year with flower-buds (*or* gems)'. Tate writes: "She shines
the tarnished year with glowing buds." He cannot have simultaneous bud-jewels as in Latin, and therefore ingeniously
returns the jewelry to the scene by having Venus polish silver.
The image is closer to the Latin implications than is apparent
at first reading, because *purpura* is a color ranging from crimson through purple to a purplish brown. Merely by changing
purpurantem from active to passive, Tate arrives at his image.

The nineteenth century saw no translation of "Pervigilium
Veneris," but was content to reprint Thomas Parnell's (1679–
1718); the 1920s saw a spate of verse translations.[42] Among
them was a translation by Frank L. Lucas (1894–1967). He
treats the Latin as follows:*

> She it is that paints the springtide, flower-bejewelled,
>   purple-drest,
> She that swells the young bud's bosom with low
>   whispers from the west,
> Till it breaks in balmy blossom; She that in the wake of
>   night,
> O'er the fields where darkness flung them, spreads the
>   dewdrops' liquid light.
> See how, trembling, all but falling, each one glitters
>   like a tear!
> Yet they fall not—in its station clings so fast each tiny
>   sphere.
> See, the Rose comes forth in crimson, shows her blush
>   of maiden shame!
> Dew, that through the windless midnight from the
>   starry Heavens came,

---

*The order of lines differs so markedly from Tate's because Lucas was following the
extant corrupt manuscript, rather than Mackail's conjectural rearrangement into quatrains with a repeated refrain.

Bathes tomorrow morn her bosom, strips its mantle
    dank and green;
Venus bids at morn tomorrow wed shall every Rose be
    seen.
Child of kisses Love hath given, born of blood the
    Cyprian shed,
Bred of gem's and flame's refulgence, of the sun's own
    crimson bred,
Then the Rose shall rend the splendour of the bridal
    veil she wore
And her life's one wedlock show her flushed with the
    beauty no man saw.
Loveless hearts shall love tomorrow, hearts that have
    loved shall love once more.[43]

Lucas makes a few minor changes for the sake of rhyme: for instance, he adds "green" to rhyme with "seen." Faced with bud-gems, and bud-breasts, Lucas separates the Latin nouns into several words: "flower-bejewelled," "young bud's bosom." *Rubor* becomes "blush of maiden shame." Lucas apparently understands all the implications of the Latin, but because he is unwilling to use meaning spread non-locally, his translation fails to present a criticism of the way in which the Latin poem intricately intermingles flowers and bodies. Lucas's Rose becomes an allegory.

Tate, on the other hand, is able to maintain the Latin effect. Because he was not inhibited by a theory of translation which forbade the addition of meanings entailed by non-local criticism, he was able to go beyond mere denotation and concentrate on how the poem expresses its meanings.

Substituting for the Devices of the Original

Until now, the discussion has centered on non-local imitation of devices present in the original poem: pun for pun, allusion for allusion, meaning spread for meaning spread. How-

ever, when translating a foreign language, the poet will
eventually come upon a device for which there exists no ready
equivalent in English. The Victorian reaction was simply to
lose the effect. Pound counselled that the translator substitute
a device derived from the special abilities of English. He suggested, for example, that rather than try to reproduce the
plethora of feminine rhyme in Guido Cavalcanti's *canzoni,* the
translator rely on "our concealed rhymes [meaning half-
rhymes and consonant rhymes] and our semi-submerged
alliteration."[44]

The Latin language has inherent in it at least two rhetorical
devices not readily reproducible in English: manipulation of
word order and submerged metaphor. Rolfe Humphries, a
classical scholar and translator, discusses the effects possible to
a writer of Latin through manipulation of word order:

> Latin, an inflected language, makes possible effects that
> are impossible in our word-order English. Words not in
> agreement can be placed side by side for ironic effect;
> images can carry from one word to the next, the mem-
> ory, the lingering overtone of the first making a chord,
> or a prism, with the second; the line, or the stanza, can
> be full of ambiguities or surprises, matters held in sus-
> pense, judgment on them changed as we go along, and
> the resolution not coming till the very end. Horace is the
> master of these effects and the utter despair of all
> translators. . . .[45]

Submerged metaphor depends on the comparative generality
of Latin words. The writer of Latin could employ five or six
words with unconnected primary meanings, but with related
secondary meanings concerning, say, gardening, and thereby
create a gardening metaphor without once overtly mentioning
the subject.

Pound warned against trying to reproduce literally the
effects of Latin in English:

> By latinization I mean here the attempt to use an unin-
> flected language as if it were an inflected one, i.e. as if

each word had a little label or postscript telling the reader at once what part it takes in the sentence, and specifying its several relations. Not only does such usage—with remnants of Latin order—ruin the word order in English, but it shows a fundamental miscomprehension of the organism of the language. . . .[46]

Pound did not mean that translators should not strive to re-create the effects of the great Roman writers, merely that they should use the resources of English.

Translators have begun to explore and to theorize about the compensations English offers. Dudley Fitts, for instance, finds that the English translator should accommodate the genius of his language by distilling the particular out of a Latinate general. He so reasons in the discussion of John Peale Bishop's translation of "Tuércele el cuello al cisne engañoso plumaje," by the Mexican poet González Martínez. Fitts writes:

. . . there is nothing in the Spanish about the reeds' green soul or the mute cry of stone. These are Bishop's own ideas. . . . The translator felt . . . that a Latin language can be more persuasive than English in dealing with such quasi-particularities as "the soul of things" and "the voice of the landscape," and that in order to achieve something comparable to this incantatory force . . . the English demands a harder, more urgent kind of particularity. *El alma de las cosas* is too vague; let's specify a natural "thing" and give it a soul. *La voz del paisaje* could suggest anything from a billboard to a hungry vicuña; let's particularize a part of the landscape and by oxymoron—"mute cry"—provide it with a voice.[47]

Fitts is noting that English speakers seem much less comfortable with abstractions than the speakers of Romance languages. In part, this may be due to the nature of English vocabulary. English possesses a larger vocabulary than any other language. It abounds in so-called synonyms, which actually differ at least slightly from each other in denotation and connotation. For instance, "Blood ran down his arm" is simply a statement. "Gore ran down his arm" implies action on a brutal plane. "Ichor ran down his arm" suggests inflation of the incident, or a wounded science-fiction insectoid. Thus, when an English speaker chooses a word, differences in denotation frequently force him to make a more specific statement than the speaker of a language with fewer words.

But if the English speaker is forced to be specific, that very specificity is a strength of his language. Differences in connotation allow the translator to make fine distinctions in tone.

Pound did not write about the wealth of English vocabulary, but he did demonstrate how to use the specificity of English to compensate for losses. Propertius, in Elegy 3. 16, writes that he has received a summons from Cynthia, but he is afraid to walk the Roman streets at night. He gives himself encouragement:

> quisquis amator erit, Scythicis licet ambulet oris,
> nemo adeo ut noceat barbarus esse volet.
> luna ministrat iter, demonstrant astra salebras,
> ipse Amor accensas praecutit ante faces,
> saeva canum rabies morsus avertit hiantis:
> huic generi quovis tempore tuta via est.
> sanguine tam parvo quis spargatur amantis
> inprobis? ecce, suis fit[48] comes ipsa Venus?[49]

(Anyone who will be a lover may walk on Scythian shores: no one will be so barbarous as to harm him. The moon attends to his path, the stars show the rough patches, Love himself carries a flaming torch before him, turns aside the savage madness of dogs' gaping bites: for such a one all roads are safe at any time. Who is so wicked he would be wet with the worthless blood of a lover? See, among his men, Venus herself is an attendant [*and/or* companion].)

Propertius here compares walking in Rome to walking in the wilds of Scythia. Accompanying Propertius will be such potent personages as the moon, the stars, Cupid, and Venus; this august company to be devoted to protecting him from mad dogs and potholes. Such hyperbole can easily be transferred from one language to another. But Propertius is also joking in ways not so easily duplicated in English. He has created a submerged metaphor with *ministrat* and *comes*. *Ministrare* is "to attend to," or "to serve, as at table." *Comes* is "a companion or comrade," or "the suite attendant on an individual." Together the words suggest, without actually saying so, that Venus is Propertius's hired servant or dependent relative.

When Pound set about recasting the humor of the above passage, he turned away from Latin devices toward English resources:

> If any man would be a lover
>   he may walk on the Scythian coast, . . .
> The moon will carry his candle,
>   the stars will point out the stumbles,
> Cupid will carry lighted torches before him
>   and keep mad dogs off his ankles.
> Thus all roads are perfectly safe . . . ;
> Who so indecorous as to shed the pure gore of a
> suitor?!
>   Cypris is his cicerone.[50]

Pound could have said, "Venus is his guide." To do so would have completely lost the humor expressed by the Latin means of submerged metaphor. Therefore, Pound turned to the peculiarities of English and found a very specific kind of guide, a tourist guide, which is funny in sound and meaning: "Cypris is his cicerone."

Pound made no attempt to match Propertius's manipulation of word order. Propertius shows an exaggerated fear of mad dogs by saving *hiantis* for the end of the line: *saeva* 'savage' *canum* 'of dogs' *rabies* 'madness' *morsus* 'of bites' *avertit* 'he turns aside'; but just as the lover seems safe, Propertius tosses in the adjective modifying "bites," *hiantis* 'gaping'. Pound added "off his ankles" for a touch of humor, but he did not try to copy this joke. Instead, he used the great variety of diction levels available in English to achieve the ludicrous touch. Mincing polysyllables are contrasted with forthright monosyllables: 'Who so indecorous as to shed the pure gore of a suitor?!" Not only does the diction level of "indecorous" clash with that of "gore," but "pure" in English practically demands to be followed by "blood." Incongruity of situation is matched by incongruity of language. Clashes in diction level, made possible by the specificity of English, substitute for the word order suspension and sly generality of Latin.

These devices employed by Pound have been used by several contemporary translators from Latin, among them James Clancy and James Michie. In their translations there is a marked tendency to bring metaphors submerged in the Latin into the open and to compensate, via shades of diction, for the delicacy thus lost. How their practice differs from the Victorian can be seen by comparing James Clancy's modern translation of Horace's Ode 1. 4 with Thomas Charles Baring's earlier one.

James Clancy makes specific a concealed metaphor at the beginning of the ode:

> Winter's fists unclench at the touch of spring and
> western breezes,
>   dried-out keels are drawn down to the waves. . . .[51]

Thomas Charles Baring (1831–1891) translated the same lines:

> Sharp winter melts with Spring's delicious birth;
> The ships glide down on rollers to the sea. . . .[52]

The Latin reads:

> Solvitur acris hiems grata vice veris et Favoni
>   trahuntque siccas machinae carinas. . . .[53]

(At the pleasing return of spring and the west winds, harsh winter thaws and cranes draw forth the dried-out keels.)

Solvere 'to melt' takes up columns of dictionary explanation. Its primary meanings are "to loosen, to relax, especially from austerity." When used in conjunction with ships, *solvere* can also mean "to set or to unfurl sails."[54] And, according to Rolfe Humphries's exposition of the effects of Latin word order, although ship is not here the grammatical object of *solvere,* its proximity to *solvere* still colors the meaning. Thus, *solvere* in this poem suggests relaxing from a state of tension, snow-thaw, and unfurling sails. Baring follows usual Victorian practice by choosing the primary and most general meanings. Clancy's translation exemplifies the new tendency to distill the more particular meaning of the metaphor. He does this by supplying "fists," never mentioned in Horace, for winter to "unclench."

Later in his translation of the same ode, Clancy chooses not to re-create a submerged metaphor, but to parallel its tone by shifts in diction. As Horace talks of the vicissitudes of spring and winter, life and death, he develops a metaphor of gambling. The italicized words in the passage below can be associated with dicing:

> pallida Mors aequo pulsat pede pauperum tabernas
>   regumque turris. o *beate* Sesti,
> vitae *summa* brevis *spem* nos vetat *incohare* longam.
>   iam te *premet* nox fabulaeque Manes
> et domus exilis Plutonia; quo simul mearis,
>   nec regna vini *sortiere* talis,
> nec tenerum Lycidan mirabere, quo calet iuventus
>   nunc omnis et mox virgines tepebunt.
>
>   *(italics mine)*

(Pale Death knocks with the same rhythm at poor men's hovels and kings' towers. O *lucky* Sestius, the *sum* of short life forbids us *to take in hand* far-reaching *expecta-tions;* now night and storied Shades and Pluto's meager dwelling *press* [or *dun*] you; once you go there, such a man as you will not *dice* for the toastmastership, nor wonder at tender Lycidas, for whom each young man now burns, and the girls will soon be warm.)

Only *sortiere* 'to dice' deals directly with gambling. The other italicized words take on their undertones of gambling only because of its presence.

Thomas Charles Baring translated the above passage:

> Pale Death alike knocks at the poor man's house
> And the King's palace. Happy Sextius! Few
>   And brief the hopes our little day allows;
> Dark night brings on apace the shadowy crew
>   Of Pluto's dismal reign; once thou art there,
> The mastership of toasts thou ne'er wilt get,
>   Nor look on Lycidas, whose beauty rare
> Now the young men, and soon the girls will pet.[55]

Such a translation ignores the ironic humor with which Horace tempers his image of Pluto's encroachments, in effect saying, "All of life is a gamble. Only death is a certain bet."

But Clancy does not unearth the gambling metaphor either. Instead, he replaces its irony with ironic clashes of diction:

> Death with his drained-out face will drum at destitute
>   cottage
>   and royal castle. You have been lucky, Sestius:
> all of life is only a little, no long-term plans are
>   allowed.
>   Soon night and half-remembered shapes and drab
>
> Pluto's walls will be closing in; enter his halls and
>   you're done with
>   tosses of dice that crown you toastmaster,
> marveling glances at slim young Lycidas, for whom all

> the boys are
>   now burning, and the girls will soon catch fire.[56]

"Drum" and "destitute," which come from subtly different levels of diction, clash with each other. After the didactic pronouncement that "all of life is only a little," Clancy drops into the jargon of credit: "no long-term plans are allowed." These contrasts undercut solemnity, just as Horace's submerged metaphor creates a low-keyed irony. Clancy is following Pound's advice to replace the effects particular to Latin with effects particular to English.

James Michie, too, relies on the specificity of English, but, unlike Clancy, he prefers to excavate implied Latin metaphors. Michie translates from Horace:

> Don't ask (we may not know), Leuconoe,
>   What end the gods propose for me
>   Or you. Let Chaldees try
>   To read the ciphered sky;
>
> Better to bear the outcome, good or bad,
>   Whether Jove purposes to add
>   Fresh winters to the past
>   Or to make this the last
>
> Which now tires out the Tuscan sea and mocks
>   Its strength with barricades of rocks.
>   Be wise, strain clear the wine
>   And prune the rambling vine
>
> Of expectation. Life's short. Even while
>   We talk Time, grudging, runs a mile.
>   Don't trust tomorrow's bough
>   For fruit. Pluck this, here, now.[57]

In 1866, Charles Stuart Calverley translated the end of this same poem:

> Be thou wise: fill up the wine-cup; shortening,
>   since the time is brief,

Hopes that reach into the future. While I
  speak, hath stol'n away
Jealous Time. Mistrust To-morrow, catch
  the blossom of To-day.[58]

Just as Michie has added a bough and some fruit to Tomorrow's appurtenances, Calverley has added "a blossom of To-day" to be plucked. Moreover, the phrase is an allusion to Tennyson.[59] Calverley shows himself to be a more forward-reaching translator than his contemporary Baring, whose translation of the same ode is quoted earlier. Yet, Calverley's use of added (or revealed) metaphor is still slight when compared to Michie's. Note how much more sustained and concrete the metaphor has become in Michie: "prune the rambling vine"; "Don't trust tomorrow's bough / For fruit." Michie's metaphor exists in Horace, but as an undertone to much more general terms. Horace says *vina liques* 'strain the wines', *spem longam reseces* 'cut short *or* cut back long hope', and *carpe diem* 'pluck the day'. Once *vinum* 'wine' is mentioned, other phrases have secondary reference to grape growing. Michie, by adding a bough, fruit, and a vine, and by using "prune," a word specific to vine trimming, has made Horace's metaphor in the more concrete fashion typical of English poetry. In Calverley's treatment, the underlying connection between wine, hope, and plucking is lost. Wine cup and blossom remain unconnected.

    Another comparison between Michie and Calverley is apt. Calverley imitated, with some success, an effect of Latin word order:

dum loquimur, fugerit invida
aetas

While I
speak, hath stol'n away
Jealous Time.

Michie makes no attempt to use this Latin effect. Instead, he draws on a grammatical peculiarity of English, making "of expectation" both a subjective and objective genitive which could modify either "wine" or "vine." Michie is saying, on the one hand: "Strain the wine, expectation," and "Prune the vine, expectation," and on the other: "Strain expectation out of the wine," and "Prune expectation off the vine." Michie thus adds new, but suitable, meanings to Horace.

Michie also plays with diction levels. He takes a phrase, "this here now," usually relegated to incorrect status, and with two commas lifts it to the level of the rest of his language in the poem. He returns to the phrase the desire to convey immediacy which must have engendered it.

For another ode, Michie partially compensates for the loss of Horace's deft manipulation of word order through carefully chosen nuances in denotation and subtle shifts in diction. Ode 1. 9 was precisely the example used by Rolfe Humphries to illustrate the effects of Latin word order impossible to duplicate in English. Humphries uses the last verse to illustrate:

> *Nunc et latentis* (somebody's hiding) *proditor* (somebody's betraying) *intimo* (something here about intimacy—betrayed?) *gratus* (the betrayer is welcomed, or maybe pleasing) *puellae* (to the girl, or maybe it's the betrayer of the girl) *risus* (Oh! now we see it's the girl's laugh giving her away) *ab angulo* ([from the corner] and now it's clear and we see how *intimo* [secret corner] fitted in).[60]

The verse continues:

> pignusque dereptum lacertis
> aut digito male pertinaci.[61]

(and a token of love is snatched from an arm or an unsuccessfully clinging finger.)

Michie treats the last verse and a half of this ode as follows:

> . . . for now is the
> Right time for midnight assignations,
>   Whispers and murmurs in Rome's piazzas
>
> And fields, and soft, low laughter that gives away
> The girl who plays love's games in a hiding-place—
>   Off comes a ring coaxed down an arm or
>   Pulled from a faintly resisting finger.[62]

There is no way in English to separate "pleasing laughter, betrayer of the girl" so that "betrayer" comes an ambiguous and slightly threatening first, while "laughter," humorously delayed, will finally explain that the girl has betrayed her hiding place herself. Michie instead turns to the diction levels and sounds of English to convey the aura of teasing sexuality. Michie used "pulled" for its long, drawn-out sound, which matches the sound of *male,* and he uses "coaxed" which is more specific than any Latin verb is likely to be. Latin *blandiri* 'to coax', includes the ideas of fawning and flattery; *permulcēre* includes "to charm or to please." Between the sound of "pulled" and the meaning of "coaxed," Michie returns the idea of teasing delay to the poem.

Michie also lets minor diction surprises add a sportive note. There are the slightly formal "assignations" and the slightly foreign "piazzas" to contrast with the colloquial tone of "gives away." Michie's diction rings changes almost as subtle as Horace's word order.

In contrast, C. S. Calverley's translation of 1866 uses only one level of diction:

> Park and public walk
>   Attract thee now, and whispered talk
>   At twilight meetings pre-arranged;
>
> Hear now the pretty laugh that tells
>   In what dim corner lurks thy love;
>   And snatch a bracelet or a glove
> From wrist or hand that scarce rebels.[63]

Like Horace's diction, Calverley's is neutral, neither formal nor informal. Calverley plays with word order, placing "scarce rebels" in the same position as *male pertinaci*. Unfortunately, mimicking Horace's word order does not in this instance produce Horace's effect.

Towards a Larger Understanding of Meaning

Calverley's translation does not sound, as John Peale Bishop complained of others, as if it were English which were foreign to him. But neither does it sound as if Calverley had available to him all the resources of his language. This was a choice on his part: to translate by paraphrase, seeking to imitate what Horace did by the means Horace did it, even when those means are not congenial to English.

Calverley's translations illustrate that in the most progressive non-Wardour Street Victorian translations, concern remained with the language of the original. This was the concern which motivated Matthew Arnold when he gave way to a passion for literality for once even greater than Newman's:

> . . . Mr. Newman calls Xanthus [Achilles' horse] *Chestnut,* indeed, as he calls Balius *Spotted,* and Podarga *Spryfoot;* which is as if a Frenchman were to call Miss Nightingale *Mdlle. Rossignol,* or Mr. Bright *M. Clair.*[64]

In rebuttal, one can remark that an argument against translating inherited surnames does not apply to translating animal names given, in all probability, to describe physical characteristics. Further, in translating fictional surnames, the question arises whether the author intended the names to have a meaning. In an allegory such as *Pilgrim's Progress,* the characters' names are the characters' qualities, and must be translated. Then there are names, like so many of the names of Charles Dickens' characters, carefully chosen for resonance with

meaning. Perhaps a Frenchman should translate "Mr. Murd-
stone" as *M Meurteroc.* To return to the animal kingdom, perhaps an American should translate *Rosinante* as "Nagina."

In many current translations, the emphasis is on the language *into which* the translation is being made. For F. W.
Newman to translate the names of horses was a bold step;
William Arrowsmith, a modern translator, casually translates
the names of minor sea-nymphs. D. S. Carne-Ross, who com-
missioned Arrowsmith's translation for part of a BBC radio
Iliad, contends that if, near the opening of Book 18, the Ner-
eids' names are not translated, "one is left with an unreadable
piece of enumeration. . . ."[65] Yet, this has been the practice of
three centuries of translators. In 1611, Chapman was writing:

> There Glauce and Cymodoce and Spio did attend,
> Nesaea and Cymothoe and calme Amphitoe,
> Thalia, Thoe, Panope and swift Dynamene,
> Actea and Limoria and Halia the faire. . . .[66]

Alexander Pope (1688–1744) at least added a few qualifiers:

> *Thalia, Glauce,* (ev'ry wat'ry Name)
> *Nesaea* mild, and Silver *Spio* came.
> *Cymothoe* and *Cymodoce* were nigh,
> And the blue Languish of soft *Alia's* Eye.
> Their Locks *Actaea* and *Limnoria* rear,
> Then *Proto, Doris, Panope* appear. . . .[57]

William Cullen Bryant (1794–1878) can only list:

> There came
> Glaucè, Thalia, and Cymodocè,
> Nesaea, Speio, Halia with large eyes,
> And Thoa, and Cymothöè; nor stayed
> Actaea, Limnoreia, Melita,
> Amphithöè, Iaera, Agavè,
> Doto, and Proto, and Dynamenè.[68]

In the translation jointly by William Benjamin Smith (1850–1944) and Walter Miller (1864–1949), the lines read:

> Glauce, namely, was there and Cymodoce, also Thalia,
> Spio, too, and Nesaea, the ox-eyed Halia, Thoë,
> Limnorea, Actaea, the fair, and Cymothoë with them;
> Melite also, Iaera, Amphothoë, too, and Agave,
> Doto, Proto, and fair Dynamene, also Pherusai, . . .
> Other Nereids also that dwelt in the depths of the salt
>   sea.[69]

D. S. Carne-Ross produced William Arrowsmith's translation as a counterexample:

> Then, out of his grief and anguish, Achilles cried aloud,
> a terrible, awful cry, and his goddess mother heard him
> where she sat in the depths of the sea at the side of her
>   agèd father,
> and she too gave a cry, and the goddesses gathered
>   around her,
> all those who were daughters of Nereus in the depths
>   of the sea—
> Seagreen and Shimmer, the goddesses Blooming and
>   Billow
> and those who are names of islands, those who are
>   called for the caves,
> and She-who-skims-on-the-water, and Spray with the
>   gentle eyes
> like the gentle eyes of cattle, naiads of spume and the
>   shore,
> the nymphs of marshes and inlets and all the rocks
>   outjutting,
> and Dulcet too was there and Wind-that-rocks-on-the-
>   water
> and Grazer-over-the-sea and she whose name is Glory,

and the naiads Noble and Giver, and lovely Bringer,
  and Nimble,
and Welcomer too, and Grace, and Princess, and
  Provider,
and she who is named for the milk, the froth of the
  curling breakers,
glorious Galateia, and the famous nymphs of the surf,
and Infallible and Truth, true daughters of their father,
and goddesses over the sand, and she who runs from
  the mountains
and whose hair is a splendor, and all the other
  goddesses
who are daughters of Nereus along the deep floor of
  the sea.[70]

Carne-Ross believes that Arrowsmith's translation is the result of a revolution in translating Greek begun and encouraged by Ezra Pound.[71] It is easy to see why. Arrowsmith does not take great liberties with the meaning, but his translation is definitely a creative translation, rather than a paraphrase. He makes a single nymph, *Glauke,* over into both "Seagreen" and "Shimmer," since her name carried both meanings. Similarly, *Nesea* 'Island' is pluralized as "those who are names of islands," and *Speio* 'Cave' becomes "those who are called for the caves." *Halia* 'Breath' becomes "Spray," and *Kymothoë* 'Spume', the "naiads of spume."[72] As Carne-Ross explains:

> . . . in Greek . . . [the names] are not really proper names at all; as one reads the passage in Homer, the firm outlines of these mythological young persons dissolve into a glimmering sequence of images, all the delicate play of wind and light and rock and shore. William Arrowsmith . . . recreated in English the fluid succession of sea pictures which rise up before the mind's eye in the original Greek. . . .[73]

Arrowsmith's translation is an example of the kind of faithfulness in freedom sought by creative translators of the twentieth century. These translators believe that what a poem means is dependent on how it expresses that meaning. Translation by analogy is directed towards rescuing those meanings which depend not on denotation but on tone, style, verbal ambiguity, and cultural background.

The Poet's Intuition

The idea of creative translation and the various strategies it suggests have caused a profound change in attitude toward translation. Victorians and Edwardians were primarily interested in the accuracy of the translation. They placed great stress on the ability of the translator to read the original language correctly. Matthew Arnold counselled the translator of Greek to submit his translation to "the scholars, who possess . . . a knowledge of Greek. . . . They are the only competent tribunal in this matter. . . . Let him [the translator] not trust to his own judgment of his own work."[74] In this century, the intuition of the poet-translator is more prized. We have Carne-Ross's statement that "the right kind of poet . . . can *guess* what the original is like from a crib. . . . Only a poet . . . can translate poetry."[75]

This recovered reliance on the poet's intuition is in part based on the inspired intuitions in the translations of Ezra Pound. Pound translated *Cathay* from the kind of crib Carne-Ross suggests. Wai-Lim Yip marvels:

One can easily excommunicate Pound from the Forbidden City of Chinese studies, but it seems clear that in his dealing with *Cathay,* even when he is given only the barest details, he is able to get into the central consciousness of the original author by what we may perhaps call a kind of clairvoyance.[76]

Today, freed by Pound's example, translation has moved away from syllable counting and dictionary equivalence. The poet-translator is asked to express his insights into the many aspects of the original poem: its sense, its tone, its style. Translators make their criticisms more freely, searching out the resources of English to render "mimetic homage"[77] to their originals.

Part Three
The Creative Translation as New Poem

11

New Tastes for Old

On the title page of *Make It New,* appear the Chinese characters

They mean "make it new, day by day, make it new."[1] The two middle signs are the ideogram for the sun. The top and bottom signs contain at their left the ideogram for tree, and at their right the ideogram for axe. Thus, this evocation of renewal includes pruning away dead wood so that the live wood can grow.[2]

Make It New collects most of Pound's important essays dealing with critical theory and with translation. In it is the essay "Dateline," which states that translation is a form of criticism and also that the two functions of criticism are excernment, "the general ordering and weeding out of what has actually been performed. . . . so that the next man (or generation) can most readily find the live part of it,"[3] and the formulation of a "forward reach of co-ordinating principle," which in art Pound believed was more likely to occur in "the demonstration," rather than in commentary. In fact, he comments that "the most intense form of criticism" is "criticism in new composition."[4] These juxtapositions imply that Pound intended criticism by translation to perform both functions of criticism.

Pound's "excernments" were not guided by the excellence of the original works in themselves; he looked for what he thought would improve contemporary writing. He admitted the greatness and enjoyability of many books not on his critical lists, but warned the would-be writer "not [to] confuse enjoyment with . . . preparation for writing."[5]

Since Pound's translations were "preparation for writing," he sometimes criticized not only original poems in his translations, but contemporary poetry as well. This led to distortions, not in the service of the original poem, but in the service of Pound's own poetic and political concerns. At this point, creative translation passes over into imitation. But Pound believed that in one sense all good criticisms of the past must be imitations because a really new look at the past changes the conception of the past, which is in turn a change in the present. By a happy paradox, the reinterpretation of the past helps create what is modern.

Pound, together with Yeats and Eliot, defined "modern" in British and American poetry for the twentieth century. Yet, ironically, in the field of translation, where Pound's labors began, it took much longer for his preferences to be assimilated. Translation choice and style remained largely governed by older tastes until sometime after 1950.

J. P. Sullivan points out that Pound had an instinct for perceiving what in the heritage of the past is, or is about to be, modern:

> Some authors feel "modern," like Rochester and Petronius (and this modernity is a matter of style, feeling, and subject); other authors, and these are often greater, are not so "modern" in tone (such are Shakespeare, Pope, and Tennyson). Others again can be made "modern," for behind their "period" and "classic" interest there is a sensibility which needs only a critic's insight to reveal it in all its contemporary relevance (Donne and Propertius). "Modern," of course, is not meant here as an evaluation but as a description; nevertheless, to perceive that quality and bring it to light is a critical triumph of a sort.[6]

In style, feeling, and subject, Pound made a change, which he called a change from "the soft" to "the hard." He used these terms in an essay which began:

> I apologize for using the semetaphorical terms 'hard' and 'soft' in this essay, but after puzzling over the matter for some time I can see no other way of setting about it. By 'hardness' I mean a quality which is in poetry nearly always a virtue—I can think of no case where it is not. By softness I mean an opposite quality which is not always a fault.[7]

By hard, Pound seems to have meant several different things: first, a diction which stresses consonants, rather than vowels and semi-vowels; second, precision of statement, rather than vague allusiveness, and concrete presentation, rather than abstract; third, literary realism, a dealing with harsh truths, rather than pleasant ones; fourth, ironic distance, rather than sentimentality. These tastes he learned and fostered through translation.

Concrete Presentation and
Consonantal Diction

Pound stated his preference for concrete presentation in the Imagiste "manifesto" of 1912, the first principle of which is:

Direct treatment of the 'thing' whether subjective or objective.[8]

Pound explains:

Don't use such an expression as 'dim lands *of peace*'. It dulls the image. It mixes an abstraction with the concrete. It comes from the writer's not realizing that the natural object is always the *adequate* symbol.
Go in fear of abstractions.[9]

Pound did not mean that by avoiding abstractions he wished to eschew symbols, but that he wanted symbolic meanings to arise from objective meanings, and not to exist independent of them. He said:

I believe that the proper and perfect symbol is the natural object, that if a man use 'symbols' he must so use them that their symbolic function does not obtrude; so that *a* sense, and the poetic quality of the passage, is not lost to those who do not understand the symbol as such, to whom, for instance, a hawk is a hawk.[10]

In Pound's practice, the natural objects were used in a technique of "superposition," in which the connection between the human emotion and the natural object is not expressed verbally, but suggested by juxtaposition.

According to "A Retrospect," Guido Cavalcanti and the troubadour Arnaut Daniel taught him the concrete style:

In the art of Daniel and Cavalcanti, I have seen that precision which I miss in the Victorians, that explicit rendering, be it of external nature, or of emotion. Their testimony is of the eyewitness, their symptoms are first hand.[11]

Victorians either did not see or did not prize this characteristic in Arnaut Daniel; they concerned themselves with the sincerity of the troubadours' romantic love. Of the troubadours, Guilhem de Cabestanh appealed to them most, as much for his apocryphal biography as for his writing.* Francis Hueffer, whose book *The Troubadours* (1878) introduced the troubadours to the English-speaking public, stated:

> . . . we cannot . . . refuse our sympathy to a passion so pure and so intense as that reflected in the *canzos* of Guillem de Cabestanh. Only seven of his poems have been preserved to us, but these rank amongst the highest achievements of Provençal literature. . . . Guillem's songs are comparatively simple in structure, and contain few of those marvelous *tours de force* of rhyme and metre which most troubadours delight in.
>
> Such artificialities would, indeed be ill adapted to the extreme simplicity of his theme, which is nothing but the deepest passion for the beloved object. There is in his poems no fickleness, no variation of mood, and if his literary remains were voluminous, the uniformity of his passion would pall on us. As it is, this very monotony adds to the intensity of our impression. Guillem is a patient lover, a male type of the nut-brown maid.[12]

---

*He was supposed to have been slaughtered by a jealous husband, who then fed Cabestanh's heart to the lady in question. When told what she had eaten, the lady declared, "It was so good and savory that never shall any other meat take its sweetness from my mouth," and jumped from the window to her death. This story is told in Hueffer, pp. 152–58.

Hueffer then prints "Lo jorn, qeus vi domna, premiera-men," and follows it with his own translation, which begins:

> The day when first I saw you, lady sweet,
> When first your beauty deigned on me to shine,
> I laid my heart's devotion at your feet;
> No other wish, no other thought were mine.
> For in my soul you wakened soft desire;
> In your sweet smile and in your eyes I found
> More than myself and all the world around.
>
> Your tender speech, so amorous, so kind,
> The solace of your words, your beauty's spell
> Once and for ever have my heart entwined,
> No longer in my bosom it will dwell.
> Your worth to cherish it shall never tire.
> Oh! then, your gentle grace let me implore;
> My all I gave you, I can give no more.

and ends:

> The hour will come, O lady, well I know,
> When from your yielding mercy I may claim
> The one word 'friend.' I ask no other name.[13]

There is not in the whole translation, nor in the original, one concrete image.

On the other hand, Hueffer dislikes two troubadours who used concrete images often. He finds Arnaut Daniel mannered and obscure,[14] and Guilhem IX, comte de Peiteus and duc d'Occitan, witty but immoral.[15]

A later Victorian critic, John Frederick Rowbotham, was even less sympathetic. He calls Arnaut Daniel "ambiguous," "fantastic," and "artificial."[16] Guilhem IX is

> flagrantly and vulgarly immodest. The coarse and brutal terms in which he invariably alludes to women recall

rather the bluff spirit of the pre-crusading baronage than speak of that delicate and over-refined timorousness of amorous sentiment which was to be the marked character of the troubadours.[17]

In the above condemnation, Guilhem de Peiteus is not recognizable as the man Pound found "the most 'modern' of the troubadours. . . . Guillaume . . . is just as much of our age as of his own."[18] Nor is obscurantist Arnaut Daniel recognizable as the poet Pound praised for the precision and explicitness of his descriptions, and for his perception that "the beauty" of rhymes "depends not upon their multiplicity, but upon their action the one upon the other."[19]

For these reasons, Pound praised Arnaut's "L'aura amara," in which he heard "the chatter of birds in autumn. . . ."[20] Pound said:

> . . . the onomatopoeia obviously depends upon the '-utz, -etz, -encs, and -ortz' of the rhyme-scheme, seventeen of the sixty-eight syllables of each strophe. . . .[21]

No doubt he also admired the fact that the birds' complaint against the cold, which opens the poem, is thus continually recalled throughout the lover's plaint and praise. No overt comparison is made; no "like" or "as" compares the cold birds and the lover, merely their co-presence.

These rhymes also demonstrate another trait of Arnaut's poetry which Kenner says attracted Pound: a crisp, consonantal diction.[22] Victorian taste tended toward a line rhyming heavily on the long vowels and semi-vocalic consonants m, n, ng, l, r, w, y). Kenner quotes "The moan of doves in immemorial elms" as the quintessence of the style.[23] Pound, he believes, sought correctives to this excess of sonority in Arnaut, whose poetic texture emphasized "the exploitation of consonantal boundaries, their sharp discrimination of word from word."[24]

Yet, Pound's intuitions about Arnaut Daniel were not realized in his translations of 1910 or 1912 or 1917, nor in anyone else's before 1950. Pound's convolutions overrode his insights:

> When faint leaf falleth
>   From the high forky tips,
> And cold appalleth
>   The parching shoots and slips
> And stills sweet quips
>   Of birds so that none calleth,
> Still are my lips
>   For Love, howe'er he galleth.[25]

Pound himself called these translations "English dither."[26] Yet, as Peter Schneeman remarks, "there is something *there* despite the straining."[27] Concealed in Wardour Street language is:

> Faint leaves fall
> from the high forked tips
> and cold appalls
> the parching shoots and slips
> and stills the quips
> of calling birds—
>   my cold-galled lips
>   are still
>   for love.
>   (*my rearrangement*)

The superposed, precise images are there; there, too, are the consonantal boundaries of "quips" and "tips"; but both are hampered by -*eths* and by too literal an imitation of the rhyme scheme.

Not until the 1950s, again with the translations of Paul Blackburn, did this particular view of the modernity of the troubadours re-enter translation. Blackburn re-created the sharp sounds and the concrete, natural objects the troubadours used as symbols. He mimicked the "form of canzoni where stanza answers stanza not boisterously, but with a subtle, persistent echo."[28] He displayed this appreciation in his translation from the "most 'modern' of the troubadours," Guilhem IX:

> In the new season
> when the leaves burgeon
> and birds
> sing out the first stave of new song,
> time then that a man take the softest joy of her
>> who is most to his liking.
>
>> But from where my joy springs
>> no message comes:
> the heart will not sleep or laugh nor dare I go out
> till I know the truth, if she will have me or not.
>
>> Our love is like top
>> branches that creak
>> on the hawthorn at night
>> stiff from ice
>> or shaking from rain. And tomorrow
>>> the sun
> spreads its living warmth through the branches and
>   through
> the green leaves on the tree.
>
> Remembering
> the softness of that morning we put away anger,
> when she gave me her love, her ring
>> as sign,
>> remembering the softness,
> I pray to God I live to put my hands
> under her cloak, remembering that.
>
> And I
> care not for the talk
> that aims to part
> my lady from me;

for I know how talk runs rife and gossip spreads
from empty, rancid mouths that, soured
   make mock of love.
  No matter. We are the ones, we have
   some bread, a knife.[29]

In Blackburn's translation, the ring given for remembrance rings audibly through the full and partial rhymes: "sing," "liking," "springs," "shaking," "living," and "remembering" (repeated three times in the same stanza with "ring"). A series of important words runs a vowel-gamut from high to low, each word ending in a decisive k: "creak," "shak(ing)," "cloak," "talk," "mock." Blackburn evidently remembers that Pound said that Arnaut Daniel's rhymes were good, not because of their multiplicity, but because of their "action one upon the other," for Blackburn rhymes "bread" with "spreads" and "knife" with "rife," counteracting the gossipers in the very rhymes. Guilhem de Peiteus did so himself, rhyming *coutel* 'knife' with *s'espel* 'spreads'.

The hawthorn tree, as Blackburn shows, is meticulously observed: it is a non-deciduous tree, whose tough leaves curl when cold and unfurl when warm. It tends to be more bush-like than treelike, and therefore is particularly creaky when ice-laden.

Because the hawthorn tree is offered as a simile for the joys and despairs of love, it is not entirely the type of imagery Pound preferred. Pound wanted similes implicit, rather than explicit; he wanted symbols to be natural objects juxtaposed (or "superposed") with each other to generate comparison and emotion in the mind of the reader. But nothing could be more like the symbols Pound was urging than the bread and the knife of the last line. Guilhem does not explain these objects, or use a conjunction of comparison. He merely presents them. Bread and a knife to cut it indicate a sufficient feast. The knife has sexual overtones (even stronger in Guilhem, who calls the bread *pessa* 'a piece'). The bread has religious overtones, and either bread or a knife will suffice to stop a mouth.

Francis Hueffer and Paul Blackburn, translating a century apart, evidently admire very different qualities in the troubadours. Hueffer appreciated generally stated, sentimental love poems; these appealed to his nineteenth-century sensibilities; Blackburn admired the concrete images and exact observation of nature which Pound insisted were to be found in Provençal verse. This change in taste is not, of course, simply a preference for subtly echoing stanzas or for concrete description, but is also bound up in a change in choice of subject and viewpoint. The scholar James J. Wilhelm writes:

> Let us not delude ourselves into thinking that the troubadours are divorced from the twentieth-century sensibility. . . . Scholars of the nineteenth century . . . at the very same time that they were embracing [these poets] . . . laid [them] to rest with the inscription COURTLY LOVE. . . . The brilliant, potentially dangerous ladies of southern France, fantastic women like Malbergion and Dangerose and the Countess of Dia and the great Eleanor herself, dissolved into weeping, swooning damoiselles. Romantics like Sir Walter Scott and Alfred Lord Tennyson . . . ignored the simple fact that the lady in Provensal verse is as often a bitch-goddess as she is a sweet, sugary belle.[30]

Wilhelm's statement results from the twentieth-century penchant for realism. It is as much a product of what we wish to see as was Hueffer's view. Guilhem de Cabestanh's idealized lady and unrequited love are as much a part of the Provençal landscape as the exactly observed hawthorn tree. The realism of many of the troubadours, which co-existed with their idealizations, was not appreciated by the Victorians, but Pound admired Arnaut Daniel as "a very real, very much alive young man,"[31] who writes of "no gardens where three birds sing on every bough."[32]

The twentieth-century appreciation of realism in poetry can not be laid at the door of any one man, not even Ezra Pound, but he was among the first to nurture it in twentieth-century poetry and to demand it in twentieth-century translation.

A Preference for Realism

From the age of Pope to the time of the Edwardians, a popularly held poetic theory decreed that poetry should "elevate," that it should deal with noble souls and noble deeds. Wordsworth, during the Romantic revolution, added that poetry ought to deal with the common, everyday experiences of the common man, but he meant to show what was ennobling in such experiences. Thus, although one can realistically describe noble, heroic, and joyous events, realism as a literary program came to stand for unflinching descriptions of scandalous, ignoble, and degrading experiences, particularly the experiences of the poor.[33] The first push for realism came in the novels of the late nineteenth century, those of Flaubert, Zola, George Meredith, and Thomas Hardy.

Realism was slower to enter English poetry. Edwardian poetry was enervatingly and consistently pretty. Pound and Eliot, declares Warner Berthoff, were the great forces for realism in poetry.[34] The advent of realism in original poetry occurred almost immediately. The poetry of such highly different poets as William Carlos Williams, Marianne Moore, e. e. cummings, and Hart Crane all bear witness to the fact. However, realism, like concrete presentation and ironic distance, took longer to make its way into translation.

For Pound, if one poet in the tradition was the cynosure of realism, it was François Villon. Pound's essay of 1910, "Montcorbier, *alias* Villon," insists on Villon's ability to describe objectively the harsh and ugly realities of gutter life. Pound wrote:

Villon has the stubborn persistency of one whose gaze cannot be deflected from the actual fact before him: what he sees, he writes.

Villon's is a voice of suffering, of mockery, of irrevocable fact.

His poems . . . treat of actualities, they are untainted with fancy. . . . In Villon filth is filth, crime is crime; neither filth nor crime is gilded.

He has sunk to the gutter, knowing life a little above it; thus he is able to realize his condition, to see it objectively, instead of insensibly taking it for granted.[35]

Pound's two 1908 translations of Villon are rather romantic. As N. Christoph de Nagy remarks, they are very much Villon seen through the eyes of Rossetti and Swinburne.[36] Translators influenced by Pound to translate Villon realistically had to cull their hints from "Montcorbier *alias* Villon" and *The ABC of Reading.* Perhaps that is why realistic translations of him took so long to appear.

If literary realism is concerned with describing in unflinching detail scandalous, ignoble, or degrading situations, this program is carried out to the letter in Villon's Ballade of Pardon; yet it seems to be this *ballade* which excited the Victorian John Payne to write:

One cannot help loving the frank, witty, devil-may-care-poet, with his ready tears and his as ready laughter, his large compassion for all pitiable and his unaffected sympathy with all noble things. Specially attractive is the sweetness of his good-humour: so devoid of gall is he that he seems to cherish no enduring bitterness against his most cruel enemies, content if he can make them the subject of some passing jest or some merry piece of satire. . . . Thibault d'Aussigny, the author of his duresse in Meung gaol, and François Perdryer, at the nature of whose offence against him we can only guess, are the only ones he cannot forgive, and his invectives against the former are of a half-burlesque character, that permits us to suspect a humorous exaggeration in their unyielding bitterness.[37]

Payne's attempt to find nobility of the Victorian sort in Villon induced him to translate the *ballade* in question as follows:

Ballad Crying All Folk Mercy

I

Frères, be they white or be they grey;
  Nuns, mumpers, chanters awry that tread
And clink their pattens on each highway;
  Lackeys and handmaids, apparellèd
  In tight-fitting surcoats, white and red;
Gallants, whose boots o'er their ankles fall,
  That vaunt and ruffle it unadread;
I cry folk mercy, one and all.

III

Save only the treacherous beasts of prey,
  That garred me batten on prison bread
And water, many a night and day.
  I fear them not now, no, not a shred;
  And gladly (but that I lie a-bed
And have small stomach for strife or brawl)
  I'd have my wreak of them. Now, instead,
I cry folk mercy, one and all.

Envoi

So but the knaves be ribroastèd
  And basted well with an oaken maul
Or some stout horsewhip weighted with lead,
  I cry folk mercy, one and all.[38]

The translation does not sound romantic (as opposed to realistic) if one does not know what Villon had written—but that is because Villon is so full of particularizing detail that it is difficult to make him sound vague in anything close to a paraphrase. Examination of subsequent translations will show how much Payne omitted as coarse and ignoble.

By 1924, John Heron Lepper is using a euphemism for Villon's projected fart (which Payne eliminated), but shares Payne's delusion that Villon is forgiving:

Ballade
Wherein Villon Cries All Folk Mercy

[III]

... No, those vile dogs I'll not excuse
Who robbed my belly of its ease!
I'd shame them with a downward
    sneeze,
But, sitting, I can summon none:
Well, well, then, to avoid a breeze,
I cry you mercy, every one!

[Envoi]

Their fifteen ribs I fain would grease
With cudgel-oil, and senses stun
With bullets or such balls as these:
I cry you mercy, every one![39]

By 1946, H. G. McCaskie is not afraid to call a fart a fart, but shrinks from calling a turd a turd:

Ballade

[III]

But you false curs who, night and day,
   Filled me with hard crusts to my chin,
To you alone I do not pray,
   Nor do I fear you now one pin:
   A belch or fart from me you'd win
But sitting down it can't be done.
   Oh, well; why let a row begin?
Pray you forgive me, every one.

[Envoi]
If your fifteen ribs are driven in
    By hammers weighing half a ton,
Or lead balls from a culverin,
    Pray you forgive me, every one.[40]

McCaskie has also been willing to concede that if Villon said he would rather see his torturers tortured than forgiven, he meant it.

In the 1960s, some extremely literal translations appeared. Literality returned realism to Villon, however many other effects were lost. Galway Kinnell's earlier translation of Villon was of this type:*

Ballade

[I]
To Carthusians and Celestines,
To Mendicants and Devotes,
To stargazers and clock-pattens,
To serving girls and pretty sluts
In jackets and tight-fitting coats,
To cocky beaux fainting with love
Happily fitted with tawny boots,
I cry to all men pardon.

[III]
Except to the sons-of-bitches
Who made me shit small and gnaw
Crusts many a dusk and dawn,
Who don't scare me now three turds:
I'd raise for them belches and farts
But I can't for I'm sitting down,
Instead, to prevent riots,
I cry to all men pardon.

*So, too, was Anthony Bonner's *Villon* Translation of 1960, some lines of which are quoted earlier.

[Envoi]
May their fifteen ribs be mauled
With big hammers heavy and strong
And lead weights and similar balls,
I cry to all men pardon.[41]

Kinnell declared that his intention was to be realistic:

> . . . ever since the nineteenth-century translations, a kind
> of romantic perfume has clung to the English versions of
> Villon. . . . I have tried to keep the poetry factual, harsh
> and active, hoping thus to find a tone of voice which
> might better suit the great original.[42]

At last a fart is a fart, a slut a slut, a turd is a turd, and Villon's voice, while deprived of its consistent rhymes on "the
strong word,"[43] is, as Pound insisted, "a voice of suffering, of
mockery, of irrevocable fact."[44]

Ironic Distance

Pound put irony to uses especially characteristic of the
twentieth century. In his hands, irony can convey the author's
knowledge of the unreliability of his speaker, or even of the
speaker's *own* knowledge of his unreliability. Such irony is a
form of self-criticism,[45] which corrects sentimentality and self-
pity, and which gains a larger, more "objective," perspective
on the subjective speaker. The use of irony to criticize the
speaker is an offshoot of this century's concern with the unreliable narrator (hence the unreliable author). This concern
dominates Ford Maddox Ford's novel *The Good Soldier,* whose
narrator is frighteningly untrustworthy, and is a factor in
James Joyce's *Ulysses* and *Dubliners,* where many narrators and
super-narrators crowd the pages. Instead of eventually offering
the reader a "true" picture, with errors cancelled out, Joyce
gives evidence that the reader can not have the "facts" of the

fictional occurrence.[46] T. S. Eliot, in *The Wasteland,* presents a similar mob of speakers.

Victorians and Edwardians were resistant to the use of self-critical irony in translation. They found it incompatible with their conception of the classics as dignified and noble; furthermore, as dignified and noble in the Victorian sense. H. A. Mason uses Matthew Arnold's *On Translating Homer* to point out just where, by twentieth-century notions, the Victorian definition of nobility jars. He quotes Arnold's translation of *Aeneid* xii, 435–36: "From me, young man, learn nobleness of soul and true effort, / learn success from others." Arnold had cited this as a touchstone for determining nobility. Mason comments:

> The priggish-melancholy note of Aeneas, oh so conscious in his modesty of the nobility of the example he is setting his son, is exactly what the Victorians found 'edifying'. They are welcome to it. . . . Newman was, of course, right in insisting that Homer was continually lapsing from the Victorian standard of noble decorum. But just as Arnold failed to appreciate these 'lapses', he also failed to see what was Homer's true dignity. Homer's dignity is quite another thing than Victorian dignity. Like Shakespeare's and Dante's, it is compatible with a great deal of low-level coarseness. For failure to see that it is not a blemish in the highest poetry to use expressions which are in everyday life vulgar or coarse, Arnold's Homer resembles Bowdler's Shakespeare.[47]

The Victorian distaste for mixing irony with dignity or passion also sprang from their conception of the speaker in poetry. Victorians tended to see poetry as the direct expression of the unadulterated feelings of the author.[48] They did not stress a concept of a speaker or persona or mask through which the poet speaks.[49] This notion of poetry as coming directly from the experience of the author is behind the biographic approach the Victorian critics took to poetry. Of course, Browning's dramatic monologues do not fit into such a simplified explanation, but there is still a connection. George Wright explains the difference between the twentieth-century speaker (or persona) of the poem and Browning's:

> ... Eliot, Yeats, and Pound ... characteristically detach themselves from their personae and invite the reader to share with the poet a fuller consciousness of the poem. ... The poetry of these men is as "personal" as any poetry.
>
> Yet the way in which it is personal is different from most nineteenth-century verse, and its difference rests in its abandonment of the persona as the center of the poem (and, implicitly, of the world). ... Even Browning resembles his nineteenth-century contemporaries in using his poetry to present person after person; the era sometimes seems an endless (and fascinating) parade of people, experience piled on experience, life piled on life. The three poets whose work has been the subject of this study do not present people as people. They present situations inhabited by people.[50]

To put the case in slightly different terms, Pound and Eliot insert an emotional distance between poet and speaker and insist on the consideration of that distance. The speaker of Browning's "My Last Duchess" is clearly not the poet. However, the reader of "My Last Duchess" proceeds to analyze the speaker as if he were a real person. But with Pound's *Hugh Selwyn Mauberley* and Eliot's *Wasteland,* one begins to ask questions such as: Who is the speaker? How far does the speaker represent the poet? Does the poet see things that the speaker does not?

In twentieth-century poetry, in addition to considering the poet's distance from the speaker, the reader must consider the speaker's emotional distance from himself. The reader can ask: How much of what the speaker says does he intend ironically? Howevermuch the situation and the speaker are at odds in "My Last Duchess," the speaker seems to be taking himself quite seriously. Victorians understood that poet and speaker might be separate, but they did not question the terms of that distance, nor did they normally expect the speaker to be portrayed as doubting the validity of his own feeling. But twentieth-century speakers are usually full of such doubts. They are likely to see not only their own emotional response to the situation, but to make an attempt to see themselves as others see them. A twentieth-century speaker is not likely to be able unselfconsciously to say, "Learn from me nobleness of soul and true effort; learn success from others." A vision of his priggish appearance to others would stop him. He would be far more likely to say, "Well, son, you'll never learn success from me."

Pound's first major use of distancing irony came in translation. Peter Schneeman points out that Pound learned irony by imitating classical, particularly Latin, epigrams[51] and that these were exercises leading up to *Homage to Sextus Propertius.*[52] The *Homage* is pervaded by irony which the speaker directs at himself. For example, when a drunken Propertius pays a surprise visit to Cynthia in the wee hours, Pound translates:

And Cynthia was alone in her bed.
                      I was stupefied.
I had never seen her looking so beautiful
     No, not when she was tunick'd in purple.
Such aspect was presented to me, me recently emerged
     from my visions,
You will observe that pure form has its value.
"You are a very early inspector of mistresses.
"Do you think I have adopted your habits?"
     There were upon the bed no signs of a
       voluptuous
              encounter,
No signs of a second incumbent.
She continued:
     "No incubus has crushed his body against me,
     "Though spirits are celebrated for adultery.

"And I am going to the temple of Vesta . . ."
                                                    and so on.
Since that day I have had no pleasant nights.[53]
                                        (ellipsis Pound's)

Pound's Propertius, however deep in love, is capable of self-mockery and of cynicism. There is the yawn of "and so on," humorously implying a lengthy tirade; there is the clever use of "incumbent," with its connotations of both "present possessor" and "one who lies in bed"; and in the midst of all this, there is the art-appreciator's aside of "You will observe that pure form has its value."* In this translation, the reason for Propertius's stupefaction dangles ambiguously between Cynthia's solitary state and her beauty. Propertius knows that Cynthia may well be unfaithful. He knows he cuts a ridiculous figure checking up on her in the wee hours of the morning. This Propertius has enough objectivity to see himself as he appears both to Cynthia and to his reader, and therefore the tone of this passage is not self-pitying, but ironic.

Pound's *Homage* enraged those critics who saw the world with Victorian eyes. Both the absence of Victorian dignity and the presence of distancing irony offended them. The very first review of *Homage to Sextus Propertius,* written by W. G. Hale (1848–1929), Professor of Latin at the University of Chicago, ranted:

> Mr. Pound is often undignified or flippant, which Propertius never is. . . . Such renderings [as "I shall have my dog's day"] pervert the flavor of a consciously artistic, almost academic, original.[54]

Robert Nichols, a minor poet and dramatist, complained:

> . . . [Pound is] one who seems to think that vulgarity is an aid to incompetence, more especially if used to gal-

*This is a nearly literal translation of the Latin: *En quantum per se candida valet.*

vanize a poet of 'melancholy remembrance and vesperal' into a fox-trot quickness. . . . In place of the quiet and tender irony we are accustomed to see upon the face of Thomas Campion's favorite Latin poet we behold a mask of mordant gaiety and elegiac irony, sometimes almost saturnine. . . . Let Mr. Pound stick to the mask. It disguises him just sufficiently and gives to his utterances that slight softness of poetry which he in himself does not possess. . . . In himself Mr. Pound is not, never has been, and almost, I might hazard, never will be, a poet. He is too hard; too clever; he has yet to learn that poetry does not so much glitter as shine.[55]

The battle over Pound's Propertius has raged to the present day, but by 1935 it was possible for a critic to appreciate the very effect of distancing so disturbing to many of the poem's first readers. John Speirs (b. 1906) in 1935 wrote in *Scrutiny*:

The sophistication of the verse here [in the *Homage*] is no surface thing. It indicates the deeper sophistication of one who is 'expert from experience'—centuries of experience. A critical self-knowledge is his reward:

For I am swelled up with inane pleasurabilities
                    and deceived by your reference
To things which you think I would like to believe

is, of course, said ironically. The constant 'inspection' of his experience is indicated, also, by the frequent employment of non-emotive words. . . . [In Part IX] The intensity of concern . . . is not mitigated . . . by the apparent levity. . . .[56]

Speirs is rejecting the Victorian contention that irony and levity detract from intensity of emotion.

Just as critics were slow to appreciate the irony in the *Homage,* translators were slow to take it up. Irony quickly became

an important tool of such diverse poets as William Carlos
Williams and e. e. cummings, but remained hard to find in
translations. In 1937, Arthur S. Way, a well-known classical
translator,[57] was still trying to take Propertius seriously despite
the poet's vigorous resistance:

> True is it that all Rome through do men cry shame on
> thee,
>> And that thou art living in wantonness unto all
>> folk known?
> This have I looked for?—deserved? I will punish thy
> perfidy!
>> To a new port, Cynthia, now shall my sail by the
>> wind be blown. . . .
>> Ah, then too late wilt thou weep who vainly wert
>> loved so long! . . .
> But, by those sweet laws of Heaven's Queen Juno's
> ordinance born,
>> O let not thy reinless passions, my life, to thyself
>> bring harm!
> Not only the bull will thrust at a foe with crescent
> horn,
>> Even a wounded ewe will resist an assailant's arm.
> Fear not; from thy faithless form thy vesture will I
> never tear,
>> Nor yet shall thy doors close-barred be battered
>> down by me,
> Never I in mine anger will disarrange thy braided hair,
>> Nor ever my cruel fist shall deal one blow unto
>> thee!
> Such shameful combat as this let some boor brutally
> dare,
>> Around whose brows twined never the ivy of
>> poesy.
> Nay, this will I write—and thine whole life shall not
> efface the shame—
>> "Cynthia peerless in beauty—Cynthia faithless of
>> speech."

Believe me, howe'er thou dost scorn the whisper of evil
   fame,
      Cynthia, the line with bloodless pallor thy cheek
      shall bleach.[58]

Way's interminable lines, with their strange inversions, are
at odds with the ironic humor informing Propertius's account
of his revolt. " . . . vesture will I never tear," says Way, and
"Ah, then too late wilt thou weep who vainly wert loved so
long." But this elegy is the revolt of the wounded sheep:

   at tu per dominae Iunonis dulcia iure
      parce tuis animis, vita, nocere tibi.
   non solum taurus ferit uncis cornibus hostem,
      verum etiam instanti laesa repugnat ovis.[59]

(But you, [my] life, by the sweet law of [our] mistress
Juno, forbear to harm yourself by your pride [or, in your
soul]. Not only the bull strikes his assailant with curved
horns; even a wounded sheep resists her oppressor.)

Despite his protestations of non-violence, ewe-like Propertius
feels a sneaking envy of the lout who would simply beat
Cynthia.

Not until 1957 do the introductions to translations begin to
recognize Pound's revision of Propertius criticism. In that
year, L. R. Lind presented translations of Propertius by Frances
Fletcher. Lind noted:

   Propertius, for all his stature, is unknown to those who
   cannot read Latin because there has never been an adequate English verse translation of his elegies. Pound's
   "Homage to Propertius" is not, and was never intended
   to be, a translation. Yet for all its oddity (and it is made
   of as much Pound as of Propertius) it gives us the tem-
   perament of the poet in the chief elements of its neurotic
   complexity. Mingled with his frank sexual passion there
   is also an irony of objective self-analysis.[60]

Frances Fletcher's Propertius is presented free of *eths, -is'ts,* and added sentimentality:

> Is it true, Cynthia, that throughout Rome you are
>   notorious,
> That your scandalous living is no secret thing?
> Have I merited this culmination? You'll pay, deceiver:
> I'll ride the wind elsewhere. . . .
> But, by imperial Juno's gentle laws, take care, Cynthia,
> That you do not, through caprice, bring disaster upon
>   yourself!
> Not only does the bull charge his enemy with low-
>   curved horns:
> Even the sheep, when disturbed, strikes back at the
>   offender.
> I'm not going to tear the clothes from your perjured
>   body;
> Nor will my anger beat down your barred door:
> Nor shall I, in a rage, pull out your braided hair;
> Nor pommel you black-and-blue with my hard fists.
>
> But I'll write—words you cannot, no,
> Not in your lifetime, un-write:
>   "Cynthia, compelling in beauty; Cynthia,
>   frail in honesty."
> Scorn as you will, Cynthia, the gossiping tongues,
> This verse—believe me—will put the fear of God in
>   you.[61]

Unfortunately, Fletcher is not enough of a poet to catch the speaker's blend of self-contempt and pride.

At last, in 1972, a translation appeared which was able to convey Propertius's irony in the light Pound saw it so long before. Warden comments in his Introduction:

> [Propertius's] tone is a curious blend of irony and inten-
> sity. The central theme of this poetry, his love affair with
> Cynthia, is presented throughout from this double per-

spective: there is irony in the passion and passion in the irony.[62]

Warden has the poetic means to express his critical insight:

> Listen to what they say:
>> Cynthia the city whore
>> all Rome's her beat.
> Is it true? could you do that? you'll pay for it you
>> traitor;
>> I too can set my sail to another breeze. . . .
>
> Oh Cynthia
> tell me by Juno mistress of our common bondage
> whose tender sacraments we shared
> why must you hurt yourself like this my darling?
> I'll grant I am no bull
> to charge and toss my foe on crooked horn,
> but wounded and at bay
> even a sheep fights back.
> There'll be no vulgar brawling—
> I'll not strip naked your cheating body
>
> nor break down the door that will not let me in
>
> nor grab in anger at your braided hair
>
> nor bruise you (god forbid) with rough fists
>
> I am a poet—not a peasant.
> And so I'll write a poem
> which will mark you till your dying day;
> scorn as you will
> the mutterings of reputation
> these words will make you blench:
>
> IN BEAUTY CYNTHIA EXCELS
> (but you should hear the lies she tells).[63]

Warden captures Propertius's complex emotions. The speaker is both shamed and proud that he cannot simply hit out. He knows his verbal revenge is childish and weak; yet he is also conscious that a poet's revenge will indeed be repeated twenty centuries later.

Pound's sense of the ironic objectivity and self-criticism in Propertius took some fifteen years to be accepted critically, and another forty to be expressed by a second poet, just as Pound's attempts to resurrect natural symbols and realism in translation had encountered prolonged resistance. Yet, Pound's campaign for these elements of a new sensibility had an immediate impact on original poetry, as study after study attests.[64] Just why translation proved more resistant to change is difficult to determine. Pound himself found it so, as many of his own translations demonstrate. However, after a forty-year gestation period, tastes in translation began to reflect the modern revolution in poetry.

12

Changing the Present

Distorting the Original Poem

Pound stated quite frankly in a letter of 1931 that he had distorted the poetry of Sextus Propertius:

> . . . [the *Homage*] presents certain emotions as vital to me in 1911, faced with the infinite and ineffable imbecility of the British Empire, as they were to Propertius some centuries earlier, when faced with the infinite and ineffable imbecility of the Roman Empire. These emotions are defined largely, but not entirely, in Propertius' own terms.[1]

J. P. Sullivan distinguishes where the terms are Propertius's and where they are Pound's:

> Clearly he [Propertius] could have nothing like the attitude toward the Roman Empire that Pound had toward the British Empire; any sign of that indeed might have brought him even shorter shrift than Ovid's offense against Augustan moral reforms. . . . The objections to war and soldiering were [expressed in terms] personal rather than political. . . . Of course, contrary to Pound's reading of ii. 34, Propertius *does* admire Virgil. . . . Nevertheless, Book iv does offer some evidence that Pound's view is not entirely mistaken. Propertius does

not feel that he can sincerely . . . write the sort of court poetry so many Augustan poets wrote. . . . Pound has made the irony more obvious for his own purposes. . . .[2]

Thus, some of Pound's distortions were made to illuminate Propertius, but some changed Propertius to express Pound's own political and artistic credos.

Wai-lim Yip felt that Pound had made similar distortions of the poems in *Cathay*. Yip says that many of Pound's "philological mistakes . . . are done deliberately to heighten artistic intensity, and some, for a less defensible reason, are conditioned by his own obsessions as a practicing poet."[3]

According to Yip, one of these obsessions was the technique of superposition, which, Pound explained, "is one idea set on top of another."[4] In superposition, juxtaposition alone creates associations among a series of images. Yip points out that Pound imposed superposition on many poems in *Cathay*, notably "Leave-Taking near Shoku," "The City of Choan," and "The River Song."[5] Yip concludes:

> In a loose sense, all the poems in *Cathay* are, to some extent, Poundian, because the cuts and turns of the mind in the original poems are either overemphasized or modifed according to his own peculiar gestures of expression.[6]

Yet, Yip admires the added superposition in

Surprised. Desert turmoil. Sea sun.

which was Pound's translation of

驚	沙	亂	海	日
Startling	sand	derange confound	sea (i.e. sun above the "Vast Sea," ancient name for the Mongolian Desert)	sun[7]

Yip enthuses:

> . . . Pound isolates the word "Surprised," causing it to
> mean simultaneously "to be seized by the barbarians'
> unexpected attack" and "to be taken suddenly by the
> sandstorm." This word has become . . . the "node" into
> which two planes of action, relentless killing and natural
> hazards, merge."[8]

Yip feels that here and elsewhere in *Cathay* Pound has grasped
how in Chinese poetry the philosophical and cosmological
principal of *yin* and *yang* lie behind and inform all action, so
that the acts of human beings and the forces of nature com-
plement each other, often ironically.[9]

The Classics as Living Influences

Yip approached the paradox which underlies Pound's translations. In concerning himself with those parts of the poems
which touch on his present concerns, and in manipulating the
poems to propagandize* his beliefs, Pound nonetheless came
closer to the "central consciousness" of the poems than previous translators. Perhaps that is because, by believing that
classical poems contained material relevant to his contemporary concerns, Pound was turning a critical eye on their very
greatness—their timelessness in Eliot's sense: "This historical
sense, which is the sense of the timeless, as well as of the temporal and of the timeless and of the temporal together, is what
makes a writer traditional."[10] Pound, always less inclined to
metaphysics, put his concern with the classics this way:

> We await, *vei jauzen lo jorn,* the time when the student
> will be encouraged to say which poems bore him to tears,

---

*In this context, it is interesting to remember that *propaganda* was once simply literature disseminated for the increase of faith, and later acquired its meaning of political
lie.

and which he thinks rubbish. . . . if the first question asked were: "Gentlemen, are these verses worth reading?" instead of "What is the mood of 'manet'?" . . . the professor . . . might . . . meet from his class a less persistent undercurrent of conviction that all Latin authors are a trial.[11]

Despite his admittedly biased readings, Pound at least assumes the poem has something to say to him. Presumably, the function of a translation of poetry into poetry is to give the reader who can not understand the original a sense of why the original has importance *for him.* Burton Raffel, who has been heavily influenced by Pound, insists:

I do not think many people know how to read a translated poem. . . .
    The lay reader, who does not know the original, who usually cannot and will not read anything written in the language of the original, must not deal in . . . expert terms. He cannot be concerned, beyond a bare minimum, with questions of fidelity and accuracy. Is it good? he needs to know. Does it speak with a different voice from those he hears and reads in his own tongue, but at the same time with a voice he is capable of understanding— and enjoying? How does it illuminate the literature he knows? How might it illuminate him? . . . Whatever a translation of Baudelaire may mean to the French is not basically his affair; the French do not have to read Baudelaire in translation.[12]

These concerns are not scholarly concerns. G. S. Fraser makes the distinction:

Academic scholars are able to get an objective view of a text by dissociating it as far as possible from their own contemporary sensibility, which is what the poetic critic and translator . . . dare not do.[13]

Fraser and Raffel stand Matthew Arnold's dictum on its head. They believe that the translator is properly not concerned with what Homer meant to the Greeks, but with what Homer means to him. Not that Fraser or Raffel advocate that the translator shall be ignorant (indeed, they wish him as knowledgeable as possible), but his knowledge is used to a different purpose. In the new view of translation introduced by Pound, the knowledge of the translator is at the service of his instinct for what is modern. He goes to the past seeking poets whose affinities with his own tastes will illuminate, redefine, and confirm his own perspectives.

This principle of translation is in part a return to the concept of imitation. From classical times through the Middle Ages and the Renaissance, the notion of taking ideas and ornaments from other poets was approved. Ben Jonson was writing about a centuries-old method of working when he said:

> The third requisite in our *Poet,* or Maker, is *Imitation,* to be able to convert the substance or riches of another *Poet,* to his own use. To make choise of one excellent man above the rest, and so to follow him, till he grow very *Hee:* or, so like him, as the Copie may be mistaken for the Principall. Not, as a Creature, that swallowes what it takes in, crude, raw, or indigested; but, that feedes with an appetite, and hath a Stomacke to concoct, divide, and turne all into nourishment.[14]

The Romantic era, with its insistence on originality, laid this tradition temporarily to rest.[15]

Not every critic has been delighted at the re-emergence of imitation. John Hollander, who calls it "interpretive translation," defines its aims very well as he complains:

> Any translation might . . . do the work of an "interpretive" one [for the reader] by showing him something in an argument that he had not previously seen, as looking through a mirror at an unfinished painting lets one per-

ceive relationships that habitual observation had tended to obscure. But the literary sort of "interpretive translation" differs from this in being more like a peculiarly constructed sort of distorting mirror, or a carefully chosen ratio of enlargement or reduction, aimed always at selecting particular features of the original for emphasis, or even for being rendered visible at all.[16]

Pound emphasized in translation those elements in previous literatures which he could use to create and correct modern poetry. Consequently, modern poetry changed and, following it, translation style. Very few translators were able, as Pound did, to go to the past and find something new in it for themselves, although the principle of using the past for renewal is surely more important than the specific renewal Pound made out of it. However, at least one poet-translator since Pound has turned to the past with "a Stomacke to concoct, divide, and turne all into nourishment": Robert Lowell has turned to the poetry of the past to discover ways of presenting an attitude lost to modern poetry.

Robert Lowell's Distortion of Villon

Robert Lowell is known to have been aware of Pound's work.[17] He was on the committee which awarded Pound his controversial Bollingen prize in 1948. Lowell seems to have been influenced by Pound in his choice of authors and in his conception of translation. His translations from classical and medieval literature are from Homer, Sappho, Propertius, Der Wilde Alexander, and François Villon. Pound, in discussing Imagism, often paired the names of Sappho and Villon,[18] and chose Homer and Sappho as *the* two Greek authors to read.[19]

When Lowell chose Villon to translate, he was not only influenced by Pound in choice of author: his specific selections from Villon display close knowledge of Pound's Villonauds and "Montcorbier, *alias* Villon." Lowell opens his translation with the first line of the Great Testament and a few lines from the Little Testament:

> I am thirty this year,
> near Christmas, the dead season,
> when wolves live off the wind.[20]

Pound opens his "Villonaud for this Yule," a condensation of the *ubi sunt* sections of the Great Testament, with the same few lines from the Little Testament:

> Towards the Noel that morte saison
> *(Christ make the shepherds' homage dear!)*
> Then when the grey wolves everychone
> Drink of the winds their chill small-beer. . . .[21]

Pound based "A Villonaud: Ballad of the Gibbet" on the sections of the Great Testament which refer to Villon's connections to the Paris gangs[22] and combined this theme with lines based on "Freres humains qui après nous vivez,"[23] a ballad not contained in either the Little or Great Testaments. Lowell ends his selection from Villon with "Freres humains."

Within his selections from the Great Testament, Lowell displays his close acquaintance with "Montcorbier, *alias* Villon." Stanzas 2 and 3 in Lowell's translation are of Villon's Stanzas 29 and 30, which Pound had translated into prose and praised.[24] A few pages later, Lowell uses Stanza 22, also praised by Pound.[25] Lowell's translation of line 179, "less ripe than black," closely follows Pound's interpretation, "more black than ripe."[26]

Although Pound singled out for praise the Ballade of Dead Ladies, Villon's Prayer for His Mother, and "Freres humains," one can hardly say that Pound's influence caused Lowell to translate such famous poems. However, it is interesting to note that Lowell follows Pound's *misquote* of a Rossetti translation. Rossetti wrote

> Mother of God, where are they then? . . .
> But where are the snows of yester-year?[27]

Pound recalled this as:

> Mother of God, *where are they, where?*
> But where are the snows of yester-year![28]
> *(italics mine)*

Lowell translates:

> Where are they, where? Oh, Virgin,
> where is last year's snow?[29]

Perhaps Lowell even took the hint for his theme from Pound. In "Montcorbier *alias* Villon," Pound mentioned Villon's lines *Je suis pecheur, je le sçay bien; / Pourtant ne veult pas Dieu ma mort* 'I am a sinner, I know well, but God does not wish my death'.[30] Lowell chose to concentrate on Villon's ability to combine absolute realism with a serene faith in God. In this, he departs from Pound's view of Villon. Despite his admiration of the above lines, Pound was not recommending Villon's religion, but his realism, a realism Pound felt to be almost agnostic:

> Villon never lies to himself; he does not know much, but what he knows, he knows: man is an animal, certain things he can feel. There is much misery, man has a soul about which he knows little or nothing.[31]

The realism embraced by the twentieth century does not easily come to grips with Villon's type of religious faith. T. S. Eliot, when expressing *his* religious faith, did so through a persona fraught with doubts, clinging to faith with difficulty when confronted with the ugly facts of mortal existence. In Flannery O'Connor's stories and novels the realism never embraces faith. The apocalyptic vision which could make sense of her novels' events is *outside* of her novels, implied by the need her stories generate for the vision. For most twentieth-century writers, realism and unshakable faith are opposed perspectives. Therefore, when Robert Lowell chose to emphasize the religious elements in the Great Testament, he was using Villon to re-create a religious attitude in the same way that Pound used Propertius to re-create an ironic anti-imperialism.

Lowell's selections and arrangement of Villon display the compatibility of realism and faith. He takes from the Great Testament those portions in which Villon meditates on mis-spent youth, decaying age, and the certainty of death. Lowell includes none of the bequests and the individual characteriza-tions which go with them. Yet, these cuts reveal how thor-oughly realism is engrained in Villon. When only Villon's general theme remains, realism is still present. Villon medi-tates on death, and death is presented in terms of precisely observed, unpleasant symptoms: "Feet cramp, the nostrils curve. . . ."[32] Should Villon meditate on old age, old age is par-ticularized by a real woman, the Old Armoress, a former cour-tesan well-known to Villon's companions:[33]

> "This is how beauty dies:
> humped shoulders, barrenness
> of mind; I've lost my hips,
> vagina, and my lips.
> My breasts? They're a retreat!
> Short breath—how I repeat
> my silly list! My thighs
> are blotched like sausages."[34]

As Lowell's selections point out, in Villon an unflinching cat-alogue of unpretty details sets the stamp of realism on the most general topic.

Lowell's selections also reveal how deeply a serene religious faith informs Villon. Verse after verse contains lines like

God save those still alive!	(line 232)[35]
God grant / they do good works	(241–42)
They're dead, God rest their souls!	(1760)

Jesus, absolve their souls!   (1767)

God rest their souls!   (279)

My father (God have mercy!) / is in the
    ground   (299–300)

Yet, these lines do not strike the reader as mere formulae, since Lowell demonstrates their direct connection to Villon's Prayer for His Mother and the Ballade of the Hanged (called "Villon's Epitaph" by Lowell).

Villon's faith in God's mercy is also realistic. Lowell renders the second stanza of Villon's Prayer for His Mother as follows:

> "I am a woman—poor, absurd,
> who never learned to read your word—
> at Mass each Sunday, I have seen
> a painted paradise with lutes
> and harps, a hell that boils the damned:
> one gives me joy, the other doubts.
> Oh let me have your joy, my Queen,
> bountiful, honest and serene,
> by whom no sinner is condemned—
> in this faith let me live and die."[36]

Villon, as Lowell makes clear, knows how ignorance limits his mother's faith: her understanding of heaven and hell derives from the pictures she sees in church. Yet, both Lowell and Villon affirm the transcendent reality of that faith: God's mercy includes her with her limitations.

Lowell closes his selections from Villon with the Ballade of the Hanged, which is not in the Testaments. The speakers are hanged thieves. His translation begins:

> "Oh brothers, you live after us,
> because we shared your revenue.
> God may have mercy upon you,
> if you have mercy upon us.
> Five, six—you see us tied up here,

the flesh we overfed hangs here,
our carrion rots through skin and shirt,
and we, the bones, have changed to dirt.
Do not laugh at our misery:
pray God to save your souls and ours!

We hang in chains to satisfy
your justice and your violence,
brother humans—surely, you see
that all men cannot have good sense!
Here no man may look down on us—
Oh Child of Mary, pity us,
forgive our crimes—if dying well
saved even the poor thief from hell,
the blood of Christ will not run dry:
pray God to save your souls and ours!"[37]

In this poem, in the original and in the translation, both the
religious faith and the absolute realism are stongly expressed,
but Lowell, for his own purposes, has also changed the poem.
For instance, Villon says:

> Se freres vous clamons, pas n'en devez
> Avoir desdaing, quoy que fusmes occix
> Par justice.[38]

(If we call you brothers, don't be disdainful, even though
we have been killed by justice.)

Lowell changes this to

> We hang in chains to satisfy
> your justice and your violence. . . .

He is adding, or exaggerating, the implication that even
human justice is not free of sin. Lowell also changes the

refrain. He writes "pray God to save your souls and ours!" But Villon wrote *Mais priez Dieu que tous nous vueille absouldre* 'But pray God will absolve us all'. Villon neither limits this prayer for God's mercy to the hanged men, nor explicitly extends it to all men. Lowell explicitly makes the prayer take in all mankind.

More fundamentally, Lowell has slanted his version of Villon by ending with "Freres humains." Villon ended the Great Testament with the following *ballade:*

> Icy se clost le testament
> Et finist du pauvre Villon.
> Venez a son enterrement,
> Quant vous orrez le carillon,
> Vestus rouge com vermillon,
> Car en amours mourut, martir:
> Ce jura il sur son couillon,
> Quant de ce monde voult partir. . . .
>
> Il est ainsi, et tellement,
> Quant mourut n'avoit qu'ung haillon:
> Qui plus, en mourant, mallement
> L'espoignoit d'Amours l'esguillon;
> Plus agu que le ranguillon
> D'ung baudrier luy faisoit sentir
> (C'est de quoy nous esmerveillon),
> Quant de ce monde voult partir.[39]

(Here closes and ends the testament of poor Villon. Come to his burial when you hear the bells. [Come] dressed in vermillion, for he died a martyr in love. This he testified on his testicle as he would leave this world.

It was this way, so much that when he died he had only a rag. What's more, while he was dying the spur of love was pricking him on. He felt it more sharply than the tongue of a belt-buckle. It's this that we marvel at as he would leave this world.)

These lines concentrate, not on Heaven's mercy, but on the human condition of love. Galway Kinnell says that this *ballade* is

> ... a farewell to love, [which] becomes virtually a hymn in praise of love—or, anyway, of the pain of love. This is one of poetry's amazing acts of transcendence and transformation, like the celebration of the mudbanks in the culminating pages of *Walden,* for already in *The Testament* are indications that in Villon's case the pain of love consists, at a minimum, of disease and impotence. The beauty, even the sense of a certain blessedness, which pervades this last *ballade,* in which the "spur of love" stabs the poet once more as he dies, is not disspelled by the realization that the spur is not only sexual desire but perhaps also venereal disease.[40]

Robert Lowell chose to close his selections from Villon, not with a praise of human love, but with a prayer for the mercy of God. Lowell's theme is "Pourtant ne veult pas Dieu ma mort." It is a theme definitely represented in Villon. Robert Lowell chose it at the expense of other themes because he was looking to Villon for a voice not present in twentieth-century poetry, a voice which could express a religious faith in complete harmony with a realistic perspective. In so doing, he followed Ezra Pound's injunction to make it new.

13

Changing the Past

The Observer Modifies the Thing Observed

Matthew Arnold, F. W. Newman, and other nineteenth-century critics who considered the problem of poetic translation realized the impossibility of creating a complete equivalent of the original work; but they did not imagine that in approaching their goal they *changed* the original work. Ezra Pound and T. S. Eliot thought just that. In so thinking, they were elaborating a metaphysical application of the physical principle expressed by Werner Heisenberg in 1925, one form of which is: "the process of observation modifies the thing observed." Pound, when writing the *Homage to Sextus Propertius* in 1917, could not have had Heisenberg's theory in mind; but Pound always had an uncanny intuitive grasp of the Zeitgeist. Buckminster Fuller remembered that

> Heisenberg said that observation alters the phenomenon observed. T. S. Eliot said that studying history alters history. Ezra Pound said that thinking in general alters what is thought about. Pound's formulation is the most general, and I think it's the earliest.[1]

In mentioning T. S. Eliot, Fuller was probably referring to Eliot's famous essay of 1919, "Tradition and the Individual

Talent," which said:

> ... what happens when a new work of art is created is something that happens simultaneously to all the works of art which preceded it. The existing monuments form an ideal order among themselves, which is modified by the introduction of the new (the really new) work of art among them. The existing order is complete before the new work arrives; for order to persist after the supervention of novelty, the *whole* existing order must be, if ever so slightly, altered; and so the relations, proportions, values of each work of art toward the whole are readjusted; and this is conformity between the old and the new. Whoever has approved this idea of order, of the form of European, of English literature will not find it preposterous that the past should be altered by the present as much as the present is directed by the past.[2]

Presumably, Eliot was talking about "original" art, but the above statement has far-reaching implications for translation. J. P. Sullivan remarks that Pound "In both his criticism and his practice ... has stressed translation as one of the threads that link the individual talent to the poetic tradition."[3] John Hollander also noted the connection, commenting sourly:

> ... [This] has been an eclectic age, tirelessly committed to exhuming the artifacts of the literary and artistic past, and yet intent on maintaining a synoptic view of the present. Such an age depends upon a jealous and uneasy friendship with literary translation as almost no other age has, all the while purporting to remain under few illusions as to the fidelity of the comrade in question. ... translation has come to the brink of identification with the process of literary invention as such. ... (the job of the poet as outlined in T. S. Eliot's "Tradition and the Individual Talent" is strangely like that of an Ideal Translator).[4]

Logopoeia as Metalanguage

Pound's theories about the modification of the original by translation can be inferred from his uses of logopoeia. Pound began by using logopoeia to bridge differences of language and of culture, but gradually moved towards using logopoeia to discuss those differences.

Stuart Y. McDougal points out that by using words like "plasmatour" and "venust" in his later translations from Provençal

> Pound creates a new language to express the unified sensibility of medieval Provence and thereby affirms the importance of this sensibility to the modern world.[5]

But "plasmatour" and "venust," in addition to expressing the sensibility of Provence, are newly revived archaisms which draw attention to themselves and their new-old quality. They stand out of the poem in a way the words they "translate" never do. In *Homage to Sextus Propertius* and in *The Cantos,* Pound began to use such strangeness to draw the reader's attention to the questions raised by the process of translation. Logopoeia became simultaneously language and metalanguage. Pound could, and did, in the very translation itself, discuss the process of translation, compare one period of history with another, and discuss the history of translation and the evolution of literature. George T. Wright explains in *The Poet in the Poem* that Pound wrote as if

> . . . the translator shares the interests, the outlook, the feelings, of his author, but further, he becomes, in a sense, the twentieth-century self of his author. In assuming the mask of the old poet he becomes both writers at once, and through the contemporary idiom of the words an intelligence speaks which is greater than the single-dimensional intelligence of either. . . . Gradually in Pound's work the emphasis shifts from the re-creation of

character to the significance of the re-creation, and . . .
from the point of view of the persona to the point of
view implied by the augmentation of the persona.[6]

In a sense, by creating a greater intelligence, compounded
of the original poet and his modern voice, Pound achieved a
Hegelian synthesis. The ideas of the original poet are seen to
have implications beyond those he himself could have seen,
because these ideas have been absorbed into a larger context.
J. P. Sullivan argues that the augmentation of Propertius is a
benefit:

> . . . it is impossible for us to be as *inward* with a dead civ-
> ilization and a dead language as with our own. Yet inso-
> far as we are at all inward with Greek and Latin authors,
> it is through their absorption into the English tradition.
> Their poetic tradition is alive insofar as it is viable. . . .
> . . . the great translations are . . . the regrounding of
> the original in a contemporary sensibility. . . .[7]

Sullivan adds that Pound's observation of Propertius not only
changed Propertius, but modern poetry:

> . . . for the twentieth century, Pound's *Homage* is the only
> part of Propertius which lives for the common reader in
> the way a poet would wish to live, and it is this vital
> strength that draws him to our attention as a poet and
> not simply as a text or a subject for research. Propertius
> *required* Pound's reinterpretation (and even distortion) to
> bring him within our own frame of reference as a poet.
> And that frame of reference had also to be reinterpreted
> and distorted to come to terms with Propertius (the tech-
> nical originality of the *Homage* is obvious).[8]

Thus, like the spiral of history in *Die Phänomenologie des
Geistes,* translation winds round to the Elizabethan notion of
imitation, but with a difference. The Elizabethans believed

that the writers of the ancient world were men like themselves, sharing the same world view. Elizabethan translators obliterated distance in time and ignored real differences in Weltanschauung. The Victorians ignored similarities. When Pound returned to Elizabethan translation practice, he could not return to the naive Elizabethan view. Instead, Pound reached for a synthesis of the two views. To repeat Eliot's words, he tried to present "the past in its place with its definite differences from the present, and yet so lively that it shall be as present to us as the present."[9] Hugh Kenner writes of the way in which Pound translates the past into the present:

> Nothing we know the mind to have known has ever left us. Quickened by hints, the mind can know it again, and make it new. Romantic Time no longer thickens our sight, time receding, bearing visions away. . . . Translation, . . . after Ezra Pound, aims neither at dim ritual nor at lexicographic lockstep, but at seeming transparency, the vigors of the great original—Homer, Kung [i.e., Confucius]—not remote but at touching distance, though only to be touched with the help of all that we know.[10]

Time Layers

By means of logopoeia, Pound directs the attention of the reader to the significance of the augmented personae who speak in his poems. A startling phrase or unusual verse form may cause the reader to examine the relationship of the translated passage to the present and to other times. For instance, the *Homage to Sextus Propertius* contains passages deliberately rendered in the style of a rough-draft, literal translation; *The Cantos* open with a passage from the *Odyssey* cast in the style of Pound's "Seafarer." In each case, the unexpected choices convey more information than a straightforward translation; they allude to literary and extra-literary concerns outside the scope of the original author.

Donald Davie was the first to find in the *Homage* an intentional echo of a rough-draft literal translation:

> The *Homage,* then, is written in "translatorese." In par-
> ticular Pound makes the most of the grotesque and risible
> discrepancy between the vocabularies of poetry and of
> prose, a discrepancy which is known to any one who has
> made a rough working transliteration [*sic*] from a foreign
> poem into English prose. . . .[11]

Davie then quotes:

> Me happy, night, night full of brightness;
> Oh couch made happy by my long delectations;
> How many words talked out with abundant candles;
> Struggles when the lights were taken away;
> Now with bared breasts she wrestled against me,
> > Tunic spread in delay;
> And she then opening my eyelids fallen in sleep,
> Her lips upon them; and it was her mouth saying:
> > Sluggard![12]

Davie comments:

> "Me happy" is an expression that has no home in English
> except in this schoolchild's painful transliteration [*sic*] in
> the classroom; similarly the whole of the second line
> recalls nothing but the stilted, partly comic and partly
> touching expressions that arrange themselves across the
> page of an exercise-book when foreign words are looked
> up one by one and their dictionary equivalents are writ-
> ten down. "Delectations" in particular is a word that
> exists in a dictionary, and nowhere else. It is typical of
> the Latinate syllables that trumpet mournfully and uncer-
> tainly on every page of the *Homage.*[13]

Davie points out that the irony of Pound's translation is "dis-
concertingly pervasive and undirected": it shifts from civic

affairs, to political poetry, to Propertius himself, to his young lady, and even to his art.[14] Davie believes that

> The irony begins to define something only when the pompously polysyllabic words are seen as the products of "translatorese" . . . ; the diction puts the reader in the position of one who has transliterated [sic] into his own pompous and civic English a poem that deserves to be read precisely because it derides and denies all pompous and civic pretensions.[15]

Davie is probably wrong in thinking that Pound was deriding his reader; but he is probably right about the derision of pompous civic-mindedness. Pound is inviting the reader to share his and Propertius's outrage at the civic-minded pomposity which is used to mask imperial ambition.

Pound is also mocking, in a parody of the language of translation, all those Victorian translations which took every statement of Propertius at face value, devoid of irony, and turned him into a true, if physically weak, believer in Augustus.*

Hugh Kenner explores a different dimension of translatorese. He points out that at least some of the stiltedness reflects stilted sections in the Latin. Kenner considers a section of Elegy 2. 28:

> Deficiunt magico torti sub carmine rhombi,
>   et iacet extincto laurus adusta foco,
> et iam Luna negat totiens descendere caelo,
>   nigraque funestum concinit omen avis. . . .
>   vivam, si vivet: si cadet illa, cadam.
> pro quibus optatis sacro me carmine damno:
>   scribam ego "Per magnum salva puella Iovem";
> ante tuosque pedes illa ipsa adoperta sedebit,
>   narrabitque sedens longa pericla sua.[16]

---

*For instance, J. W. Mackail wrote that "the want of self-control in his [Propertius's] poetry may reflect actual physical weakness . . ." (*Latin Literature,* p. 127).

(The noise-makers whirled to accompany the magical
chant have ceased, and the burnt laurel lies by the extin-
quished fire. And now the moon refuses to descend so
often from heaven, and a black bird prophecies an omen
of death. . . . If she lives, I will: if she dies, I will die. For
the above [prayed-for] benefits, I bind myself by a sacred
verse that I will write, "The girl was saved by mighty
Jove," and she herself will sit, veiled, before your feet,
and sitting she will tell you her lengthy dangers.)

He compares this to Pound's translation:

The twisted rhombs ceased their clamour of
     accompaniment;
The scorched laurel lay in the fire-dust;
The moon still declined to descend out of heaven,

But the black ominous owl hoot was audible. . . .
I shall live, if she continue in life.
     If she dies, I shall go with her.
Great Zeus, save the woman,
          or she will sit before your feet in a veil,
          and tell out the long list of her troubles.[17]

Kenner states:

. . . it is [now] impossible . . . to be unaware of a calcu-
lated excess of atmospherics, to miss risible implications
in the locution 'Luna negat,' or comic inflections in the
tableau of grateful loquacity presented by the last
distich.[18]

Kenner thus demonstrates that the translatorese of such
phrases as "the moon still declined to descend" and the "ominous owl hoot was audible" are rooted in language overdone
on Propertius's part.
     This is true, yet surely Pound could have conveyed these

ironic implications without translatorese. Therefore, Kenner
further explains the translatorese as an attempt by Pound to
discuss the process of transforming Latin into English. He
takes up Pound's translation of

> tale facis carmen docta testudine quale
> Cynthius impositis temperat articulis[19]

(You make such music as the Cynthian god [Apollo]
modulates, his fingers placed on the well-taught lyre.)

Pound rendered this:

> Like a trained and performing tortoise,
> I would make verse in your fashion if she should
>   command it. . . .[20]

Kenner comments:

To the mind of the unscholarly reader English associations leap unbidden ahead of Latin roots; before being
able to construe these lines, were they suddenly shoved
in front of him, he would have to brush away the irre-
levancies of testudine/turtle (via Caesar), impositis/
imposition, Cynthius/Cynthia (the imperious lady-
love), temperat articulis/temper my articulation.[21]

He concludes:

A neglected level among the layer upon layer of irony
in Pound's *Homage* is this sort of reflection of the ghosts
that dance before schoolboys' eyes. . . . there is in fact a
middle stage in learning to read Latin verse, . . . when the
magnetic affinities of random words for sophisticated but
irrational English contexts trouble the mind with contin-
ual false scents. The deliberate *collage* of pokerfaced mis-
readings performed by Pound in certain portions of this
poem should perhaps be connected with the exploration

of these zones of consciousness initiated by Joyce five years later.[22]

All of the above interpretations of the purpose of translatorese are corect. On one level, the language simply performs the function of critical interpretation; Propertius's emotions are being rendered: "Me happy, night, night full of brightness" is the touchingly comic rendition of a man so overwhelmingly, bumblingly happy that his grammar has deserted him. "The moon declined to descend" conveys the sophisticated speaker's unease with magic. At the same time, these absurd constructions are fulfilling Kenner's other claim for them: the reader is made aware of the nature of the process by which anyone who cannot think in Latin approaches the meaning of the Latin text. Furthermore, Davie's suggestion is also correct: the language mocks naive and pompous interpretations of Propertius (and other classical authors) current in Victorian and Edwardian times. By recalling past "civic-minded" interpretations in language that is obviously a parody, Pound draws attention to both his and Propertius's anti-imperial mood. Logopoeia thus becomes a means for Pound to discuss his interpretation of Propertius, the history of the interpretation of the poem, and the mental efforts by which Latin is read; all this, within the confines of the translation. Propertius is translated and Propertius is augmented, yet there was no direct discussion of Pound's additional concerns.

In Canto 1, Pound further extended the uses of the types of logopoeia found in the *Homage to Sextus Propertius*. Rather than deride previous interpretations of a poem, as he had done in the *Homage,* Pound used logopoeia to link himself with the centuries-old process of adumbrating the *Odyssey*. Canto 1 is mostly a creative translation of the opening of Book 11 of the *Odyssey*. However, Canto 1 is also the opening to the whole of Pound's long poem, and is intended to be part of a new composition, as well as a translation. It begins:

And then went down to the ship,
Set keel to breakers, forth on the godly sea, and

We set up mast and sail on that swart ship,
Bore sheep aboard her, and our bodies also
Heavy with weeping, and winds from sternward
Bore us out onward with bellying canvas,
Circe's this craft, the trim-coifed goddess.
Then sat we amidships, wind jamming the tiller,
Thus with stretched sail, we went over sea till day's
        end.
Sun to his slumber, shadows o'er all the ocean,
Came we then to the bounds of deepest water,
To the Kimmerian lands. . . .

Canto 1 then describes how Odysseus magically summoned a
crowd of ghosts in an attempt to get advice from dead Tiresias.
Finally:

        . . . Anticlea came, whom I beat off, and then Tiresias
            Theban,
Holding his golden wand, knew me, and spoke first:
"A second time? why? man if ill star,
"Facing the sunless dead and this joyless region? . . ."
            And I stepped back,
And he strong with the blood, said then: "Odysseus
"Shalt return through spiteful Neptune, over dark seas,
"Lose all companions." And then Anticlea came.
Lie quiet Divus. I mean, that is Andreas Divus,
In officina Wecheli, 1538, out of Homer.
And he sailed, by Sirens and thence outward and away
And unto Circe.[23]

    H. A. Mason offers some very interesting criticism of this
passage, on the assumption that it is intended to be a creative
translation of Homer, but one limited to the type of criticism
discussed in Part Two. He points out that additions to Homer
like "bellying" the canvas and "jamming the tiller" are
inserted "to remind us of the language used by real sailors."[24]

However, when he catches a comparison to "The Seafarer," he scolds:

> . . . it is the reverse of tonic to meet with the false archaic of the Wardour Street, Anglo-Saxon Wanderer. . . . At the very beginning I am pulled up by
>
> We set up mast and sail on that swart ship, . . .
> *(Mason's ellipsis)*
>
> If we could believe that Homer had found the paint peculiar, if he had wished to suggest something out of the way on a ship of his day, we could only applaud Pound for digging up . . . 'swart'. But as far as I can make out, Homer meant a ship painted the regulation color. . . .[25]

Mason is happy as long as Pound is focusing on "the presence of the past," but is put off by Pound's concurrent concern with "the pastness of the past." He sees the clash of styles as a lack of unity, rather than logopoeia intended to raise questions.

Pound is engaged in a larger endeavor than criticism of Homer. For one thing, he is introducing the hero of *The Cantos,* who is not Odysseus, but his analog: "A second time? why?" asks Tiresias; Homer's Ulysses delved the underworld only once. Also, the passage closes with a name never found in Homer's Hades: "Lie quiet Divus. I mean that is Andreas Divus, / In officina Wecheli, 1538, out of Homer."

Hugh Kenner asks, "What comes before 'And'?" and answers himself:

> In mankind's past, before even Homer, a foretime; a foretime even before the dark rite of confronting shades which Pound thought *older* than the rest of the *Odyssey,* reclaimed by Homer as he reclaims Homer now. In the *Odyssey,* the ten books that precede. In Ezra Pound's life, the time at Wyncote and Pennsylvania and Hamilton and Wabash, before he took ship for what was not meant

as exile. And in the history of the poem, much precedent groping and brooding, out of which mostly unspecifiable darkness the poem as we know it emerges.[26]

Kenner points out that Pound wished the beginning of *The Cantos* to comprise other beginnings: the beginnings of English (references to Anglo-Saxon poetry), the beginnings of Greek poetry (the *Nekuia*), the beginning of the Renaissance.[27] The Renaissance is referred to in "Lie quiet Divus." Andreas Divus Justinopolitanos published in 1538 in Paris *Homeri Odyssea ad verbum translata,* a line-by-line Latin version of the *Odyssey* intended as a crib for students.[28] Pound is translating, not from Greek, but from Latin, Latin of 1538. This Latin was part of the Renaissance concern with Greek classics, and in translating from it, Pound is imitating the Renaissance practice of the translation chain: Elizabethans thought nothing of translating into English a French translation of a Latin translation of a Greek text.[29] Pound is like the Elizabethans in translating a translation, but unlike them in his twentieth-century concern to specify the source.

   Pound, as Kenner points out, translated Divus's Homer into the verse form which he invented for his translation of "The Seafarer."[30] The alliteration, heavy stresses, caesuras, and diction of:

> May I for my own self song's truth reckon,
> Journey's jargon, how I in harsh days
> Harships endured oft.
> Bitter breast-cares have I abided,
> Known on my keel many a care's hold.

are all echoed in

> And then went down to the ship,
> Set keel to breakers, forth on the godly sea, and
> We set up mast on that swart ship,
> Bore sheep aboard her, and our bodies also
> Heavy with weeping. . . .

Such an echo suggests the many parallels between the cultures depicted in the Homeric and Anglo-Saxon poems.[31] Both cultures arose towards the end of a great migration. Both created a body of poetry celebrating the heroic deeds of the nobility. These poems were oral-formulaic: that is, the poet composed orally from a store of set phrases memorized by all bards.* In these poems, the heroic deeds celebrated were essentially glorified cattle raids. The heroes make formal self-inciting boasts. A lord was the head of a band of warriors bound to him by kinship and/or the receipt of ceremonial gifts of treasure and booty. Gift and countergift giving was an important economic aspect of both societies. For both the Greek and the Anglo-Saxon, the epitome of the goods of peace was a feast in the Lord's hall for the warrior band, with ceremonial gifts being parceled out, the food and wine going round, and the minstrel singing of heroic deeds. By using a verse form which recalls Anglo-Saxon poetry, Pound directs the reader to make comparisons of the two cultures.

But Pound's verse form is not the verse form of the original "Seafarer." Pound invented it in 1911, and so yet another layer of time is to be considered. Hugh Kenner says that in reading *The Cantos:*

On a given moment, layered times converge, as in Canto I the time of the subject (Odysseus), the time denoted by the style (Seafarer), the present time of writing. And ("Lie quiet Divus") there may often be a fourth, when the subject incorporates some earlier subject: Divus encompassing Homer. . . . And a fifth, the time of reading, very evident when the time of writing has itself become history.[32]

---

*Canto 1 reached its final form in 1925, so Pound could not then have known of Milman Parry's theory, first published in 1934, of oral composition from memorized formulae; but the repetition of phrase and recapitulation of story is there for anyone to see in both *Beowulf* and the *Odyssey*.

This depiction of the many layers of time and their inter-
action in the mind is Pound's unique contribution to
translation.

Using Twentieth-Century Perspectives

To date, no translator other than Pound has shown himself
interested in using logopoeia either as a metalanguage to discuss translation or to confer multiple perspectives. However,
a few translators have accepted one of the principles behind
Pound's use of logopoeia: that a translator can use the perspective of the twentieth century to advantage. For, although
the twentieth-century translator cannot fully participate in the
experience of the original poet, the intervening centuries have
granted him knowledge unavailable to the original poet.
Instead of trying to re-create the original author's structuring
of reality, the translator may deliberately reinterpret a poem
in the light of twentieth-century experience and concepts.

D. S. Carne-Ross finds an instance of such reinterpretation
in a translation made by Peter Green. The passage is from
Book 1 of the *Iliad,* just after the prophet Calchas has
informed the Greeks that the only way to placate Apollo is for
Agamemnon to return the girl Chryseis, his battle prize, to her
father, who happens to be a priest of Apollo. Green writes:

> . . . So saying, Calchas sat down, and after him the
>   noble
> Son of Atreus rose, wide-ruling Agamemnon,
> Choked black with rage, his eyes glinting like points of
>   fire.
> First he turned to Calchas, face eloquent with hatred:
>   'You long-faced quack, have you ever prophesied
>   good?
> Doom's your delight, disaster your stock-in-trade—
> Never a cheerful omen declared, much less fulfilled!

And now you stand up here with your miserable
    cantrips
And swear this plague from Apollo is all my doing—
Because I turned down rich ransom, and kept the girl
    Chryseis!
Why shouldn't I? I want her. I'd rather have her than
    my wife,
Yes, rather than Clytemnestra. She's better all around—
Prettier, nicer figure, more sense, and a damned sight
    handier
About the house. Still, even so I'm willing
To hand her back, if the public good demands it.
I have a responsibility for my men, I can't stand by
And see Achaeans slaughtered. But if I release the girl,
You'll have to find me another prize to replace her.
    How
Would it look if I was the only Argive chief among
    you
Without a share in the booty? Think of it this way,
All of you: it means that I kiss my prize goodby.'
           Then Achilles, the godlike, the swift of foot,
              replied:
'Most noble Agamemnon, high prince of covetousness,
How shall we, the Achaean warriors, find you a prize?
We are no tradesmen with a hoard of public funds;
Whatever we took when we sacked those towns has
    already
Been shared out. We cannot decently beg it
Back from its owners now. . . .'[33]

The passage is like many of the kind examined in Part One:
a modern colloquial diction contrasts with archaic concerns:
unpropitiated gods and booty-sharing. But Green has done
more than make his characters sound colloquial. Carne-Ross
explains:

    The Homer who emerges from that passage is a
    Homer with a good sense of humor, an eye for character

and an ear for the cadences of speech, a feeling for the
everyday reality of the life he is describing. A Homer, in
short, who has undergone the influence of the novel. I
think this is inevitable and quite proper. If translation is
to be more than an academic exercise, it has to be related
to living literary interests. Pope could turn the *Iliad* into
an Augustan epic because the civilization he belonged to
still believed that epic was, in Dryden's words, 'the greatest work which the soul of man is capable to perform.'
But for better or worse, the only great living form today
is the novel, and it is inevitable that we should bring to
our reading, and so to our translation, of the great narrative poetry of the past demands and preoccupations
which we have learnt from our reading of the novel.[34]

Before Ezra Pound's translations became part of the heritage, no poet would have thought to offer homage to Homer
by bringing to his narrative the "demands and preoccupations
which we have learnt from our reading of the novel." Nor is
this snatch of the *Iliad* a lone example of the deliberate imposition of the twentieth-century world-view on the poetry of
the past. Robert Lowell interprets Propertius's Elegy 4. 7 in
the light of modern psychological theory.

In 4. 7, Propertius tells of a dream he had shortly after Cynthia's funeral. Cynthia's ghost upbraids him for not attending,
asserts that she has been faithful, and makes several requests.
Propertius is to revenge her death by poisoning, and to take
care of her old nurse and another favorite slave. Finally Cynthia asks Propertius to burn his verses to her and to set up an
inscribed pillar by her grave. Cynthia then says that others
may have Propertius now, she will possess him in death.
The ghost then vanishes, leaving Propertius embracing emptiness.

To Propertius, as a Roman of the first century B.C., ghosts
existed, and in dreams they could reveal the past and predict
the future. Dreams, according to the Roman interpretation,
could be either false (arriving through the gates of horn) or
true (arriving through the gates of ivory). The ghost portrayed

by Propertius takes pains to insist that she is a true dream:

> nec tu sperne piis venienta somnia portis:
>   cum pia venerunt somnia, pondus habent.[35]

(Do not spurn dreams coming from the honest [or holy] gates; when honest [or holy] dreams come, they have weight.)

A Roman analysis of Propertius's dream would have debated such issues as whether the dream were true or false, and if true, what action Propertius should take. A more sophisticated discussion, taking the poem as a literary construct, would have discussed whether the dream was intended by the poet as true or false. Propertius's grief might also have been discussed, but the poem clearly puts this issue outside of the dream. The allusions to grief are

> cum mihi somnus ab exsequiis penderet amoris
>   et quererer lecti frigida regna mei[36]

(Since after the funeral rites of love, sleep was interrupted for me and I was lamenting the cold kingdom of my bed)

which comes before the dream, and

> haec postquam querula mecum sub lite peregit,
>   inter complexus exicidit umbra meos[37]

(As soon as she had finished convicting me with querulous argument, the shade vanished from my embrace)

which comes after the dream has ended.

Robert Lowell's treatment of Propertius departs radically from his handling of Villon. The translations from Villon select certain themes for emphasis, but those themes are treated by Lowell in ways compatible with Villon's view of reality. However, Lowell subjects Peopertius's dream to a

Freudian analysis,[38] which is incompatible with Propertius's
consciously held theories. Roman dream theory concentrated
on the prophetic nature of dreams, and held that dreams come
from outside the dreamer's mind, revealing objective truths.
Lowell holds that dreams come from inside the dreamer's
mind, and reveal subjective truths. His translation, developed
from hints present in the poem, brings out how closely Propertius associates death with sex. The first verse begins:

> A ghost is someone: death has left a hole
> For the lead-coloured soul to beat the fire:
>   Cynthia leaves her dirty pyre
>   And seems to coil herself and roll
>   Under my canopy,
>   Love's stale and public playground, where I lie
> And fill the run-down empire of my bed.[39]

Lowell's first seven lines embroider considerably. The Latin
says:

> Sunt aliquid Manes: letum non omnia finit,
>   luridaque evictos effugit umbra rogos.
> Cynthia namque meo visa est incumbere fulcro,
>   murmur ad extremae nuper humata viae,
> cum mihi somnus ab exsequiis penderet amoris,
>   et quererer lecti frigida regna mei.[40]

(Spirits are something: death does not end everything,
and the lurid shade escapes the dead funeral pyre. For
Cynthia seemed to me to lean over the foot of my bed,
[Cynthia] recently buried near the noise of a distant road,
since after the funeral rites of love, sleep was interrupted
for me and I was lamenting the cold kingdom of my
bed.)

There is nothing in the Latin suggesting shabbiness, but Lowell invents a "dirty pyre," "Love's stale and public play-

ground," and "run-down empire." Further, he turns the lurid, or pale, shade into dirty smoke: "the lead-coloured soul . . . / . . . seems to coil herself and roll / Under my canopy." All this implies that Propertius himself feels unclean and degraded by having had other women since Cynthia.

Propertius's poem offers the possibility of such interpretation to a reader even vaguely acquainted with Freudian theory. If read by such a theory, Cynthia's dream reproaches represent Propertius's own guilt feelings: *Perfida nec cuiquam melior sperande puellae* 'Faithless man, but a girl shouldn't hope for better than you', *non tamen insector, quamvis mereare, Properti* 'Still, I won't hound you, however much you deserve it, Propertius', *celo ego perfidiae crimina multa tuae* 'I conceal [when conversing with the other shades] the many crimes of your faithlessness'.[41]

Lowell goes on to suggest that Propertius fears impotence. Immediately after a near-literal translation of the ghastly aspect of Cynthia's charred ghost ("A black nail dangles from her finger-tip / And Lethe oozes from her nether lip"), Lowell begins her tirade: "Sextus, has sleep already washed away your manhood?" Probably a Roman could not have gotten a slur on Propertius's virility out of *in te iam vires somnus habere potest?*[42] Although *vires* can mean "sexual potency," the order of words goes "on you now potency sleep is able to have?" In such a word order a suggestion of loss of potency never arises.

Yet, once again, there are hints in the Latin which give some validity to Lowell's charge. Very near the end of the poem, Propertius wrote:

> nunc te possideant aliae: mox sola tenebo:
> mecum eris, et mixtis ossibus ossa teram.[43]

(Now others may have you: soon I alone will hold: you will be with me, and I will polish bone with mingled bones.)

"Polish" is the least fearsome interpretation one can give to *teram,* and is not in the center of its meaning. *Tero, terare, trivi, tritum* means "to rub to pieces, to bruise, to grind, to thresh, to polish, to visit frequently, to wear out, to exhaust." Lowell has taken up the threat of wearing Propertius away by rubbing, with its unpleasant sexual undertones, and transferred it to the present. It is this *teram* which lies behind "manhood," quoted above and also repeated in Lowell's last stanza:

> You cannot turn your back upon a dream,
> For phantoms have their reasons when they come:
>   We wander midnights: then the numb
>   Ghost wades from the Lethaean stream:
>   Even the foolish dog
> Stops its hell-raising mouth and casts its clog;
> At cock-crow Charon checks us in his log.
> Others can have you, Sextus; I alone
> Hold: and I grind your manhood bone on bone.[44]

Lowell can also justify his interpretation from the body of Propertian poetry. There is in Propertius a morbid fascination with death[45] which often is accompanied by sexual images.[46] Ronald Musker comments that in Propertius "feelings about death are so closely associated with love that he can hardly mention one without the other."[47]

Sigmund Freud in part based his theories on the evidence of past literatures. He pointed out the frequent association of love and death in the writing of all times. However, to recast Propertius in accordance with Freudian theory is circular reasoning. We may see a subconscious relationship between death and sex in his work, but Propertius was relating a "true" dream.

Nonetheless, Robert Lowell was performing a homage to Sextus Propertius. He gave him the honor of assuming that the Roman poet had gotten so much of reality into his work that it could take being interpreted *sub specie* 1946. "The Ghost" is a vision of Propertius deliberately taken from the standpoint of the present. Such a translation tells us something about ourselves, and something about Propertius, which is the point of "regrounding the original in a contemporary sensibility."[48]

Robert Lowell's method is different from Ezra Pound's. Pound tried to create by means of logopoeia a dual view of the past as it may have seemed to itself and the past as it seems to the present. He liked to throw out hints of extra-literary associations. Lowell has simply taken Propertius's poem and read it according to the perspective of his own time. Such a procedure distorts Propertius, but it also makes clear how meaningful he can be for us. This was also the object of Pound's *Homage.* "My job," Pound said, "was to bring a dead man to life, to present a living figure."[49]

New Directions

It may be that no one will ever take up logopoeia and use it as language and metalanguage. At present it seems that poets are more interested in the method of Pound's *Cantos:* John Berryman, Robert Duncan, Charles Olson, and other poets incorporate into their poems translated quotations from poets they admire and proceed to comment on them.[50]

Whether or not all Pound's practices are taken up, Pound has changed the theory and practice of translation. This is not to say that older practices are laid to rest, nor should they be. There is a place for literal translation, a place for paraphrase, and a place for creative translation, depending on the need of the person who reads the poem, and the person who translates it. There is a place for translations which emphasize the affinities of the past and the present, and a place for those which emphasize the differences. But to say that there is room for all these kinds of translation is to point out the greatest single change Pound made in the theory of translation. Translators now write knowing that whatever their goal for a particular translation, it is necessarily one particular view of the poem; but set beside the original and beside translations of other times and other men, it may help illuminate the original poem. The translator, Pound demonstrated, can return what has been lost to the ongoing tradition, and become part of that tradition himself.

Notes

Chapter 1: A Renaissance for Translation

1. J. M. Cohen, *English Translators and Translations* (London: Longmans, Green & Co. for the British National Council and the National Book League, 1962), p. 29.

2. Ibid., p. 24.

3. John Dryden, Preface to *Ovid's Epistles* (1680), *The Works of John Dryden,* ed. Edward Niles Hooker and H. T. Swedenberg, Jr., 18 vols. (Berkeley and Los Angeles: University of California Press, 1956–74), 1:114–15.

4. Ibid., 1:115.

5. Ibid., 1:118.

6. Ibid., 1:116.

7. Ibid., 1:116–17.

8. Ibid., 1:119.

9. J. P. Sullivan, *Ezra Pound and Sextus Propertius: A Study in Creative Translation* (Austin: University of Texas Press, 1964), pp. 17–20.

10. Dryden, Preface to *Sylvae* (1685), *Works,* 3:3–4.

11. This idea is developed throughout *The Pound Era* (Berkeley and Los Angeles: University of California Press, 1971), but Kenner makes relatively concise statements of it on pp. 162 and 165.

12. Donald Davie, *Ezra Pound: Poet as Sculptor* (New York: Oxford University Press, 1964), pp. 5, 86–87. Kenner, "Blood for the Ghosts," in *New Approaches to Ezra Pound: A Co-ordinated Investigation of Pound's Poetry and Ideas,* ed. Eva Hesse (London: Faber and Faber, 1969), pp. 332–37, 348.

Chapter 2: The Victorian Vision of Time: Theory and Practice

1. Matthew Arnold, *On Translating Homer* (1860–1861), *The Complete Prose Works,* ed. R. H. Super, 11 vols. (Ann Arbor: University of Michigan Press, 1960–77), 1:97–98.

2. Ibid., 1:98–99.

3. Ibid., 1:100.

4. Ibid.

5. Ibid., 1:119.

6. From Newman's translation of Sarpedon's speech to Glaucus, *Iliad,* Book 12, quoted in Arnold, 1:133.

7. Arnold, 1:164, translating from Book 6 of the *Iliad.*

8. Arnold, 1:180–81.

9. Cohen, p. 24.

10. Kenner, *Pound Era,* p. 24.

11. Dante Gabriel Rossetti, *Rossetti's Poems,* ed. and with an Introduction and Notes by Oswald Doughty (London: J. M. Dent & Sons, 1961; New York: E. P. Dutton & Co., 1961), pp. 100–101.

12. Titled, respectively, by Rossetti "The Ballad of Dead Ladies," "To Death, of His Lady," and "His Mother's Service to Our Lady" (Rossetti, pp. 100–102).

13. Text follows that in Anthony Bonner, trans. [and ed.], *The Complete Works of François Villon,* with a Bibliography and Notes, and an Introduction by William Carlos Williams (New York: David McKay Co., 1960), pp. 36, 38, hereafter referred to as Bonner, *Villon.*

14. John Payne, trans., *The Poems of Master François Villon of Paris, Now First Done into English Verse,* with a Biographical and Critical Introduction (London: The Villon Society, 1892), reprinted in John Heron Lepper, trans., *The Testaments of François Villon,* including the Texts of John Payne and Others (New York: Liveright Publishing Corp., 1924), pp. 204–5.

15. Thomas Charles Baring, trans., in *The Latin Poets,* ed. Francis R. B. Godolphin, The Modern Library (New York: Random House, 1949), p. 234.

16. Cohen, p. 29.

17. Francis Hueffer, trans., "S'al cor plagues ben for' ueimais sazos," in *The Troubadours: A History of Provençal Life and Literature in the Middle Ages* (London: Chatto & Windus, 1878), p. 258.

18. Ibid., pp. 256–57.

19. The text follows that in Hueffer, p. 257.

20. Pound, "I Gather the Limbs of Osiris, Part 5," *New Age* 10 (28 December 1911):201, quoted in Stuart Y. McDougal, *Ezra Pound and the Troubadour Tradition,* Princeton Essays in Comparative Literature (Princeton, N.J.: Princeton University Press, 1972), p. 110.

21. This translation by Pound of Arnaut Daniel's "Sols sui qui sai lo sobrafan quem sortz," appeared in "I Gather the Limbs of Osiris, Part 12," *New Age* 10 (22 February 1912):392, quoted in McDougal, p. 111.

22. Pound, "Cavalcanti" (1910, revised 1931), *Literary Essays of Ezra Pound,* ed. and with an Introduction by T. S. Eliot (New York: New Directions, A New Directions Paperbook, 1968), pp. 193–94.

Chapter 3: A New Vision of Time: Pound's Theory and Practice

1. "To A. R. Orage," April 1919, Letter 160, *The Letters of Ezra Pound, 1907–1941,* ed. D. D. Paige, with a Preface by Mark

Van Doren (New York: Harcourt, Brace & World, A Harvest Book, 1950), p. 149.

2. Pound, "To Felix E. Schelling," 8 July 1922, *Letters,* p. 179.

3. McDougal, pp. 19–20; Davie, pp. 41–42.

4. Pound, trans., *Cathay,* in *Personae: The Collected Shorter Poems of Ezra Pound* (New York: New Directions, 1971), pp. 130–31.

5. Wai-Lim Yip, *Ezra Pound's "Cathay"* (Princeton: Princeton University Press, 1969), p. 92.

6. Pound, "Cavalcanti," *Literary Essays,* p. 154.

7. Ibid., p. 199.

8. Ibid.

9. Pound, Introduction (dated 15 November 1910) to "Cavalcanti Poems" (1912, rev. 1920, 1931), *Translations,* with an Introduction by Hugh Kenner, enl. ed. (New York: New Directions, A New Directions Paperbook, 1963), pp. 19–20.

10. Pound, "Cavalcanti," *Literary Essays,* p. 200.

11. Pound, "I Gather the Limbs of Osiris, Part 3," *New Age* 10 (14 December 1911):155, quoted in McDougal, p. 76.

12. McDougal, p. 137.

13. Pound, "How to Read" (1929), *Literary Essays,* p. 25.

14. Sullivan, p. 67.

15. Pound, "How to Read," *Literary Essays,* p. 33.

16. See particularly Chapter 1 of Davie and Kenner's "Blood for the Ghosts," in Hesse.

17. Davie, p. 88.

18. Pound, trans., *The Classic Anthology as Defined by Confucius [Shih Ching],* with an Introduction by Achilles Fang (Cambridge: Harvard University Press, 1954).

19. Davie, p. 9.

20. Ibid., pp. 9–10.

21. Ibid., pp. 13–14. "Cavalier Tunes" are in Browning's *Dramatic Lyrics* of 1842.

22. Pound, *Classic Anthology*, pp. 163–64.

23. Davie, p. 11.

24. Ibid., p. 12.

25. Ibid., p. 11.

26. Ibid., p. 12.

27. Ibid., p. 13.

28. Ibid., pp. 12–13.

29. Kenner, "Leucothea's Bikini: Mimetic Homage," in *Ezra Pound Perspectives: Essays in Honor of His Eightieth Birthday*, ed. Noel Stock (Chicago: Henry Regnery Co., 1965), p. 28.

30. Pound, "A Retrospect" (1918), *Literary Essays*, p. 11.

31. T. S. Eliot, "Euripides and Professor Murray" (1920), *Selected Essays*, new edition (New York: Harcourt, Brace & World, 1964), p. 50.

32. Eliot, "Tradition and the Individual Talent" (1919), *Selected Essays*, p. 4.

33. Pound, "To Felix E. Schelling," 8 July 1922, *Letters*, p. 179.

34. Arnold Hauser, *The Social History of Art*, trans. Stanley Godman in collaboration with the author, 4 vols. (New York: Random House, Vintage Books, 1958), vol. 4: *Naturalism, Impressionism, and the Film Age*, pp. 237–39, 246. Hugh Kenner, in *The Pound Era* (pp. 29 and 143), compared Cubism with Pound's style of *Homage to Sextus Propertius* and *The Cantos*.

35. Pound, *Homage* 1; Propertius 3. 2. 11–16. As explained in the Preface, quotations from *Homage to Sextus Propertius* follow the text in Sullivan; quotations from and references to the Elegies of Sextus Propertius are based on the Loeb Classical Library edition, ed. and with an English [Prose] Translation by H. E. Butler (Cambridge: Harvard University Press; London: William Heinemann, 1967 [reprint of the 1912 ed.]. All other systems of numbering the Elegies have been converted to Butler's.

36. Kenner, *Pound Era,* p. 29.

37. Sullivan, p. 173.

38. Sir Charles Elton, trans., in *The Elegies of Propertius,* translated literally and with Notes by P. J. F. Gantillon, and with Metrical Versions of Select Elegies by [John] Nott [1782] and [Sir Charles] Elton (London: George Bell & Sons, 1884), p. 166; Propertius 2. 3. 9–22. Gantillon numbers this Elegy 2. 2. Hereafter, Gantillon's edition of the Elegies is referred to as Gantillon.

39. Pound, *Homage* 5. 2; Propertius 2. 1. 1–4, 7–10, 12–16.

Chapter 4: Pound's Influence on Historical Perspective

1. Robert Fitzgerald, trans., in *Latin Poetry in Verse Translation from the Beginnings to the Renaissance,* ed. L. R. Lind (Boston: Houghton Mifflin Co., Riverside Edition, 1957), p. 107. Reprinted by permission from *The Hudson Review,* Vol. V, No. 1 (Spring 1952). Copyright© 1952 by The Hudson Review, Inc.

2. Text follows that in *Q. Horati Flacci Opera,* ed. and with Brief Critical Notes by Edward C. Wickham, 1901, rev. H. W. Garrod, 1912, Oxford Classical Texts (Oxford: Oxford University Press, 1975). Hereafter referred to as Wickham.

3. John Warden, trans., *The Poems of Propertius,* The Library of Liberal Arts (Indianapolis and New York: Bobbs-Merrill Co., 1972), p. 49; Propertius 2. 1. 1–16.

4. Pound, *Homage* 9. 1.; Propertius 2. 28b. 10.

5. John Frederick Nims, trans., in Lind, p. 115. A later, slightly altered version of this translation appears in Nim's *Sappho to Valéry: Poems in Translation* (New Brunswick, N.J.: Rutgers University Press, 1971), p. 299. In addition to slight changes in format, the 1971 version substitutes "callous / Cupid" for "hardened / Cupid."

6. Text follows that in Wickham.

7. W. S. Merwin, *The Drunk in the Furnace,* The Macmillan Poets, 35 (New York: Macmillan Co., 1960), p. 24.

8. James Cranstoun, trans., in *Latin Literature in Translation,* ed. Kevin Guinagh and Alfred P. Dorjahn (New York, London, and Toronto: Longmans, Green & Co., 1942), p. 288; Catullus 11.

9. Pound, *Homage* 1.

10. Pound, *Translations,* p. 408; Catullus 85.

11. Pound, *Homage* 1, 1, and 4, respectively.

12. Louis Zukofsky, trans., in Lind, p. 30.

13. The discussion of Catullus's language is based on David O. Ross, Jr., *Style and Tradition in Catullus,* Loeb Classical Monographs (Cambridge: Harvard University Press, 1969), pp. 104–11.

14. Frank O. Copley, trans., *Gaius Valerius Catullus: The Complete Poetry* (Ann Arbor, Mich.: University of Michigan Press, [1957]), pp. xiv–xv.

15. Ibid., pp. 14–15.

16. Pound, "To Felix E. Schelling," 9 July 1922, Letter 189, and "To the Editor of the *English Journal,*" 24 January 1939, Letter 246, *Letters,* pp. 179, 231.

17. Ibid., Letter 189, p. 179.

18. Burton Raffel, *The Forked Tongue: A Study of the Translation Process* (The Hague and Paris: Mouton, 1971), p. 150.

19. Ibid., p. 159.

20. Raffel, trans., *Sir Gawain and the Green Knight,* with an Introduction by the translator and with an Afterword by Neil D. Isaacs (New York: New American Library, A Mentor Book, 1970), lines 815–29, pp. 73–74.

21. Ibid., lines 882–900, p. 75.

22. Ibid., lines 901–2, p. 75.

23. Raffel, Introduction to *Gawain,* pp. 19–20.

24. Ibid., p. 20.

25. Ibid.

26. R. A. Waldron, ed., Introduction to *Sir Gawain and the Green Knight,* York Medieval Texts (Evanston, Ill.: Northwestern University Press; London: Edward Arnold, 1970), p. 5.

27. Ibid.

28. Raffel, *Gawain,* lines 790–806, p. 73.

29. Ibid., lines 2270–83, p. 118.

30. *Sir Gawain and the Green Knight,* ed. by J. R. R. Tolkien and E. V. Gordon, 2d ed. edited by Norman Davis (Oxford: Oxford University Press, 1967), lines 674–83, p. 19.

31. Christine Brook-Rose, "Lay Me by Aurelie: An Examination of Pound's Use of Historical and Semi-Historical Sources," in Hesse, p. 242.

32. Kenner, *Poetry of Ezra Pound,* pp. 143–51.

33. Kenneth Rexroth, trans., in Lind, pp. 342–43.

34. Both examples are from *Homage* 1.

35. Paul Blackburn, *The Journals,* ed. Robert Kelly (Los Angeles: Black Sparrow Press, 1975), p. 108.

36. Sister [Mary] Bernetta Quinn, who was personally acquainted with Paul Blackburn, states this in *Ezra Pound: An Introduction to the Poetry* (New York and London: Columbia University Press, 1972), p. 92.

37. Davie, p. 47.

38. Pound, "Arnaut Daniel" (1920), *Literary Essays,* pp. 127–28, 130.

39. John Donne, *The Complete Poetry and Selected Prose of John Donne,* ed. Charles M. Coffin, Modern Library (New York: Random House, 1952), p. 11.

40. Ibid., "The Canonization," p. 13.

41. Christine Brooke-Rose, *A ZBC of Ezra Pound* (Berkeley and Los Angeles: University of California Press, 1971), p. 85.

42. Blackburn, trans., "Drogoman senher," by Peire Vidal, *Proensa: An Anthology of Troubadour Poetry,* selected and trans. by Paul

Blackburn, ed. and with an Introduction by George Economou (Berkeley, Los Angeles, and London: University of California Press, 1978), p. 114.

43. Blackburn, trans., "Lo dous cossire," by Guilhem de Cabestanh, *Proensa,* p. 192. "Beautiful thing" is a constant refrain in Books 2 and 3 of Williams's *Paterson* (New York: New Directions, A New Directions Paperbook, 1963).

44. The quotations are, in order, from Blackburn's translations of Guilhem de Cabestanh's "Lo dous cossire," the same, and Peire Vidal's "Plus que.l paubres," *Proensa,* pp. 191, 192, and 105, respectively.

45. *Shorter Oxford English Dictionary,* s.v.

46. Blackburn, trans., "Plus que.l paubres," by Peire Vidal, *Proensa,* pp. 105–7.

47. Blackburn, trans., "Per fin' amor m'esjauzira," by Cercamon, *Proensa,* pp. 29–30.

48. The text follows that in *Les poésies de Cercamon,* ed. Alfred Jeanroy, Les classiques français du moyen âge (Paris: Librairie Honoré Champion, 1966), pp. 26–29.

49. The quotations from Blackburn are, in order, from his translations of the Monk of Montaudon's "Molt mi platz deportz e gaieza," Cercamon's "Per fin' amor m'esjauzira," and Marcabrun's "L'iverns vai e'l temps s'aizina," *Proensa,* pp. 175, 29, and 60, respectively. The quotations from Pound are from his Arnaut Daniel translations, the first two from "Doutz brais e critz," and the third from "Sols sui," *Literary Essays,* pp. 135 and 139–40, respectively.

Chapter 5: Victorian Criticism by Translation

1. Robert Browning, Foreword to *Agamemnon of Aeschylus* (1877), *Complete Works,* from the Author's Revised Text, ed. with Introductions and Notes by Charlotte Porter and Helen A. Clarke, 12 vols. (New York: Thomas Y. Crowell & Co., 1898), 11:1.

2. Sir Thomas Herbert Warren, "The Art of Translation" (1895), *Essays of Poets Ancient and Modern* (London: J. Murray, 1909), p. 106.

3. Ibid., pp. 106–7.

4. Arnold, 1:147–48.

5. G. Heron-Allen, Foreword to *The Rubaiyat of Omar Khayyam* (Exeter: G. Lee, 1926), quoted in Sullivan, p. 15.

6. A. J. Arberry, *Omar Khayyam: A New Version Based on Recent Discoveries* (New Haven: Yale University Press, 1952), pp. 17–18.

7. Pound, "Date Line" (1934), *Literary Essays,* pp. 74–75.

8. Ibid., p. 75.

9. Warren, p. 102.

10. Ibid., p. 104.

11. Ibid.

12. Arnold, 1:102.

13. Ibid., 1:141.

14. Ibid., 1:102–3.

15. Quoted in Arnold, 1:119.

16. Warren, pp. 106–7.

17. Dryden, Preface to *Ovid's Epistles,* 1:118–19.

18. Warren, pp. 103–4.

19. Arnold, 1:98–99.

20. Ibid., 1:99.

21. Ibid.

22. Charles Stuart Calverley, "On Metrical Translation" (1868), *The Complete Works of C. S. Calverley,* with a Biographical Notice by Sir Walter J. Sendall (London: George Bell & Sons, 1901), pp. 499–500.

23. James Spedding, "English Hexameters" (1861), *Reviews and*

Discussions, Literary, Political and Historical, Not Relating to Bacon (London: C. Kegan Paul & Co., 1879), p. 328.

24. Ibid., p. 320.

25. Ibid., p. 327.

26. Arnold, 1:192.

27. Ibid., 1:197.

28. Ibid., 1:148–49.

29. The text follows that in *Poésies complètes de Bertran de Born,* ed. Antoine Thomas, Bibliothèque Méridionale, series 1, vol. 1, published for the Faculté des Lettres de Toulouse (Toulouse: Édouard Privat, 1888; reprint ed. New York and London: Johnson Reprint Corporation, 1971), pp. 133–35. Hereafter referred to as Thomas.

30. James J. Wilhelm, *Seven Troubadours: The Creators of Modern Verse* (University Park, Penn.: Pennsylvania State University Press, 1970), pp. 161–63; Anthony Bonner, trans. and ed., *Songs of the Troubadours* (New York: Schocken Books, 1972), p. 137.

31. Wilhelm, pp. 156–57; Bonner, *Songs of the Troubadours,* p. 137.

32. Hueffer, p. 206.

33. Ibid., pp. 200, 206; John Frederick Rowbotham, *The Troubadours and the Courts of Love* (London: Swan Sonnenschein & Co.; New York: Macmillan & Co., 1895; reprint ed. Detroit: Singing Tree Press, Book Tower, 1969), p. 64.

34. Rowbotham, p. 313.

35. Ibid., pp. 84–85.

36. Pound, "Proença" (1910), *The Spirit of Romance* (New York: New Directions, A New Directions Paperbook, 1968), p. 47.

37. Barbara Smythe, *Trobador Poets: Selections from the Poems of Eight Trobadors,* with an Introduction and Notes ([London: Chatto and Windus; New York: Duffield and Co., 1911; reprint ed.] New York: Cooper Square Publishers, 1966), p. 97.

38. Ibid., pp. 92–94.

39. E. g., Charles W. Jones, ed., *Medieval Literature in Translation* (New York: David McKay Co., 1950), pp. 670–75.

Chapter 6: Pound's Criticisms by Translation

1. Pound, "How I Began," *T. P.'s Weekly* (6 June 1913), p. 707, reproduced in Stock, p. 1.

2. Pound, "Sestina: Altaforte" (1909), *Personae*, pp. 28–29.

3. Pound, "Proença," *Spirit of Romance,* p. 47; Rowbotham, p. 184; Wilhelm, p. 155; Bonner, *Songs of the Troubadours,* p. 156.

4. N. Christoph de Nagy, "Pound and Browning," in Hesse, p. 114.

5. Pound, "How to Read," *Literary Essays,* p. 25.

6. Dryden, Preface to *Ovid's Epistles,* 1:119.

7. Pound, "Cavalcanti," *Literary Essays,* p. 195.

8. Pound, "I Gather the Limbs of Osiris," *Selected Prose, 1909–1965,* ed. and with an Introduction by William Cookson (New York: A New Directions Book, 1973), p. 38. Cookson includes most of the twelve-part series, but omits all the verse translations and commentary directly related to them.

9. Pound, "Cavalcanti," *Literary Essays,* pp. 168–69.

10. Ibid., p. 198.

11. Ibid., p. 199.

12. Pound, "Arnaut Daniel" (1920), *Literary Essays,* p. 116.

13. Pound, "Cavalcanti," *Literary Essays,* p. 172.

14. Pound, "French Poets" (1918), *Make It New: Essays by Ezra Pound* (New Haven: Yale University Press, 1935), pp. 159–160.

15. Sullivan, p. 36.

16. Ibid., p. 45.

17. Ibid., p. 19.

Chapter 7: Pound's Influence: Intentional Sacrifice

1. Blackburn, *Journals,* p. 129.

2. Pound, "The Seafarer" (1911), *Personae,* p. 66. The Old English text follows that in *The Anglo-Saxon Poetic Records: A Collective Edition,* ed. George Philip Krapp and Elliott van Kirk Dobbie, 6 vols. (New York: Columbia University Press; London: Routledge and Kegan Paul, 1931–42), 3:145. Hereafter referred to as Krapp and Dobbie.

3. Kenner, "Blood for the Ghosts," in Hesse, p. 333.

4. Ibid., p. 334.

5. Raffel, *Forked Tongue,* p. 108.

6. Ibid., p. 109.

7. Raffel, trans., *Poems from the Old English,* with an Introduction by the Translator and a Foreward by Robert P. Creed, 2d ed. rev. and enl. (Lincoln, Nebraska: University of Nebraska Press, A Bison Book, 1964), pp. 31–32; "The Seafarer," lines 27–46, 58–64.

8. Pound, *Personae,* p. 65; "The Seafarer," lines 58–64.

9. Raffel, *Poems from the Old English,* p. 33; "The Seafarer," lines 80–85.

10. Raffel, Introduction to *Gawain,* p. 40.

11. Ibid., p. 23. Raffel is citing a view of the poem put forth by Larry D. Benson in *Art and Tradition in Gawain and the Green Knight* (New Brunswick, N.J.: Rutgers University Press, 1965), p. 92.

12. John Gardner, trans., Introduction to *The Complete Works of the "Gawain"-Poet,* in a Modern English Version with a Critical Introduction (Chicago and London: University of Chicago Press, 1965), p. ix.

13. Ibid., p. viii.

14. Gardner, lines 1421–31, 1447–52, pp. 280–81.

15. Ibid., lines 1465–68, p. 281.

16. Text follows that in Tolkien and Gordon.

17. Gardner, lines 1481–89, 1493–99, p. 282.

18. Raffel, *Gawain,* lines 1447–54, pp. 93–94.

19. Ibid., lines 1480–84, 1496–99, pp. 94–95.

20. Text follows that in Tolkien and Gordon.

21. Pound, "Cavalcanti," *Literary Essays,* p. 172.

22. Pound, "Arnaut Daniel," *Literary Essays,* p. 116.

23. So theorizes D. S. Carne-Ross, "Translation and Transposition," in *The Craft and Context of Translation: A Symposium,* ed. William Arrowsmith and Roger Shattuck (Austin, Texas: University of Texas Press for the Humanities Research Center, 1961), p. 6.

Chapter 8: Pound's Influence: Formal Freedom

1. Gardner, Introduction to *Gawain-Poet,* p. ix.

2. John Hollander, "Versions, Interpretations, and Performances," in *On Translation,* ed. Reuben A. Brower, Harvard Studies in Comparative Literature, no. 23 (Cambridge: Harvard University Press, 1959), pp. 211–12.

3. The verse forms of the major Victorian translations of *Beowulf* are listed in the Bibliography of *"Beowulf" and "The Fight at Finnsburg,"* ed. and with an Introduction, Bibliography, Notes, Glossary, and Appendices, by Fr. Klaeber, 3d ed. with First and Second Supplements (Boston: D. C. Heath & Co., 1950), p. cxxxi. Translations known to me of other Old English poems confirm the conclusions about preferred translation forms which can be drawn from Klaeber's list.

4. An excellent short discussion of the principles of Anglo-Saxon verse can be found in *Seven Old English Poems,* ed. John C. Pope, with a Commentary and Glossary (Indianapolis and New York: Bobbs-Merrill Co., The Library of Literature, 1966), pp. 100–133.

5. Charles W. Kennedy, trans., *An Anthology of Old English Poetry, Translated into Alliterative Verse* (New York: Oxford University Press, 1960), p. 19; "The Seafarer," lines 1–9a.

6. Text follows that in Krapp and Dobbie, 3:143.

7. Brooke-Rose gives a concise, but clear, explanation of how Pound's "Seafarer" rhythms diverge from Old English practice (*ZBC*, pp. 86–88).

8. Pound, *Personae*, p. 64.

9. Michael Alexander, trans., Introduction to *The Earliest English Poems*, 2d ed. (Harmondsworth, England and Baltimore, Maryland: Penguin Books, The Penguin Classics, 1977), p. 21.

10. Ibid.

11. Ibid., p. 20.

12. Alexander, p. 74; "The Seafarer," lines 1–11a.

13. Pound, "Montcorbier, *alias* Villon" (1910), *Spirit of Romance*, p. 173. This essay is hereafter called "Villon."

14. Pound, *ABC of Reading* [2d ed.] (Norfolk, Conn.: New Directions, A New Directions Paperbook [1960]), p. 104.

15. Algernon Charles Swinburne, *The Poems of Algernon Charles Swinburne*, 6 vols. (New York and London: Harper and Brothers, 1904), 3:145.

16. Text follows that in Bonner, *Villon*.

17. Lowell, Introduction to *Imitations*, p. xii.

18. Lowell, *Imitations*, p. 14.

19. Pound, "Cavalcanti," *Literary Essays*, p. 199.

20. Pound, *Homage* 8; Propertius 2. 28. 9–16.

21. Sullivan, p. 84.

22. Pound, "A Retrospect," *Literary Essays*, p. 12.

23. J. P. McCulloch, trans., *The Poems of Sextus Propertius: A Bilingual Edition* (Berkeley, Los Angeles, and London: University of California Press, 1972), pp. 228–29; Propertius 4. 7. 15–28.

24. Warden, pp. 73–74; Propertius 2. 12. 17–20.

25. E.g., his translations of Elegies 1. 1 and 1. 3.

26. Warden, p. 171; Propertius 3. 17. 1–19.

27. Cranstoun, trans., in Godolphin, pp. 371–72.

28. Lowell, Introduction to *Imitations*, pp. xi–xii.

29. Maurice Valency, trans., "Assatz sai d'amor ben parlar," by Raimbaut d'Aurenga, in Flores, pp. 35–36.

30. Bonner, *Songs of the Troubadours*, pp. 145–46.

31. Bonner, *Villon*, p. 45; Great Testament, lines 437–44.

23. Galway Kinnell, trans., *The Poems of François Villon*, with an Introduction and Notes (Boston: Houghton Mifflin Co., 1977), pp. 53, 55. Kinnell's translation was a recipient of the Academy of American Poetry's Harold Merton Landers Award.

33. Payne, in Lepper, p. 210.

Chapter 9: Pound's Influence: Deletion and Exaggeration

1. Pound, "I Gather the Limbs of Osiris, Part 2," *New Age* 10 (11 November 1911): 131, quoted in Kenner, *Pound Era*, p. 151.

2. In Krapp and Dobbie, the arguments of various scholars who reject the end of the poem as a later addition are summarized (3:xxxvii–xxxviii).

3. Sullivan, p. 45.

4. Lind, p. 423.

5. Text follows that in *The Oxford Book of Latin Verse,* ed. H. W. Garrod (Oxford: Oxford University Press, 1912), p. 410.

6. Rexroth, trans., in Lind, p. 307.

7. Sullivan, p. 44.

8. Ibid., p. 45.

9. Pound, *Homage* 6; Propertius 2. 13A. 19–59.

10. Warden, pp. 54–55; Propertius 2. 3. 1–28.

11. David A. Campbell writes in his Notes that "Corinna is mentioned by no writer earlier than Propertius. . . ." (*Greek Lyric Poetry: A Selection of Early Greek Lyric, Elegiac and Iambic Poetry* [London, Melbourne, Toronto: MacMillan; New York: St. Martin's Press, 1967], pp. 408–9).

12. Pound, "Letter to the Editor of the *New Age*," 26 (4 December 1919): 82–83, collected in *Ezra Pound: The Critical Heritage,* ed. Eric Homberger, The Critical Heritage Series (London and Boston: Routledge & Kegan Paul, 1972), p. 164.

13. Pound, "To Felix E. Schelling," 8 July 1922, *Letters,* p. 178.

14. Mackail, *Latin Literature,* p. 126.

15. R. Y. Tyrrell, *Latin Poetry: Lectures Delivered in 1893 on the Percy Turnbull Memorial Foundation in the Johns Hopkins University* (Boston and New York: Houghton Mifflin & Co., 1895), p. 120.

16. J. Wight Duff, *A Literary History of Rome from the Origins to the Close of the Golden Age,* ed. A. M. Duff (New York: Barnes and Noble, University Paperbacks, 1963), p. 422. This edition is simply the 1909 edition with an updated Bibliography appended by A. M. Duff.

17. Sullivan, p. 29.

18. Ibid., pp. 29, 78.

19. Ibid., pp. 58–64.

20. Ibid., p. 56.

21. Pound, *Homage* 1; Propertius 3. 1. 1–8.

22. Sullivan, p. 40.

23. Propertius 3. 1. 7–8.

24. Ibid., lines 15–17.

25. Pound, *Homage* 1.

26. Sullivan, p. 100.

27. Wilhelm, pp. 154–55.

28. Thomas, p. 135; Bonner, *Songs of the Troubadours,* p. 283.

29. Wilhelm, p. 156.

30. Ibid.

31. Ibid.

32. Copley, Introducion to *Catullus,* p. xv.

33. Ibid., p. xiv.

34. Nims, p. 282.

35. Cranstoun, trans., in Guinagh and Dorjahn, pp. 288–89; Catullus 13.

36. Text follows that in *C. Valerii Catulli Carmina,* ed. R. A. B. Mynors, with Brief Critical Notes, Oxford Classical Texts (Oxford: Oxford University Press, 1958), p. 11. Hereafter referred to as Mynors.

37. Ross, pp. 105–6.

38. Ibid., pp. 105–7.

39. Copley, p. 14.

40. Ibid., pp. 14–15.

Chapter 10: Pound's Influence: Criticism by Analogy

1. Pound, "How to Read," *Literary Essays,* p. 25.

2. Sir Theodore Martin uses such footnotes in his book *The Works of Horace Translated into English Verse,* with a Life and Notes, new ed., 2 vols. (Edinburgh and London: William Blackwood and Sons, 1888).

3. Kenner, "Leucothea's Bikini," in Stock, p. 36.

4. Pound, "I Gather the Limbs of Osiris, Part 9," *New Age* 10 (25 January 1912):298, *Selected Prose,* p. 34.

5. Pound, "How to Read," *Literary Essays,* p. 25.

6. Yip, pp. 79–80.

7. Pound, Canto 95, *The Cantos of Ezra Pound* (New York: New Directions, 1972), p. 645.

8. Quoted in Kenner, "Leucothea's Bikini," in Stock," p. 27.

9. Kenner, "Leucothea's Bikini, in Stock," p. 27.

10. Pound, *Homage* 1; Propertius 3. 1. 7–8.

11. John Peale Bishop, "On Translating Poets," *Poetry: A Magazine of Verse* 62 (1943):112–13.

12. Carne-Ross, in Arrowsmith and Shattuck, p. 16.

13. Pound, *Homage* 1; Propertius 3. 2. 11–12.

14. Pound, *Homage* 12; Propertius 2. 34. 77.

15. Dudley Fitts, "The Poetic Nuance," in Brower, p. 39.

16. Fitts, *60 Poems of Martial in Translation* (New York: Harcourt, Brace & World, 1967), p. 47; Martial 11. 79.

17. Ibid., p. 11; Martial 10. 68.

18. Cranstoun, trans., in Godolphin, p. 597; Martial 10. 65. 1–4.

19. Pound, *Homage* 5. 2.

20. The Mueller edition used by Pound here reads *coccis*. Butler reads *cogis*.

21. Propertius 2. 1. 5–6.

22. *A Latin Dictionary Founded on Andrews' [Latin-English] Edition [of 1850] of Freund's Latin[-German] Dictionary,* ed. Charlton T. Lewis and Charles Short (Oxford: Oxford University Press, 1879, reprinted 1962), s.v.

23. McCulloch, p. 136; Propertius 2. 34. 27–28.

24. Smith Palmer Bovie, trans., *The Satires and Epistles of Horace: A Modern English Verse Translation* (Chicago: University of Chicago Press, Phoenix Books, 1959), p. 118; Horace *Satires* 2. 3. 175.

25. Ibid., p. 99; Horace *Satires* 2. 1. 9–10.

26. Fitts, *60 Poems,* p. 21; Martial 2. 8.

27. Ibid., p. 65; Martial 9. 15.

28. Text follows that given by Fitts, p. 64.

29. Text follows that in *Les Poésies de Peire Vidal,* ed. Joseph Anglade, Les classiques français du moyen âge, 2d rev. ed. (Paris: Librairie Honoré Champion, 1966), p. 103. Hereafter referred to as Anglade.

30. Anglade (p. 103) translates this: "Au sujet des rois d'Espagne, je suis affligé. . . ."

31. *Petit Dictionnaire Provençal-Français,* ed. Emil Levy, with the Preface of 1909, 5th ed. (Heidelberg: Carl Winter Universitätsverlag, 1973), s.v. *faire, tener, fais.*

32. Blackburn, trans., "A per pauc de chantar no.m lais," by Peire Vidal, Proensa, p. 121.

33. Allen Tate, trans., "The Vigil of Venus" (1943), *Poems, 1922–1947* (New York: Charles Scribner's Sons, 1948).

34. Mackail, trans. and ed., "Pervigilium Veneris" (1888), in *Catullus, Tibullus and Pervigilium Veneris,* The Loeb Classical Library (Cambridge: Harvard University Press; London: William Heinemann, 1962), p. 345.

35. Pound, "The Phantom Dawn" (1910), *Spirit of Romance.*

36. Pound, "Il Miglior Fabbro" (1910), *Spirit of Romance,* p. 26.

37. Tate, p. 178.

38. Ibid, pp. 187, 189.

39. Text follows that given by Tate, p. 188.

40. Tate says he has followed Mackail's bilingual edition of the text, but that he has occasionally changed the order of the quatrains (Tate, p. 183).

41. Mackail, "Pervigilium Veneris," p. 353.

42. At least, the listings in *The Union Catalogue of Books* suggest these conclusions; and so do the listings in "Latin Literature to A.D. 450" ed. Konrad Gries, in *The Literatures of the World in Translation: A Bibliography,* vol. 1: *The Greek and Latin Litera-*

tures, gen. eds. George B. Parks and Ruth Z. Temple (New York: Frederick Unger Publishing Co., 1968), p. 234.

43. Frank L. Lucas, trans., "Pervigilium Veneris," in *The Portable Roman Reader,* ed. Basil Davenport (New York: Viking Press, 1951), pp. 642–43.

44. Pound, "Cavalcanti," *Literary Essays,* p. 168.

45. Rolfe Humphries, "Latin and English Verse—Some Practical Considerations," in Brower, p. 61.

46. Pound, "Cavalcanti," *Literary Essays,* p. 169.

47. Fitts, "Poetic Nuance," in Brower, p. 38.

48. In Butler, *ecce, suis fit* reads *et cuius sit.* The former is the reading in the Mueller edition used by Pound.

49. Propertius 3. 16. 13–20.

50. Pound, *Homage* 3.

51. Joseph P. Clancy, trans., *The Odes and Epodes of Horace: A Modern English Translation* (Chicago: University of Chicago Press, 1960), p. 29; Horace Ode 1. 4.

52. Thomas Charles Baring, trans., in Godolphin, p. 231; Horace Ode 1. 4.

53. The text of the ode, here and subsequently, follows that in Wickham.

54. *A Latin Dictionary,* s.v.

55. Baring, in Godolphin, p. 232.

56. Clancy, p. 29.

57. James Michie, trans., *The Odes of Horace and the Centennial Hymn,* with an Introduction by Rex Warner (New York: Bobbs-Merrill Co., The Library of Liberal Arts, 1965), p. 24; Horace Ode 1. 11.

58. Calverley, "Translations into English" (1866), *Complete Works,* p. 250.

59. Ibid., p. 158.

60. Humphries, in Brower, p. 61.

61. Text follows that in Wickham.

62. Michie, pp. 20–21.

63. Calverley, "Translations," *Complete Works,* pp. 249–250.

64. Arnold, 1:134.

65. Carne-Ross, in Arrowsmith and Shattuck, p. 18.

66. George Chapman, trans., *Chapman's Homer,* ed. Allardyce Nicoll, vol. 1: *The Iliad;* vol 2: *The Odyssey and the Lesser Homerica,* Bollingen Series, no. 41, 2d ed. (Princeton: Princeton University Press, 1967), 1:373.

67. Alexander Pope, trans., *The Iliad of Homer,* vols. 7–8, *The Complete Poetic Works of Alexander Pope,* ed. Maynard Mack, 10 vols. (London: Methuen & Co.; New Haven: Yale University Press, 1961–67), 8:325–26.

68. William Cullen Bryant, trans., *The Iliad of Homer Translated into English Blank Verse,* 2 vols. (Boston: Houghton Mifflin and Co., 1870), 2: 165–66.

69. Benjamin William Smith and Walter Miller, trans., *The Iliad of Homer: A Line for Line Translation in Dactylic Hexameters,* illus. John Flaxman (New York: Macmillan Co., 1944), p. 386.

70. William Arrowsmith, trans., *Iliad* 18, 34–39, for BBC Radio, quoted by Carne-Ross, in Arrowsmith and Shattuck, p. 19.

71. Carne-Ross, in Arrowsmith and Shattuck, p. 7.

72. I do not know Greek. My exposition of the names of the sea-nymphs is based on the explanation given to me on June 20, 1978 by Dr. Paul Properzio, Chairman of the Department of Classical Studies at Drew University, Madison, New Jersey. Any errors no doubt arise from my having misunderstood him.

73. Carne-Ross, in Arrowsmith and Shattuck, pp. 18–19.

74. Arnold, 1:99.

75. Carne-Ross, in Arrowsmith and Shattuck, p. 15.

76. Yip, p. 88.

77. Kenner's phrase: "Leucothea's Bikini: Mimetic Homage."

Chapter 11: New Tastes for Old

1. So translated by Pound in Canto 53, *Cantos,* p. 265.

2. Information on these ideograms is based on Kenner's discussion (*Pound Era,* pp. 447–48), which in turn is based on Morrison's dictionary of Chinese characters (1815–22).

3. "Dateline" was first published in the 1934 Faber and Faber (London) edition of *Make It New.* It is now most easily available in *Literary Essays.* The comments on criticism are on pp. 74–75 of *Literary Essays.*

4. Ibid.

5. Pound, "The Renaissance" (1914), *Literary Essays,* p. 216.

6. Sullivan, p. 37.

7. Pound, "The Hard and Soft in French Poetry" (1918), *Literary Essays,* p. 285.

8. Pound, "A Retrospect," *Literary Essays,* p. 3.

9. Ibid., p. 5.

10. Ibid., p. 9.

11. Ibid., p. 11.

12. Hueffer, pp. 164–65.

13. Ibid., pp. 166–67.

14. Ibid., pp. 48–49.

15. Ibid., p. 57.

16. Rowbotham, pp. 70–71.

17. Ibid., p. 47.

18. Pound, "Proença," *Spirit of Romance,* p. 39. This comment is dated 1929.

19. Pound, "I Gather the Limbs of Osiris, Part 4," *New Age* 10 (21 December 1911):179, *Selected Prose,* p. 26.

20. Pound, "Arnaut Daniel," *Literary Essays,* p. 127.

21. Ibid.

22. Kenner, *Pound Era,* pp. 85–91.

23. Ibid., p. 85.

24. Ibid., p. 90.

25. This translation of Arnaut Daniel's "Can chai la fueilla" appeared in "I Gather the Limbs of Osiris, Part 5," *New Age* 10 (28 December 1911):201, quoted in Peter Henry Schneeman, "Ezra Pound and the Act of Translation," Ph.D. dissertation, University of Minnesota, 1972, p. 18.

26. Pound, "Arnaut Daniel," *Literary Essays,* p. 116.

27. Schneeman, p. 18.

28. Pound, "Il Miglior Fabbro," *Spirit of Romance,* p. 38.

29. Blackburn, trans., "Ab la dolchor del temps novel," by Guilhem IX, comte de Peiteus, *Proensa,* pp. 21–22. Pound's translation of this same poem first appeared in "Homage à Langue d'Oc," *Quia Pauper Amavi* (1919), and has been retained in *Personae,* p. 173.

30. Wilhelm, pp. 197–98.

31. Pound, "I Gather the Limbs of Osiris, Part 5," *New Age* 10 (28 December 1911):201, quoted in McDougal, p. 102.

32. Ibid., Part 4, *New Age* 10 (21 December 1911), quoted in Kenner, *Pound Era,* p. 87.

33. Warner Berthoff, *The Ferment of Realism: American Literature, 1888–1919* (New York: Free Press, 1965), pp. 6–9.

34. Ibid., p. 43.

35. Pound, "Villon," *Spirit of Romance,* pp. 168, 168, 173, and 176–77, respectively.

36. DeNagy, in Hesse, p. 122.

37. Payne, Introduction to *Villon,* in Lepper, pp. 179–80.

38. Ibid., pp. 266–67; Villon, "À Chartreux et à Celestins," Great Testament, lines 1968–95.

39. Lepper, p. 98.

40. H. B. McCaskie, trans., *The Poems of François Villon,* illus. Edward Ardizzone (London: Cresset Press, 1946), p. 192.

41. Kinnell, *The Poems of François Villon: A New Translation,* French-English Edition (New York: New American Library, A Signet Classic, 1965), pp. 167, 169. Kinnell's 1977 translation, some lines of which are quoted earlier, is a complete, less literal, revision of this 1965 version.

42. Kinnell, Introduction to the 1965 version, p. 19.

43. Pound, *ABC of Reading,* p. 104.

44. Pound, "Villon," *Spirit of Romance,* p. 168.

45. Kenneth Goodwin suggests this in *The Influence of Ezra Pound* (London: Oxford University Press, 1966), p. 217.

46. Arnold Goldman, *The Joyce Paradox: Form and Freedom in His Fiction* (Evanston, Illinois: Northwestern University Press, 1966), pp. 93–95; Kenner, *Joyce's Voices* (Berkeley and Los Angeles: University of California Press, 1978), p. 91.

47. H. A. Mason, *To Homer through Pope: An Introduction to Homer's "Iliad" and Pope's Translation* (London: Chatto & Windus, 1972), pp. 12–13.

48. George T. Wright, *The Poet in the Poem: The Personae of Eliot, Yeats, and Pound,* Perspectives in Criticism, no. 4 (Berkeley and Los Angeles: University of California Press, 1960), p. 160.

49. Ibid.

50. Ibid., pp. 158–59.

51. Schneeman, p. 120.

52. Ibid., p. 122.

53. Pound, *Homage* 10; Propertius 2. 29A.

54. W. G. Hale, "Pegasus Impounded," *Poetry* 14 (April 1919), in Homberger, p. 155.

55. Robert Nichols, "Poetry and Mr. Pound," *Observer* (11 January 1920), in Homberger, p. 167.

56. John Speirs, "Mr. Pound's Propertius," *Scrutiny* 3 (March 1935), in Homberger, pp. 304–5.

57. Sullivan, p. 177.

58. Arthur S. Way, trans., *Propertius* (London: Macmillan & Co.; New York: St. Martin's Press, 1937), pp. 30–31; Propertius 2. 5. 1–8, 17–30. Way is no lone holdout. E. H. W. Meyerstein's translation (*The Elegies of Propertius Done Into English Verse* [London: Oxford University Press, Humphrey Milford, 1935]) of the same elegy was written in a similar vein.

59. Propertius 2. 5. 17–20.

60. Lind, Introduction to *Latin Poetry in Translation,* p. xxix.

61. Frances Fletcher, trans., in Lind, p. 179; Propertius 2. 5.

62. Warden, Introduction to *Propertius,* p. ix.

63. Warden, pp. 59–60; Propertius 2. 5.

64. E.g., Kenner, *Pound Era;* Goodwin; Charles Olson, "Projective Verse," in *The New American Poetry, 1945–1960,* ed. Donald M. Allen (New York: Grove Press, An Evergreen Original; London: Evergreen Books, 1960), pp. 388, 393–94.

Chapter 12: Changing the Present

1. Pound, "To the Editor of the *English Journal,*" 24 January 1931, *Letters,* p. 231.

2. Sullivan, pp. 75–76.

3. Yip, p. 101.

4. Pound, "Vorticism" (1914), *Gaudier-Brzeska: A Memoir* (New York: New Directions, 1960 [re-edition of the 1916 book]), p. 97.

5. Yip, pp. 144–47.

6. Ibid., p. 148.

7. Ibid., p. 125.

8. Ibid., p. 127.

9. Ibid., pp. 96–99, 127.

10. Eliot, "Tradition and the Individual Talent," *Selected Essays*, p. 4.

11. Pound, "Notes on Elizabethan Classicists" (1917–18), *Literary Essays*, p. 240.

12. Raffel, *Forked Tongue*, pp. 103–4.

13. G. S. Fraser, "Pound: Masks, Myth, Man," in *An Examination of Ezra Pound*, ed. Peter Russell ([New York:] A New Directions Book [1950]), p. 173.

14. Ben Jonson, *"Timber: Or, Discoveries," 1641, and "Conversations with William Drummond of Hawthornden," 1619*, from the British Museum Manuscript (London: John Lane, The Bodley Head; New York: E. P. Dutton, 1923), p. 93.

15. Sullivan, p. 18.

16. Hollander, in Brower, p. 214.

17. *The Selected Letters of William Carlos Williams*, ed. and with an Introduction by John C. Thirlwall (New York: McDowell, Obolensky, 1957), p. 324.

18. Pound, "A Retrospect" and "How to Read," *Literary Essays*, pp. 7, 28.

19. Pound, "How to Read," *Literary Essays*, p. 27.

20. Lowell, *Imitations*, p. 8.

21. Pound, *Personae*, p. 10.

22. De Nagy, in Hesse, p. 117.

23. Ibid., p. 118.

24. Pound, "Villon," *Spirit of Romance*, pp. 171–72.

25. Ibid., p. 172.

26. Ibid.

27. Rossetti, p. 101.

28. Pound, "Villon," *Spirit of Romance*, p. 170.

29. Lowell, *Imitations*, p. 15.

30. Great Testament, lines 105–6, quoted in "Villon," *Spirit of Romance,* p. 170.

31. Pound, "Villon," *Spirit of Romance,* p. 171.

32. Lowell, *Imitations,* p. 14.

33. Bonner, *Villon,* p. 196.

34. Lowell, *Imitations,* pp. 19–20.

35. These line numbers refer to Villon's Great Testament.

36. Lowell, *Imitations,* p. 22.

37. Ibid., p. 23.

38. Bonner, *Villon,* p. 162.

39. Ibid., p. 128; Villon, Great Testament, lines 1996–2003, 2012–19.

40. Kinnell, Introduction to his 1965 version, pp. 17–18.

Chapter 13: Changing the Past

1. Buckminster Fuller, remark made in conversation with Hugh Kenner in December 1967, quoted in *Pound Era,* p. 162.

2. Eliot, "Tradition and the Individual Talent," *Selected Essays,* p. 5.

3. Sullivan, p. 18.

4. Hollander, in Brower, pp. 208–9.

5. McDougal, pp. 6–7.

6. Wright, p. 136.

7. Sullivan, pp. 20–21.

8. Ibid., p. 22.

9. Eliot, "Euripides and Professor Murray," *Selected Essays,* p. 50.

10. Kenner, *Pound Era,* p. 554.

11. Davie, p. 87.

12. Pound, *Homage* 8; Propertius 2. 15. 1–10.

13. Davie, pp. 87–88.

14. Ibid., p. 88.

15. Ibid.

16. Propertius 2. 28. 35–38, 42–46. Mueller's text reads *adoperta,* Butler's *operata.*

17. Pound, *Homage* 9. 1.

18. Kenner, *Poetry of Ezra Pound,* p. 147.

19. Propertius 2. 34. 79–80.

20. Pound, *Homage* 12.

21. Kenner, *Poetry of Ezra Pound,* p. 150.

22. Ibid., pp. 150–51.

23. Pound, *Cantos,* pp. 3–5; *Odyssey* 11. 1–14, 84–96.

24. Mason, p. 120.

25. Ibid., p. 121.

26. Kenner, *Pound Era,* p. 349.

27. Ibid.

28. Ibid., p. 350.

29. Theodore Savory, *The Art of Translation* (London: Jonathan Cape, 1957), p. 40.

30. Kenner, *Pound Era,* pp. 350–51 and "Blood for the Ghosts," in Hesse, p. 332.

31. The discussion of Anglo-Saxon culture is based in part on my own knowledge of *Beowulf* and the other Anglo-Saxon poems, and in part on G. A. Lester, *The Anglo-Saxons: How They Lived and Worked* (Chester, Pennsylvania: Dufour Editions, 1976), pp. 40, 65, 71. The discussion of Homeric culture is based on M. I. Finley, *The World of Odysseus* (New York: Viking Press, 1954). A detailed comparison of Homeric and Anglo-Saxon heroic poetry can be found in C. M. Bowra, *Heroic Poetry* (London: Macmillan & Co., 1952).

32. Kenner, *Pound Era,* pp. 418–19.

33. Peter Green, trans., quoted in Carne-Ross, in Arrowsmith and Shattuck, pp. 15–16; Homer *Iliad* 1. 101–19.

34. Carne-Ross, in Arrowsmith and Shattuck, pp. 16–17.

35. Propertius 4. 7. 87–88.

36. Ibid., lines 5–6.

37. Ibid., lines 95–96.

38. Robert Lowell is not alone in giving Propertius a Freudian interpretation. J. P. Sullivan, a classicist, gave Propertius a Freudian interpretation in "*Castas odisse puellas,* A Reconsideration of Propertius I-1," *Wiener Studien* 74 (1961):96–112.

39. Lowell, trans., "The Ghost: After Sextus Propertius," *Lord Weary's Castle* (New York: Harcourt, Brace & Co., 1946), p. 50.

40. Propertius 4. 7. 1–6.

41. Ibid., lines 13, 49, 70.

42. Ibid., line 14.

43. Ibid., lines 93–94.

44. Lowell, trans., *Lord Weary's Castle,* p. 52.

45. Sullivan, p. 31.

46. See especially Elegies 1. 29, 2. 8A, 2. 13A, 2. 24A, and 3. 16.

47. Ronald Musker, trans., Introduction to *The Poems of Propertius* (London: J. M. Dent & Sons, 1972), p. 26.

48. Sullivan, p. 20.

49. Pound, "To A. R. Orage," April 1919, Letter 160, *Letters,* p. 149.

50. Goodwin, pp. 208–10.

Annotated
Select Bibliography

Cross-references to other entries in this Bibliography which complete the publication information are given in parentheses, e.g., *(IV. A. 1. a)* means "Look in section *IV. A. 1. a.*"

I. Bibliographies

Brooke-Rose, Christine, comp. "Chronology" and "Bibliography." In *A ZBC of Ezra Pound,* pp. 267–80. Berkeley and Los Angeles: University of California Press, 1971.
    Useful short bibliography, especially helpful in detailing revisions and printing histories of Pound's works.

Gallup, Donald C., comp. *A Bibliography of Ezra Pound.* London: Hart-Davis, 1963.

Ferguson, Mary Anne Heyward, comp. *Bibliography of English Translations from Medieval Sources, 1943–1967.* Records of Civilization: Sources and Studies, No. 88. General Editor, W. H. T. Jackson. New York and London: Columbia University Press, 1974.

Morgan, Bayard Quincy. "A Critical Bibliography of Works on Translation: 46 B.C.—1958." In Brower, pp. 271–93 *(III. B).*

Parks, George B. and Temple, Ruth Z., comps. *The Literatures of the World in English Translation: A Bibliography.* Volume 1: *The Greek and Latin Literatures* (1968). With a section "Latin Literature to A.D. 450," edited by Konrad Gries. Volume 3: *The Romance Literatures*

(1970). New York: Frederick Ungar Publishing Co., 1968–.
Concentrates on translations after 1900, summarizes earlier ones.

II. Ezra Pound

A. Works by Pound

Pound, Ezra. *ABC of Reading* [2d ed.]. Norfolk, Conn.: New Directions, A New Directions Paperbook [1960].

———. *The Cantos of Ezra Pound.* New York: New Directions, 1972.
The most complete edition of *The Cantos.*

———, trans. *The Classic Anthology Defined by Confucius* [*Shih Ching*]. With an Introduction by Achilles Fang. Cambridge: Harvard University Press, 1954.

———. *Gaudier-Brzeska: A Memoir.* New York: New Directions, 1960.
Contains the essay "Vorticism."

———. "I Gather the Limbs of Osiris." *New Age,* 10 (30 November 1911–22 February 1912):107; 130–31, 155–56; 178–80; 201–2; 224–25; 249–51; 274–75; 297–99; 343–44; 369–70; 392–93.
The bulk of this essay is reprinted in *Selected Prose, 1909–1965 (II. A).* However, all the verse translations are omitted.

———. *The Letters of Ezra Pound, 1907–1941.* Edited by D. D. Paige. With a Preface by Mark Van Doren. New York: Harcourt, Brace & World, A Harvest Book, 1950; also in hardcover.

———. *Literary Essays of Ezra Pound.* Edited and with an Introduction by T. S. Eliot. New York: New Directions, A New Directions Paperbook, 1968.

———. *Make It New: Essays by Ezra Pound.* New Haven: Yale University Press, 1935.

———. *Personae: The Collected Shorter Poems of Ezra Pound.* New York: New Directions, 1971.

———. *Selected Prose, 1909–1965.* Edited and with an Introduction by William Cookson. New York: A New Directions Book, 1973.

_____. *The Spirit of Romance.* New York: New Directions, A New Directions Paperbook, 1968.

_____, trans. *Translations.* With an Introduction by Hugh Kenner. Enl. ed. New York: New Directions, A New Directions Paperbook, 1963.
Incomplete and lacking clarity as to the provenance of the selections.

_____, trans. *Women of Trachis.* New York: New Directions, 1957. A translation of Sophocles's *Trachiniae.*

B. Works about Pound

Brooke-Rose, Christine. "Lay Me by Aurelie: An Examination of Pound's Use of Historical and Semi-Historical Sources." In Hesse, pp. 242–79 *(II. B).*

_____. *A ZBC of Ezra Pound.* Berkeley and Los Angeles: University of California Press, 1971.
Themes in Pound's *Cantos* and their appearance in his earlier work.

Davie, Donald. *Ezra Pound: Poet as Sculptor.* New York: Oxford University Press, 1964.
Discusses Pound's use of allusion, both in the conventional sense and through manipulation of meter and form.

de Nagy, N. Christoph. "Pound and Browning." In Hesse, pp. 86–124 *(II. B).*
Considers the persona as the speaker in a dramatic monologue.

Fraser, G. S. "Pound: Masks, Myth, Man." In *An Examination of Ezra Pound,* pp. 172–85. Edited by Peter Russell. [New York:] A New Directions Book [1950].

Goodwin, K. L. *The Influence of Ezra Pound.* London: Oxford University Press, 1966.

Hale, W. G. "Pegasus Impounded." *Poetry* 14 (April 1919):52–55. In Homberger, pp. 155–57 *(II. B).*

Hesse, Eva, ed. *New Approaches to Ezra Pound: A Co-ordinated Investigation of Pound's Poetry and Ideas.* London: Faber & Faber, 1969.

Homberger, Eric, ed. *Ezra Pound: The Critical Heritage.* The Critical Heritage Series. London and Boston: Routledge & Kegan Paul, 1972.
A chronological collection of articles with emphasis on first reactions to Pound's works.

Kenner, Hugh. "Blood for the Ghosts." In Hesse, pp. 341–48 *(II. B).*

———. "Leucothea's Bikini: Mimetic Homage." In Stock, *Ezra Pound Perspectives,* pp. 25–40 *(II. B).*

———. *The Poetry of Ezra Pound.* Norfolk, Conn.: New Directions, 1951; reprint ed. Milwood, N.Y.: Kraus Reprint Co., 1974.
Explores Pound's metrics and discusses Joycean zones of consciousness.

———. *The Pound Era.* Berkeley and Los Angeles: University of California Press, 1971; available in paperback, 1973.
Discusses Pound's work as an expression of the twentieth-century Zeitgeist.

McDougal, Stuart Y. *Ezra Pound and the Troubadour Tradition.* Princeton Essays in Comparative Literature. Princeton: Princeton University Press, 1972.

Nichols, Robert. "Poetry and Mr. Pound." *Observer* (11 January 1920), p. 6. In Homberger, pp. 165–67 *(II. B).*

Norman, Charles. *Ezra Pound.* New York: Macmillan Co., 1960.
A biography.

Quinn, [Mary] Bernetta, Sister. *Ezra Pound: An Introduction to the Poetry.* New York and London: Columbia University Press, 1972.

Schneeman, Peter Henry. "Ezra Pound and the Act of Translation." Ph.D. dissertation, University of Minnesota, 1972.

Speirs, John. "Mr. Pound's Propertius." *Scrutiny* 3 (March 1936):409–18. In Homberger, pp. 302–8 *(II. B).*

Stock, Noel, ed. *Ezra Pound Perspectives: Essays in Honor of His Eightieth Birthday.* Chicago: Henry Regnery Co., 1965.

———. *The Life of Ezra Pound.* Pantheon Books. New York: Random House, 1970.

Sullivan, J. P. *Ezra Pound and Sextus Propertius: A Study in Creative Translation.* Austin: University of Texas Press, 1964.
   The best explication of the principles behind Pound's method of translation in the *Homage to Sextus Propertius.* The book includes a variorum edition of the *Homage* and gives the definitive readings. Also included are the relevant passages from the Latin text Pound used, Lucianus Mueller's 1892 edition of Propertius's Elegies.

Wright, George T. *The Poet in the Poem: The Personae of Eliot, Yeats, and Pound.* Perspectives in Criticism, no. 4. Berkeley and Los Angeles: University of California Press, 1960.
   Connects creative translation to Pound's use of personae.

Yip, Wai-lim. *Ezra Pound's "Cathay."* Princeton: Princeton University Press, 1969.

III. Translation Theory

A. Victorian and Earlier

Arnold, Matthew. *On Translating Homer* (1860–61). *The Complete Prose Works.* Edited by R. H. Super. 11 vols. Ann Arbor: University of Michigan Press, 1960–77, 1:97–216.

Browning, Robert. Foreword to *Agamemnon of Aeschylus.* In *Complete Works,* 11:1–2. From the Author's Revised Text. Edited with Introductions and Notes by Charlotte Porter and Helen A. Clarke. 12 vols. New York: Thomas Y. Crowell & Co., 1898.

Calverley, C. S. "On Metrical Translation" (1868). In *The Complete Works of C. S. Calverley,* pp. 496–503. With a Biographical Notice by Sir Walter J. Sendall. London: George Bell & Sons, 1901.

Dryden, John. Preface to *Ovid's Epistles* (1680) and Preface to *Sylvae* [*The Second Miscellany*] (1685). In *The Works of John Dryden,* 1(1956):109–19 and 3(1968):1–4. Edited by Edward Niles Hooker and H. T. Swedenberg, Jr. 18 vols. Berkeley and Los Angeles: University of California Press, 1956–1974.

Jonson, Ben. *"Timber: or Discoveries," 1641, and "Conversations with William Drummond of Hawthornden," 1619.* London: John Lane, the Bodley Head; New York: E. P. Dutton, 1923.
   From the British Museum manuscript.

Spedding, James. "English Hexameters." In *Reviews and Discussions, Literary, Political and Historical, Not Relating to Bacon,* pp. 316–35. London: C. Kegan Paul & Co., 1879.

A reprint of Spedding's Review of *On Translating Homer,* by Matthew Arnold, *Fraser's Magazine* 63 (June 1861).

Warren, Sir Thomas Herbert, "The Art of Translation" (1895). In *Essays of Poets Ancient and Modern.* London: J. Murray, 1909.

A simplified version of Matthew Arnold's theories.

B. Modern

Arrowsmith, William, and Shattuck, Roger, eds. *The Craft and Context of Translation: A Symposium.* Austin: University of Texas Press for the Humanities Research Center, 1961. Also available from Garden City, N.Y.: Anchor Books, 1964.

Bishop, John Peale. "On Translating Poets." *Poetry: A Magazine of Verse* 62 (1943):111–15.

A review of three Spanish-American poets, which Peale begins with a discussion of translation theory.

Blackburn, Paul. "Translation: Replies to a New York Quarterly Questionnaire." In *The Journals,* pp. 128–30. Los Angeles: Black Sparrow Press, 1975.

Brower, Reuben Arthur, ed. *On Translation.* Harvard Studies in Comparative Literature, no. 23. Cambridge: Harvard University Press, 1959.

Carne-Ross, D. S. "Translation and Transposition." In Arrowsmith and Shattuck, pp. 3–21 *(III. B).*

Cohen, J. M. *English Translators and Translations.* London: Longmans, Green & Co. for the British National Council and the National Book League, 1962.

Eliot, T. S. "Euripides and Professor Murray" (1920). In *Selected Essays,* pp. 46–50. New ed. New York: Harcourt, Brace & World, 1964.

Fitts, Dudley. "The Poetic Nuance." In Brower, pp. 32–47 *(III. B).*

A discussion of John Peale Bishop's translation of the sonnet "Tuércele el cuello al cisne de engañoso plumaje," by González Martínez.

Hollander, John. "Versions, Interpretations, and Performances." In Brower, pp. 205–31 *(III. B)*.

Humphries, Rolfe. "Latin and English Verse—Some Practical Considerations." In Brower, pp. 57–68 *(III. B)*.

Mason, H. A. *To Homer through Pope: An Introduction to Homer's "Iliad" and Pope's Translation.* London: Chatto & Windus, 1972.

Mathews, Jackson. "Third Thoughts on Translating Poetry." In Brower, pp. 67–77 *(III. B)*.

Raffel, Burton. *The Forked Tongue: A Study of the Translation Process.* The Hague and Paris: Mouton, 1971.

Savory, Theodore. *The Art of Translation.* London: Jonathan Cape, 1957.
    Gives a short history of translation theory. Discusses the question of suiting the translation to the audience for which it is intended.

IV. The Poems and Their Translations

A. Anthologies of Poems in Translation

Davenport, Basil, ed. *The Portable Roman Reader.* New York: Viking Press, 1951.
    Translations of prose and poetry. Mainly Edwardian and Victorian.

Flores, Angel, ed. *An Anthology of Medieval Lyrics.* The Modern Library. New York: Random House, 1962.
    Most of the translations were made especially for this book. An excellent sampling of current translation styles.

Godolphin, Francis R. B., ed. *The Latin Poets.* The Modern Library. New York: Random House, 1949.
    Mainly Victorian translations.

Guinagh, Kevin and Dorjahn, Alfred P., eds. *Latin Literature in Translation.* New York, London, and Toronto: Longmans, Green & Co., 1942.
    Translations of prose and poetry. Mainly Victorian.

Jones, Charles W., ed. *Medieval Literature in Translation*. New York: David McKay Co., 1950.
 Heavily Victorian.

Lind, L. R., ed. *Latin Poetry in Verse Translation from the Beginnings to the Renaissance*. Boston: Houghton Mifflin Co., Riverside Edition, 1957.
 Translations from many periods, including several interesting modern translations.

McClintock, William D. and McClintock, Porter Lander, eds. *Song and Legend from the Middle Ages*. The Chautauqua Reading Circle, Literature. Meadville, Pennsylvania and New York: Flood and Vincent, The Chautauqua-Century Press, 1893.

Ross, James Bruce and McLaughlin, Mary Martin, eds. *The Portable Medieval Reader*. New York: Viking Press, 1949.
 Translations tend to be Victorian.

Storrs, Ronald, ed. *"Ad Pyrrham": A Polyglot Collection of Translations of Horace's Ode to Pyrrha (Book 1, Ode 5)*. London, New York, Toronto: Oxford University Press, 1959.
 Translations from c. 1610 to c. 1940 arranged chronologically.

Van Doren, Mark, ed. *An Anthology of World Poetry in English Translation by Chaucer, Swinburne, Dowson, Symons, Rossetti, Waley, Herrick, Pope, Francis Thompson, E. A. Robinson, and Others*. New York: Albert and Charles Boni, 1928.

B. Greek

1. Translations

a. Edwardian and Earlier Modes

Bryant, William Cullen, trans. *The Iliad of Homer Translated into English Blank Verse*. 2 vols. Boston: Houghton Mifflin and Co., 1870.

Chapman, George, trans. *Chapman's Homer*. Edited by Allardyce Nicoll. Volume 1: *The Iliad;* volume 2: *The Odyssey and the Lesser Homerica*. Bollingen Series, no. 41. 2d ed. Princeton: Princeton University Press, 1967.

Pope, Alexander, trans. *The Iliad of Homer*. Vols. 7–8, *The Complete Poetic Works of Alexander Pope*. Edited by Maynard Mack. 10 vols.

London: Methuen & Co.; New Haven: Yale University Press, 1961–1967.

Smith, Benjamin William and Miller, Walter, trans. *The Iliad of Homer: A Line for Line Translation in Dactylic Hexameters.* Illustrated by John Flaxman. New York: Macmillan Co., 1944.

b. Modern Mode

Arrowsmith, William, trans. Lines from *Iliad* 18 for BBC radio. Quoted by D. S. Carne-Ross in Arrowsmith and Shattuck *(III. B)*.

Green, Peter, trans. Lines from *Iliad* 1 for BBC radio. Quoted by D. S. Carne-Ross in Arrowsmith and Shattuck *(III. B)*.

Lattimore, Richmond, trans. *The Iliad of Homer.* Chicago: University of Chicago Press, Phoenix Books, 1951; also in hardcover.

Logue, Christopher, trans. *Patrocleia [Iliad* 16]. N. p.: Scorpion Press, 1962.
    Free adaptation. Impressive.

2. Texts

Homer. *The Iliad.* Edited and with an English Prose Translation by A. T. Murray. Loeb Classical Library. 2 vols. Cambridge: Harvard University Press, 1924.
    Greek and English on facing pages.

————. *The Odyssey.* Edited by W. B. Stanford. With a General and a Grammatical Introduction, Commentary, and Indexes. 2 vols. London: Macmillan & Co.; New York: St. Martin's Press, 1965.
    Greek text with notes in English.

3. Critical Works

Finley, M. I. *The World of Odysseus.* New York: Viking Press, 1954.

C. Latin

1. Translations

a. Edwardian and Earlier Modes

Baring, Thomas Charles, trans. Horace Odes 1. 4. and 1. 11. In Godolphin, pp. 231–32, 234 *(IV. A)*.

Calverley, C. S. "Translations into English" (1866). In *The Complete Works of C. S. Calverley*, pp. 158–252 *(III. A)*.
A high level of Victorian translation.

Cranstoun, James, trans. Catullus 11 and 13. In Guinagh and Dorjahn, pp. 288, 288–89 *(IV. A)*.

———, trans. Martial 10. 65. In Godolphin, p. 597 *(IV. A)*.

———, trans. Propertius 3. 17. In Godolphin, pp. 371–72 *(IV. A)*.

Elton, Sir Charles, trans. Selected Elegies of Propertius. In *The Elegies of Propertius*, pp. 141–42, 154–55, 165–87. Translated Literally and with Notes by P. J. F. Gantillon. With Metrical Versions of Select Elegies by [John] Nott [fl. 1782] and Sir Charles Elton [b. 1778–d. 1853]. London: George Bell & Sons, 1884.

Lucas, Frank [b. 1894–d. 1967], trans. "Pervigilium Veneris." In Davenport, pp. 642–47 *(IV. A)*.

Martin, Sir Theodore, trans. *The Works of Horace Translated into English Verse*. With a Life and Notes. New ed. 2 vols. Edinburgh and London: William Blackwood and Sons, 1888.

Way, Arthur S., trans. *Propertius*. London: Macmillan & Co.; New York: St. Martin's Press, 1937.

b. Modern Mode

Bovie, Smith Palmer, trans. *The Satires and Epistles of Horace: A Modern English Verse Translation*. Chicago: University of Chicago Press, Phoenix Books, 1959.

Clancy, Joseph P., trans. *The Odes and Epodes of Horace: A Modern English Translation*. Chicago: University of Chicago Press, 1960.

Copley, Frank O., trans. *Gaius Valerius Catullus: The Complete Poetry*. Ann Arbor: University of Michigan Press [1957].

Fitts, Dudley, trans. *60 Poems of Martial in Translation*. New York: Harcourt, Brace & World, 1967.

Fitzgerald, Robert, trans. Horace Ode 1. 25. In Lind, p. 107 *(IV. A)*.

Fletcher, Frances, trans. Selected Elegies of Propertius. In Lind, pp. 179–83, 184–217 *(IV. A)*.

Lowell, Robert, trans. "The Ghost: After Sextus Propertius." *Lord Weary's Castle*, pp. 50–52. New York: Harcourt, Brace & Co., 1946.

McCulloch, J. P., trans. *The Poems of Sextus Propertius: A Bilingual Edition*. Berkeley, Los Angeles, and London: University of California Press, 1972.

Merwin, W. S., trans. Catullus 11. In *The Drunk in the Furnace*, p. 24. The Macmillan Poets, 35. New York: Macmillan Co., 1960.

Michie, James, trans. *The Odes of Horace and the Centennial Hymn*. With an Introduction by Rex Warner. New York: Bobbs-Merrill Co., The Library of Liberal Arts, 1965.

Nims, John Frederick, trans. Horace Ode 2. 8. In Lind, p. 108 *(IV. A)*.

Raffel, Burton, trans. *The Essential Horace: Odes, Epodes, Satires, and Epistles*. With a Foreword and an Afterword by W. R. Johnson. San Francisco: North Point Press, 1984.

Rexroth, Kenneth, trans. "Rumor letalis" attributed to Peter Abelard, and "Omne quod Natura parens creauit" by Sulpicius Lupercus Servasius Iunior." In Lind, pp. 342–343, and 307 (IV. A).

Tate, Allen, trans. "Pervigilium Veneris" (1943). In *Poems, 1922–1947*, pp. 184–201. New York: Charles Scribner's Sons, 1948.

Warden, John, trans. *The Poems of Propertius*. The Library of Liberal Arts. Indianapolis and New York: Bobbs-Merrill Co., 1972.

Zukofsky, Louis, trans. Catullus 8. In Lind, p. 30 *(IV. A)*.

_____and Zukofsky, Celia, trans. *Catullus: Gai Valeri Catulli Veronensis Liber*. London: Cape Goliard Press; New York: Grossman, 1969.
    Attempt to mimic Latin sounds with minimal attention to sense.

2. Texts

Catullus. *C. Valerii Catulli Carmina*. Edited and with Brief Critical Notes by R. A. B. Mynors. Oxford Classical Texts. Oxford: Oxford University Press, 1958.
    Latin only.

Horace. *Q. Horati Flacci Opera.* Edited and with Brief Critical Notes by Edward C. Wickham, 1901. Revised by H. W. Garrod, 1912. Oxford Classical Texts. Oxford: Oxford University Press, 1975.
Latin only.

Martial. *Marci Valerii Martialis Epigrammata.* Edited and with Brief Critical Notes by W. M. Lindsay. Oxford Classical Library. 2d ed. Oxford: Oxford University Press, 1929; reprinted 1959.
Latin only.

"Pervigilium Veneris." Edited and Translated by J. W. Mackail. In *Catullus, Tibullus and Pervigilium Veneris.* The Loeb Classical Library. Cambridge: Harvard University Press; London: William Heinemann, 1966. First printing 1913.
English and Latin on facing pages.

Propertius. Edited and with an English [prose] Translation, Preface, Biography of Propertius, and Bibliography, by H. E. Butler. The Loeb Classical Library. Cambridge: Harvard University Press; London: William Heinemann, 1967. A reprint of the 1912 edition.
Respectable edition of the text, with a pseudo-archaic prose translation, purportedly literal.

Servasius, Sulpicius Lupercus, Iunior. "Omne quod Natura parens creauit." in *The Oxford Book of Latin Verse,* p. 403. Edited by H. W. Garrod. Oxford: Oxford University Press, 1912.

3. Critical Works

Dronke, Peter. *Medieval Latin and the Rise of the European Love-Lyric.* Volume 1: *Problems and Interpretation;* volume 2: *Latin Texts.* Oxford: Oxford University Press, 1965.

Duff, J. Wight. *A Literary History of Rome from the Origins to the Close of the Golden Age.* Edited by A. M. Duff. New York: Barnes and Noble, University Paperbacks, 1963.
This is the 1909 edition with an updated Bibliography appended by A. M. Duff.

Hadas, Moses. *A History of Latin Literature.* New York: Columbia University Press, 1952.

Mackail, J. W. *Latin Literature.* New York: Charles Scribner's Sons, 1904 [1st printing, 1895].

Ross, David O., Jr. *Style and Tradition in Catullus*. Loeb Classical Monographs. Cambridge: Harvard University Press, 1969.
    An analysis of the levels of diction in the poetry, with special attention paid to the element of high-society slang.

Tyrell, R. Y. *Latin Poetry: Lectures Delivered in 1893 on the Percy Turnbull Memorial Foundation in the Johns Hopkins University*. Boston and New York: Houghton Mifflin & Co., 1895.

D. Old and Middle English

1. Translations

a. Edwardian and Earlier Modes

Banks, Theodore Howard, Jr., trans. *Sir Gawain and the Green Knight*. New York: F. S. Crofts & Co., 1929.

Kennedy, Charles W., trans. "The Seafarer." In *An Anthology of Old English Poetry, Translated into Alliterative Verse*, pp. 19–26. New York: Oxford University Press, 1960.

b. Modern Mode

Alexander, Michael, trans. "The Seafarer." In *The Earliest English Poems*, pp. 74–77. 2d ed. The Penguin Classics. Harmondsworth, England and Baltimore, Maryland: Penguin Books, 1977.
    A dual-language edition of this book was published by the University of California Press in 1970.

Gardner, John, trans. "Sir Gawain and the Green Knight." In *The Complete Works of the "Gawain"-Poet*, pp. 221–324. In a Modern English Version with a Critical Introduction. Chicago: University of Chicago Press, Phoenix Books, 1965.

Raffel, Burton, trans. *Sir Gawain and the Green Knight*. With an Introduction by the Translator and an Afterword by Neil D. Isaacs. New York: New American Library, A Mentor Book, 1970.
    A creative translation emphasizing the structures and emotions of the original.

———, trans. "The Seafarer." In *Poems from the Old English*, pp. 31–34. With an Introduction by the Translator and a Foreword by Robert P. Creed. 2d ed. rev. and enl. Lincoln, Nebraska: University of Nebraska Press, A Bison Book, 1964.
    Good, creative translation.

2. Texts

Sir Gawain and the Green Knight: An Alliterative Romance-Poem (AB. 1360 A.D.). Re-edited from Cotton. MS. Nero, A. x. by Richard Morris. 2d ed. rev. 1869. London: N. Trübner & Co. for the Early English Text Society, 1864.

_____. Edited by J. R. R. Tolkien and E. V. Gordon. 2d ed. rev. by Norman Davis. Oxford: Oxford University Press, 1967; corrected 1968.

_____. Edited by R. A. Waldron. York Medieval Texts. Evanston, Ill.: Northwestern University Press; London: Edward Arnold, 1970. Text, glossary, and helpful notes.

"The Seafarer." In *The Exeter Book, The Anglo-Saxon Poetic Records* 3(1936): 143–47. Edited by George Philip Krapp and Elliott van Kirk Dobbie. 6 vols. New York: Columbia University Press; London: Routledge and Kegan Paul, 1931–1942.

3. Critical Works

Benson, Larry D. *Art and Tradition in Gawain and the Green Knight.* New Brunswick, N.J.: Rutgers University Press, 1965.

Bowra, C. M. *Heroic Poetry.* London: Macmillan & Co., 1952.
A comparison of the heroic poetry of various ages and literatures.

Klaeber, Fr., ed. *Beowoulf and The Fight at Finnsburg.* With an Introduction, Bibliography, Notes, Glossary, and Appendices. 3d ed. With 1st and 2d Suppl. Boston: D. C. Heath & Co., 1950.

Lester, G. A. *The Anglo-Saxons: How They Lived and Worked.* Chester Springs: Pennsylvania: Dufour Editions, 1976.

Pope, John Collins, ed. *Seven Old English Poems.* Indianapolis and New York: Bobbs-Merrill Co., The Library of Literature, 1966.

E. Provençal

1. Translations

a. Edwardian and Earlier Modes

Hueffer, Francis, trans. "S'al cor plagues ben for' ueimais sazos" and Guilhem de Cabestanh's "Lo jorn, qeus vi domna, premieramen."

In *The Troubadours: A History of Provençal Life and Literature in the Middle Ages,* pp. 258, 166–67. London: Chatto & Windus, 1878.

Rowbotham, John Frederick, trans. "Bem platz lo gais temps de pascor" by Bertran de Born. In *The Troubadours and Courts of Love,* pp. 84–85; reprint ed. Detroit: Singing Tree Press, Book Tower, 1969.

Smythe, Barbara, trans. "Bem platz lo gais temps de pascor" by Bertran de Born. In *Trobador Poets: Selections from the Poems of Eight Trobadors,* pp. 92–94. With an Introduction and Notes. [London: Chatto & Windus; New York: Duffield & Co., 1911; reprint ed.] New York: Cooper Square Publishers, 1966.

b. Modern Mode

Blackburn, Paul, trans. *Proensa: An Anthology of Troubadour Poetry.* Edited and with an Introduction by George Economou. Berkeley, Los Angeles, and London: University of California Press, 1978.

Bonner, Anthony, trans. "Un sirventes cui motz no falh" by Bertran de Born. In *Songs of the Troubadours,* pp. 145–47. New York: Schocken Books, 1972.

Valency, Maurice, trans. "Assatz sai d'amor ben parlar" by Raimbaut d'Aurenga. In Flores, pp. 35–36 *(IV. A).*

Wilhelm, James J., trans. "Bem platz lo gais temps de pascor" by Bertran de Born. In *Seven Troubadours: The Creators of Modern Verse,* pp. 154–56. University Park, Pennsylvania and London: The Pennsylvania State University Press, 1970.

2. Texts

Arnaut Daniel. *Les poésies d'Arnaut Daniel.* Edited by René Lavaud. Critical Edition following Canello. With French Translation and Notes. Toulouse-Périgeux: 1910; reprint ed., Geneva: Slatkine Reprints, 1973.

Bernart de Ventadorn. *Bernard de Ventadour, troubadour du XIIᵉ siècle: chansons d'amour.* Edited by Moshé Lazar. Critical Edition with French Translation, Introduction, Notes, and Glossary. Bibliothèque française et romane. Series B: Critical Editions of Texts, no. 5. Published by Centre de Philologie romane de la faculté des Lettres de Strasbourg. Paris: Librairie C. Klincksieck, 1966.

Bertran de Born. *Poésies complètes de Bertran de Born.* Edited by Antoine Thomas. With the Original Text, an Introduction, Notes, and Glossary, and unpublished Extracts from the Cartulaire de Dalon. Bibliothèque Méridionale. Series 1, vol. 1. Published under the auspices of the Faculté des Lettres de Toulouse. Toulouse: Imprimerie et Librairie Édouard Privat, 1888; reprint ed., New York and London: Johnson Reprint Corporation, 1971.

Cercamon. *Les poésies de Cercamon.* Edited by Alfred Jeanroy. Les classiques français du moyen âge. Paris: Librairie Honoré Champion, 1966.

Guilhem IX, comte de Peiteus. *Les chansons de Guillaume IX, duc d'Aquitaine (1071–1127).* Edited by Alfred Jeanroy. Les classiques français du moyen âge. 2d rev. ed. Paris: Librairie Honoré Champion, 1967.

Marcabrun. *Poésies complètes de troubadour Marcabru.* Edited by J.-M.-L. Dejeanne. With French Translation, Notes, and Glossary. Bibliothèque Méridionale. Series 1, vol. 12. Published under the auspices of the Faculté des Lettres de Toulouse. Toulouse: Imprimerie et Librairie Édouard Privat, 1909; reprint ed., New York: Johnson Reprint Corporation, 1971.

Peire Vidal. *Les poésies de Peire Vidal.* Edited by Joseph Anglade. Les classiques français du moyen âge. 2d rev. ed. Paris: Librairie Honoré Champion, 1966.

Raimbaut d'Aurenga. *The Life and Works of the Troubadour Raimbaut d'Orange.* Edited and translated by Walter Pattison. Minneapolis: University of Minnesota Press, 1952.

3. Critical Works

Bonner, Anthony, trans. and ed. *Songs of the Troubadours.* New York: Schocken Books, 1972.
    Fairly literal translations accompanied by interesting comments on the poems and the various troubadours. Many references to Pound's translations and *Cantos* in the notes.

Goldin, Frederick. *Lyrics of the Troubadours and Trouvères: An Anthology and a History.* With Translations and Introductions. Garden City, New York: Doubleday, Anchor Books, 1973.

Short introductions to the poets. Selected lyrics with literal translations on facing pages.

Hueffer, Francis. *The Troubadours: A History of Provençal Life and Literature in the Middle Ages.* London: Chatto & Windus, 1878.
 Includes some verse translations by Hueffer, One of the first major Victorian studies of the troubadours.

Rowbotham, John Frederick. *The Troubadours and Courts of Love.* London: Swan Sonnenschein & Co.; New York: Macmillan & Co., 1895; reprint ed. Detroit: Singing Tree Press, Book Tower, 1969.
 Criticism and some translations of his own.

Wilhelm, James J. *Seven Troubadours: The Creators of Modern Verse.* University Park, Pennsylvania: The Pennsylvania State University Press, 1970.
 Critical introductions to fairly literal translations. Acknowledges Pound.

F. French

1. Translations

a. Edwardian and Earlier Modes

Lepper, John Heron, trans. *The Testaments of François Villon.* Including the texts of John Payne and others. New York: Liveright Publishing Corp., 1924.
 Lepper's version is poor and in the Victorian mode. Payne's 1892 version is included in its entirety, as are all of Rossetti's and Swinburne's translations, plus one by Arthur Symons and Pound's two Villonauds.

Payne, John, trans. *The Poems of Master François Villon of Paris, Now First Done into English Verse.* With a Biographical and Critical Introduction. London: The Villon Society, 1892. Reprinted in John Lepper's translation of *The Testaments of François Villon,* pp. 114–292 *(IV. F. 1. a).*

Rossetti, Dante Gabriel, trans. Three Poems by François Villon (1870). In *Rossetti's Poems,* pp. 100–102. Edited and with an Introduction and Notes by Oswald Doughty. London: J. M. Dent & Sons; New York: E. P. Dutton & Co., 1961.

Swinburne, Algernon Charles, trans. Ten poems by François Villon. In *The Poems of Algernon Charles Swinburne*, 3:139–47. 6 vols. New York and London: Harper and Brothers, 1904.

   Swinburne himself oversaw this edition, the last in his lifetime.

b. Modern Mode

Bonner, Anthony, trans. *The Complete Works of François Villon (IV. F. 2).*

Kinnell, Galway, trans. *The Poems of François Villon: A New Translation.* New York: New American Library, A Signet Classic, 1965.

   Emphasis on Villon's realism. Very literal. French and English on facing pages.

————, trans. *The Poems of François Villon.* With an Introduction and Notes. Boston: Houghton Mifflin Co., 1977.

   A complete revision of Kinnell's 1965 version. Less literal, more lyric, but still forceful and direct. French and English on facing pages.

Lowell, Robert, trans. Poems of François Villon. In *Imitations*, pp. 8–24. New York: Farrar, Straus & Giroux, 1961.

   Book includes creative translations of Sappho, Heine, Baudelaire, et al.

McCaskie, H. G., trans. *The Poems of François Villon.* Illustrated by Edward Ardizzone. London: Cresset Press, 1946.

   Rhymed, uneven quality. English and French on facing pages.

2. Texts

Bonner, Anthony, trans. [and ed.] *The Complete Works of Françqis Villon.* With a Bibliography and Notes. Introduction by William Carlos Williams. New York: David McKay Co., 1960.

   Text and translation on facing pages. Best text for English speakers. Based on the 4th rev. ed. (1932) of A. Longnon's work, emended according to Burger, and with notes based on Burger and P. Champion.

V. Related Themes in Modern Literature

Berthoff, Warner. *The Ferment of Realism: American Literature, 1888–1919.* New York: Free Press, 1965.

Elliot, T. S. "Tradition and the Individual Talent" (1919). In *Selected Essays*, pp. 3–11 *(III. B)*.

Goldman, Arnold. *The Joyce Paradox: Form and Freedom in his Fiction.* Evanston, Ill.: Northwestern University Press, 1966.

Hauser, Arnold. *The Social History of Art.* Translated by Stanley Godman in collaboration with the author. 4 vols. New York: Random House, Vintage Books, 1958. Vol. 4: *Naturalism, Impressionism, the Film Age.* Published in 2 vol. hardcover by Alfred A. Knopf.

Kenner, Hugh. *Joyce's Voices.* Berkeley and Los Angeles: University of California Press, 1978.

Olson, Charles. "Projective Verse." In *The New American Poetry, 1945–1960*, pp. 386–97. Edited by Donald M. Allen. New York: Grove Press, An Evergreen Original; London: Evergreen Books, 1960.

Index of Terms

Index of Names and Titles